In order to understand where we are today, one must comprehend the long journey we took to get here.

—*Andrea Zagato, third-generation designer and coachbuilder*

ITALIAN SPORTS CARS

WINSTON GOODFELLOW

FOREWORD BY SERGIO PININFARINA

MBI Publishing Company

Dedication

To my late uncle, Lloyd Swayne Jr. He was a true aficionado of all types of sports cars, who possessed that type of crushing cool that never goes out of style. Uncle Lloyd indoctrinated me to Italy's sports cars' on-road magic by letting this long-haired, lanky teenager first drive his Ferrari 330 2+2, then his 308 GT4. Needless to say, Italian sports cars had me hooked.

First published in 2000 by MBI Publishing Company, 729 Prospect Avenue, PO Box 1, Osceola, WI 54020-0001USA

MBI Publishing Company books are also available at discounts in bulk quantity for industrial or sales-promotional use. For details write to Special Sales Manager at Motorbooks International Wholesalers & Distributors, 729 Prospect Avenue, PO Box 1, Osceola WI, 54020 USA.

Library of Congress Cataloging-in-Publication Data

Goodfellow, Winston.
    Italian sports cars / Winston Goodfellow.
       p. cm.
    Includes index.
    ISBN 0-7603-0819-5 (hardbound : alk. paper)
    1. Sports cars–Italy–History.   I. Title.
TL236 .G65 2000
629.222'1'0945–dc21   00-056850

On the front cover: One of the most spectacular cars from the 1960s was Alfa Romeo's 33 Stradale. Alfa based the machine's mechanicals on the race car of the same name and wrapped them in a ravishing Franco Scaglione design. The body was constructed at Carrozzeria Marazzi, a small coachbuilder on the outskirts of Milan. Just eighteen 33 Stradales were built from 1967 to 1969.

Endpaper: Distinguished by its V-shaped radiator, Alfa Romeo's RLSS (Super Sport) debuted in 1925. Here, one is seen in 1927 as it participates in Italy's *Mille Miglia*. Although an OM won that first running of the famed 1,000-mile race, Alfa Romeo dominated it and numerous other venues over the next ten years.

On the frontispiece: The distinctive speedometer of the Lamborghini 350 GT is characteristic of Carrozzeria Touring's design. When asked to reflect on why Lamborghini's first car was one of the finest GTs of its day, former company chief engineer Gianpaolo Dallara simply stated, "I would have to say it involved some luck . . . We really didn't know any better!"

On the title page: At the 1976 Paris Auto Show, Ferrari introduced the 512 BB. Ferrari had enlarged its flat-12 engine to 5 liters, enabling it to deliver smoother midrange acceleration. When *Road & Track* tested the Ferrari in 1978, it recorded 0–60 miles per hour in 5.5 seconds and 0–100 miles per hour in 13.2 seconds and the estimated top speed at 180-plus miles per hour. The Countach LP400 remained the magazine's fastest car, however it noted that, "the Ferrari 512 Boxer wins a more important award, as the best all-around sports and GT."

On the back cover: (Left) When Iso and Bizzarrini parted ways in late 1965, the latter kept producing the competition-minded Grifo A3 under his own name, calling it the Bizzarrini Strada or GT America. Its sleek shape and front "mid-engine" design shows how he valued performance above all else. Like Iso's products, a Corvette V-8 powered the Bizzarrini Strada. This 1967 Strada 5300GT bears the serial number "262".

(Center) Ferrari's 355 was one of the 1990s most beautiful road cars, and is a perfect example of how far the performance envelope moved in two decades. This V-8 model was faster and quicker than a number of Ferrari's previous "mass produced" 12-cylinder benchmarks: the 275 GTB/4; the Daytona, the Boxer, and Testarossa.

(Right) Lamborghini's Miura was the model that brought the mid-engine configuration to the fore of production car design and engineering. It was first shown as a naked chassis at the Turin Show) in November 1965, then reappeared in March 1966 covered with a sensational Bertone body. The model shown here is the last and best of the Miuras, the SV.

Edited by John Adams-Graf
Layout by Jim Snyder and Katie Sonmor
Designed by Tom Heffron
All photographs, unless otherwise noted, are supplied by the author, Winston Goodfellow.

Printed in Hong Kong

Contents

	Author's Note and Acknowledgments	6
	Foreword	7
	Introduction	8
Section I	**Laying the Foundation**	9
Chapter 1	Sowing the Seeds (1900–1929)	11
Chapter 2	Convergence (1930–1939)	17
Section II	**The Recovery**	25
Chapter 3	Conflict, Compression, and First Steps (1940–1947)	27
Chapter 4	Release (1948–1952)	37
Chapter 5	The Boom (1953–1955)	49
Section III	**Prosperity**	57
Chapter 6	Capitani d'Industria (1956–1960)	59
Chapter 7	The Ferrari Factor (1961–1965)	71
Chapter 8	The Hot Years Begin (1966–1967)	87
Section IV	**The Decline**	97
Chapter 9	Twilight of the Goddesses (1968–1973)	99
Chapter 10	Via Crucis (1974–1983)	113
Section V	**Revolt and Rebirth**	125
Chapter 11	Backlash, Boom, and Bust (1984–1996)	127
Chapter 12	Return to Roots (1996–Today)	137
Bibliography		146
Appendix A	Italy's Sigificant Postwar Sportscar Manufacturers and Models	148
Appendix B	A Brief Guide to Italy's Postwar Designers, Engineers, Entrepreneurs, and Managers	151
	Index	155

Author's Note and Acknowledgments

The most difficult task in researching and writing Italian sports Cars was determining which models to include and which to leave out. The astute reader will note that built-for-competition-only models, such as Ferrari's 250 GTO, Alfa's TZ-2, and Maserati's 450 S are thus only mentioned in passing, usually when applying it to a street car's history or an engineer's or designer's career.

One of the greatest joys in writing this book was hearing firsthand the memories and insights of those who lived Italy's illustrious automotive history. I was able to get a perspective from all sides of the equation, for assembly line workers, company chiefs, designers, engineers, and test drivers were most generous with their time.

This would prove critical when tackling the big picture influences such as political and economic climates, let alone finding out the *real* stories behind many cars' creations. I just wish this book was several times this size so I could relate everything these individuals had to say.

There are six people in particular who should be noted for their help: Carlo Felice Bianchi Anderloni, Valentino Balboni, Giordano Casarini, Sergio Pininfarina, Piero Rivolta, and Tom Tjaarda. You were always as gracious as could be, making yourselves available to my constant smattering of questions, or pointing me in the proper direction to find an answer. Sergio Pininfarina also gave me the best dinner conversation I had in 1999 when we actively debated what the "Car of the Century" should be.

Others I have drawn heavily from are Giulio Alfieri, Giotto Bizzarrini, the late Carlo Chiti, Gian Paolo Dallara, Marcello Gandini, the late Girolamo Gardini, Adolfo Orsi, Pierluigi Raggi, Sergio Scaglietti.

Over the years, many others have made themselves available, frequently for more than one interview. For sharing their stories and insights, I would like to thank Peter Agg, Anna Bianchi Anderloni, C. Rino Argento, Remo Barbieri, Ron Barker, Helmut Becker, the late Aurelio Bertocchi, the late Nuccio Bertone, Rosanna Bizzarrini, Peter Brock, Milt Brown, Al Burtoni, Ian Callum, Mr. & Mrs. Guiseppe Caso, Engineer Cavallero, Francesco Colombo, Ermanno Cozza, Robert Cumberford, Venazio Di Biase, Salvatore Diomante, The Duke of Aosta, Piero Ferrari, Mauro Forghieri, Paul Frère, Tom Gale, Mike Gammino, Gene Garfinkle, the late Dante Giacosa, Fabrizio Giugiaro, Giorgetto Giugiaro, David Gooding at Christie's, Nori Harada, Peter Kalikow, Brandon Lawrence at Sports Car Italiano, Giovanni Lazzarini, the late Franco Lini, Daniele Lorenzon, Bob Lutz, Mario Marazzi, Franco Martinengo, the late Ron Miller, Giorgio Molinari, Luigi Molli, Bill Moore, Sandro Munari, Roberto Negri, the late Luigi Oriani, Horacio Pagani, Ivo Pera, Erminia Perego, Mike Perry, Lorenza Pininfarina, Giuliano Pizzi, Enzo Prearo, Bruce Qvale, Lorenzo Ramaciotti, Gino Recalcati, Frank Reisner, Paula Fray Reisner, Marion Rivolta, Rachele Rivolta, Piero Sala, Filippo Sapino, Giovanna Scaglione, Maria Luisa Scaglione, Ubaldo Scarzi, Paolo Stanzani, Romolo Tavoni, Orazio Veggian, Brenda Vernor, Count Giovanni Volpi di Misurata, Bob Wallace, Andrea Zagato, Elio Zagato, Maurizio Zanisi. I would also thank those who wished to remain anonymous.

It was a treat living their adventure while composing this book. Their memories greatly enriched my life, and for that I am eternally grateful.

Others were also helpful, particularly those who jumped through hoops on short notice to let me photograph their cars, or provide historic material. Three people in particular came through with the latter item: John Ling, and Lorenza Pininfarina and Francesco Pagni of Pininfarina SpA. Francesco was especially helpful, for I am sure I gave him more than one gray hair when asking for a wide range of material at the drop of a hat, no mean feat when Pininfarina was in the midst of preparing for the Turin Auto Show.

I would also like to thank Gian Beppe Panicco and his secretary Elizabeth at Carrozzeria Bertone, and Walter Miller. Panicco & Company provided some key photos, while Walter cracked the whip on his staff to make sure my urgent literature orders were handled properly.

Several people deserve special mention for providing cars. They are Bruce Trenery of Fantasy Junction, who had five cars available in the blink of an eye; Craig Davis, who provided another four in the same time span; Alfa fanatics Ken and Jeri Shaff for their dizzying array of Giuliettas and other "goodies"; John Mozart and Mike Hemus, with the latter shaking off a recent operation to come to my aid; and Italian collector extraordinaire Mario Righini, who let me stay way past my welcome when taking photos of his magnificent (and the only remaining) Auto Avio Costuzioni 815.

Additional cars were kindly provided by The Blackhawk Museum, John Bookout, Scott Borman, Alfredo Brener, Joe Brilando, Stephen Block, Milt Brown, Al Burtoni at Milano Imports, Bob Butler, Nicolas Cage, Todd Coady, Tom Coady, Rob Cole, De Tomaso SpA, Scott Emsley, Dennis Glavis at Ferrari of Los Gatos, Ray Jones, John Ling, Automobili Lamborghini, Brandon Lawrence at Sport Cars Italiano, Maserati SpA, Norb McNamara, Pagani Srl, Frank Palmer, Pininfarina SpA, Dane Prenovitz, Qvale Modena SpA, Piero Rivolta, Kevin Romak, Fred Roth, Tom Shaughnessy, Jon Shirley, Bob Smith of Bob Smith Coachworks, David Sydorick, Symbolic Motorcars.

Others who helped in locating cars, making sure my Italian was reasonable, translating, and god knows what else were Richard Adatto, Antonio Ferreira de Almeida of Maserati SpA, Alberto Armaroli of Automobili Lamborghini, *Automobile Quarterly* Archives, John Bagioli at Fiorano Motors, Mr. & Mrs. Pino Baldessari, Marjorie Bartlett, Henia Burtoni, Carlo Fiorani at Ferrari/Maserati USA, Dick Gale, Rick Gale, Liz Gardini, Graham Gauld, Ed Gilbertson, Guiseppe Greco at Automobili Lamborghini, John Hart at the Blackhawk Museum, Kurt & Leslie Hunter, Antonella Lunghi-Wemple, Lea Janeczko, Mark Ketcham, Gordon McCall, Norb McNamara, Sabra McNamara, Dick Merritt, Otis Meyer, Walter Miller, Glenn Mounger, Mr. & Mrs. Giorgio Nada, Sergio Nada, Stefano Nada, Jack Oliver, Grazia Pasvogel, Mike Perry, Mr. & Mrs. Walter Pittoni, Marella Rivolta, Renzo Rivolta, *Road & Track* Archives, Carl P. Schmitt, Julie Summerville, Federica Zanisi, Eugenio Zigliotto.

I am further indebted to Carlo Anderloni, Tom Tjaarda, Jonathan Stein of *Automobile Quarterly*, Matt Stone of *Motor Trend*, and Denise Hunter. The first four kept me honest by volunteering to proof the manuscript, and make sure there were no glaring errors or omissions. Miss Hunter put up with me being a stranger for a number of weeks, compliments of many late nights at the office.

Finally, special thanks go to my editor John Adams-Graf, Zack Miller, and Tim Parker at MBI Publishing Company. It was most pleasing that they believed in this "historical" approach, rather than the typical "bore, stroke, and dates" formula that is seen much too often.

If I have overlooked anyone, the omission is accidental, and I apologize.

Foreword

This book uses a novel approach to the history of the Italian sports car. As expected, it covers the landmark models from Ferrari, Alfa Romeo, Maserati, Cisitalia, and others.

What makes it different from other books is the way it makes the connection between these cars and the economic and social reality that existed at the time. It also explores Italy's history and ambiance.

Impressing me the most was the way Winston broke our history into distinct periods. How he was able to accomplish this I don't know, for his analysis in choosing the years to define each period is most impressive.

I applaud what he has done, and am most sincere when I say this is the best approach an author or researcher can use.

Sergio Pininfarina
Chairman, Pininfarina SpA

Introduction

New Yorker Peter Kalikow was a headstrong teenager in 1958. Well versed in America's burgeoning sports car movement, the future real estate magnate felt he knew them all and could rattle off specifications of 'Vettes, Jaguars, Mercedes, or Porsches without hesitation.

Kalikow's whole outlook changed when he stumbled upon Luigi Chinetti's Ferrari stand at the New York Auto Show. There stood a Series I 250 cabriolet—a car so staggeringly beautiful, so awe-inspiring, the astounded youth felt it existed on an entirely different plane from the world he knew.

It took Kalikow an hour to break the Ferrari's hypnotic spell. He excitedly returned home to convince his well-to-do father to visit the show and purchase the car. When the elder Kalikow learned its price tag was $12,000, "Why should I even consider something that doesn't have air conditioning and costs several times more than my Cadillac?" he chided the salesman.

But young Peter understood why. There were sports cars, then there were *Italian* sports cars. The more he researched, the more he realized that the southern European nation was the epicenter of the sports car universe.

So powerful, so influential was that perception that 11 years later he was in Italy, talking with many of the men he so admired about designing and manufacturing his new Chevrolet-powered gran turismo, the Momo Mirage. "It was the only place to go if you wanted to produce something sporty," Kalikow mused many years later.

Tom Tjaarda also had a life-altering experience in 1958. Then a junior at the University of Michigan, he had every intention of becoming an architect after graduation. Little did he realize a challenge thrown down by a professor would radically alter his career path.

The gauntlet was simple: Make a model of a new car. Although Tjaarda had no formal training in automotive design, he instinctively referenced what he felt were the world's most beautiful shapes—the slinky, perfectly proportioned sports cars of the "Italian school" that had dominated the international automotive magazines since the early 1950s.

Several months later, Tjaarda presented his professor with a scale model of a sports station wagon. So amazed was the teacher at its refinement and surface development that he immediately contacted Luigi Segre, head of the coachbuilding firm Ghia in Turin, Italy.

Without so much as an interview, Segre hired the young student. Four decades and 80-plus automotive designs later, Turin remains Tjaarda's home.

Flash forward to 1997, when Ian Callum was making a name for himself with Aston Martin's sensational DB7. That year, the famed British sports car manufacturer approached the talented Scottish designer to make a true supercar, a prototype that would serve notice to Ferrari that Aston meant business.

Wanting something that was beautiful yet forceful in personality, Callum naturally referenced landmark designs—Aston's own DB4 GT Zagato, a model designed in Italy in 1960, and a classic Ferrari of the same vintage, the 250 SWB. The result was Aston Martin's Project Vantage showcar, a beautiful bolide that captivated the international new car show circuit throughout 1998.

Spread over 40 years, these anecdotes succinctly illustrate that Italian sports cars have a special hold on us, influencing us like no other. Yet all too often writers, historians, and enthusiasts fall into the trap of focusing solely on the emotive "end product," the cars themselves.

An amazing story thus goes completely overlooked: one of a country and its people decimated by war that, within two decades, were basking in the automotive spotlight. But as the world beat a path to numerous doors in Turin, Milan, and Modena, Italy's burgeoning sports car and GT industry experienced a precipitous decline. Today, these same constructors and designers are making a concerted effort to return to the fore.

To truly comprehend what lies behind these seminal machines and their heritage, it is necessary to not only explore the cars but to learn about their creators, their historic ups and downs, and the macro- and micro-economic events that influenced them.

That epic tale is told in this book.

Section I
Laying the
Foundation

Sowing the Seeds

1900 - 1929

Italy's ascent to the world's sports car spotlight began decades before its golden postwar years. In the early 1900s, Italian performance cars were rudimentary, large displacement, front-engined machines made by companies such as Fiat, OM, SCAT, and Isotta-Fraschini. Successful in races at home and abroad, their torpedo-shaped bodies and competition raison d'etre made them generally unsuitable for road use.

Their development and production ceased when Italy entered World War I in 1915. At the end of hostilities four years later, for the great majority of the nation's populace, the automobile remained an object beyond their comprehension, financial reach, and, most important, imagination.

That started to change when Milan hosted Italy's first postwar motor show in 1921. The following year, Fiat completed construction of its large Lingotto factory (complete with a 2/3-mile-long test track on the roof) on the outskirts of the industrial city of Turin. Still, the automobile had a long way to go before entrenching itself in the national psyche.

Italy remained politically fragmented after World War I, the cessation of wartime production causing its underlying economic shortcomings to reappear with a vengeance. Lockouts, strikes, and violence were common, as were banking and corporate failures.

The ongoing turmoil and lack of decisive leadership brought former left-wing journalist Benito Mussolini to power. Riding a large wave of groundswell support in the working class in October 1922, he was appointed prime minister by King

Fiat is the granddaddy of all Italian manufacturers. Founded in 1899 by Giovanni Agnelli and two counts, the name stands for "Fabbrica Italiana Automobili Torino." By the mid-1920s, Fiat was the country's dominant industrial concern. During the company's formative years, Fiats actively campaigned around the world, and were quite successful in competition on both sides of the Atlantic. These early competition roots led to many Fiat production sports cars.

This 1913 Isotta-Fraschini KM4 typifies early sporting machinery: all engine and little else. The KM's four-cylinder powerplant displaced more than 10 liters and propelled the car to 80-plus miles per hour. The fenders have been removed by the owner because of vibration at high speeds on long-distance jaunts.

Vitorio Emanuele. For the next several years, Mussolini called upon Italians to devote themselves to national goals while he quietly but efficiently eliminated political opposition.

In January 1925, Mussolini declared Italy a Fascist state, appointing himself as dictator. Over the next decade, *Il Duce* and his government would periodically use its power to benefit the automotive industry.

One such recipient was Italy's famed endurance race, the Mille Miglia. Because long-distance competition was gaining prestige in the eyes of the world's manufacturers and public as a way to demonstrate reliability and test new ideas, the Mille was to be run on public roads from Brescia to Rome and back, covering a 1,000-mile distance (thus, the "Mille Miglia" title).

One of the race's four fathers was Giovanni Canestrini, an influential journalist and decorated airman. After the idea was hatched in his apartment in December 1926, Canestrini announced its formation in Italy's widely read *Gazzetto dello Sport* newspaper, the headline declaring "The Mille Miglia . . . Will Be the Most Important Manifestation of Italian Motor Sport Ever." After great public outcry, the Fascist government's second-in-command, Secretary-General Arturo Turati, quelled vocal opposition by enlisting the cooperation of the police, civil, and military authorities.

The initial race was held on March 26, 1927, and positive reaction was immediate. "Motorsport . . . was now making headway with the general public," author Luciano Greggio wrote in his tome on the coachbuilding firm Bertone, observing that first Mille Miglia "set the seal on motor racing as a popular spectacle."

As interest in racing increased, a quiet revolution transformed the way Italy manufactured personal transportation. "When someone wanted a car, they bought a complete running chassis at the factory," noted Carlo Felice Bianchi Anderloni, who was then a young boy who would rise to automotive prominence as a manager and designer in the late 1940s. "The owner then went to a *carrozzeria*, an independent coachbuilder that made the body for his car." As these types of firms had been making horse-drawn carriages since the late 16th century, "they were an important side of the production process," Anderloni continued, "for they were the ones who actually finished the car."

The profound changes in production efficiency started at Fiat in the first half of the 1920s. Influenced by Ford's modern assembly line methods, not only did Italy's lone mega-manufacturer start producing more chassis and bodies in-house, but as new manufacturing techniques spread throughout the industry the coachbuilders were forced to examine their production methods as well. Because long-established production techniques were not efficient for series production, steel and aluminum started taking the place of wooden body panels.

This gave rise to "panel-beating" departments, sections where skilled craftsmen hand-formed panels to cover the car's wooden frame. Spray painting also became a prerequisite, replacing the brush.

The second element of change came from France and also dramatically affected car body construction methods. Because chassis were not particularly rigid, in the early 1920s airplane designer Charles Weymann developed a method using a wooden frame joined by small strips of metal; the "Weymann system" also featured rubber bushings between the body and chassis and special screws. Car bodies now had "elasticity," allowing them to adjust as the chassis flexed. This produced a boom in reliability and, more important, eliminated the mandatory use of 90-degree angles necessary with wood construction.

Coachbuilders and manufacturers from Turin to Milan embraced the system and were soon using it under license. By the late 1920s, the Italians would develop their own manufacturing techniques, allowing their inherent design talent to blossom.

The country's expanding middle class also fueled change. With public interest in competition—and the offshoot desire for sporting cars—increasing, "Something was ripening," Battista "Pinin" Farina noted in his autobiography, *Born with the Automobile*. Then an important figure in his brother Giovanni's firm, Carrozzeria Farina, Pinin observed "a new market, one comprised of young people and women especially, was coming to know the car. . . . The convertible came into fashion . . . (and) there was the introduction of the (financing) method of buying." Emotion-based advertising in magazines also started appearing, further feeding the public's burgeoning interest.

Companies moved in to meet demand. The upstart Maserati brothers produced their first three cars in Bologna in 1926, while

established Brescia-based manufacturer OM swept the top three spots in the first Mille Miglia. On the street, sporty-looking cars such as Fiat's 519 S and 509 S and Lancia's swoopy Lambda Sport by Carrozzeria Ca.Sa.Ro were starting to be seen.

If there was one true benefactor of these changes, it was the company that would bring international prominence to Italy's nascent sports car revolution, Alfa Romeo. Founded in June 1910 on the outskirts of Milan, the firm was originally named A.L.F.A. (Anonima Lombardo Fabbrica Automobili). In its earliest days, it manufactured airplane engines and large, sturdy cars.

An A.L.F.A. first competed in April 1911 at the 1,500 kilometer, five-stage Modena Trials. Thanks to its class-winning showing, competition would become a cornerstone of the company. Soon, A.L.F.A.s were participating in other events such as Sicily's grueling Targa Florio.

Yet Alfa's rise to sports car stardom was not without problems. Strikes from 1912 to 1914 caused great hardship, for the concern was suffering from insufficient operating capital, a malady afflicting numerous automotive firms.

In August 1915 industrialist Nicola Romeo became A.L.F.A.'s majority shareholder. Then 39, Romeo was born in the province of Naples. He graduated from the Naples Politechnic with a civil engineering degree, then moved to Leige to obtain a degree in electrical engineering. In 1902 he migrated to Milan and became a powerful industrialist over the next decade, producing mining machinery and portable compressors.

From a cash flow perspective, Romeo's involvement with A.L.F.A. was perfectly timed. When Italy entered World War I, the company's automotive production was replaced by munitions,

Alfa Romeo's sporting heritage can be traced back to its very first cars. This 24 HP Tipo Corsa dates from 1910, the year the company was founded as A.L.F.A. (Anomima Lombarda Fabbrica Automobili; the Romeo name was added in 1915). The 24 HP's four-liter, four-cylinder engine produced 42 horsepower at 2,200 rpm.

A.L.F.A.'s 40-60 HP was introduced in 1913 to satisfy those clients who felt that 24 horsepower wasn't sporty enough. Its 6-liter, four-cylinder engine was good for 70 horsepower and gave the car a listed top speed of approximately 75 miles per hour. While a Corsa (competition) is pictured here, the chassis was versatile enough to be fitted with more luxurious coachwork.
Automobile Quarterly Publications

war materiel, and tractors, and its workforce ballooned to 2,500. A surge in operating revenue followed.

After the war, the company changed its name to Alfa Romeo, and automotive production resumed. Almost immediately, Alfa was haunted by the return of cash flow problems and labor strife. Although cars managed to trickle out of the factory in Portello, the firm was brought to its knees in 1922 when one of its largest creditors failed.

In 1923 the crisis was resolved in part by intervention from Mussolini, and the company debuted its first true postwar car, the R.L. In addition to the Normale, Alfa manufactured a handful of R.L. Sports. Having a 3-liter engine that produced 71 horsepower at 3,500 rpm, an R.L. Sport won 1923's Targa Florio race.

By 1924, Alfa was a magnet for talented personnel, its payroll boasting names such as engineers Luigi Bazzi and Vittorio Jano and drivers Enzo Ferrari, Guiseppe Campari, and Antonio Ascari. This enthusiastic cadre of men and the Targa Florio victory convinced Nicola Romeo that continual participation in international competition was the best way to promote the company.

Helping secure Alfa Romeo's road to sports car fame—and acting as a harbinger of what was to come in Italy—was Portello's close relationship with Carrozzeria Zagato. Founded in 1919, the driving force behind the coachbuilding firm was Ugo Zagato.

Described by his son Elio as "the man I most admired and respected; he was full of good ideas, able to contemplate and foresee the future," Ugo was born in 1890, the youngest of five children. At age 15 he left his impoverished home environment to work at a foundry in Germany.

He returned to Italy four years later for military duty and was discharged within two months. Zagato then worked at Carrozzeria Varesina in Milan for six years and was sent to Turin in 1915 to assist in the design and construction of airplanes when Italy entered World War I.

Upon the war's conclusion, Zagato returned to Milan to start his own carrozzeria, his mind filled with aeronautic construction techniques. Recalling why he desired his own company, "It is better to be a small owner than an important employee," he once noted. Early commissions included bodies on Fiat, Diatto, and Alfa's R.L. chassis.

In the mid-1920s, Alfa chief engineer Vittorio Jano instructed one of his test drivers to pay Zagato a visit with the prototype 6C 1500. After designing and constructing its beautifully proportioned lightweight aluminum body, the Zagato Alfa proved incredibly durable in 10,000-plus kilometers of testing. "(It) was a fantastic car," former Alfa test driver Giovanbattista Guidotti told Italian journalist Michele Marchiano. "It seemed like it was glued to the road even when we encountered stretches of gravel. Driving it gave me a new feel: that of total security. To look at her was like looking at a work of art. . . ."

And so started a long-standing collaboration between the two firms. With Alfa now Zagato's principal client, the coachbuilder moved next to the Alfa factory in 1928. Within months, Zagato-bodied Alfas were dominating sporting events such as the Mille Miglia, and the relationship became an instrumental part in creating Italy's enviable global reputation for producing outstanding "dual-purpose" cars: those that could be used successfully in serious competition by top drivers and appeal to the sportsman (such as Zagato-Alfa owner Mussolini) who wanted to compete or drive quickly on the street.

Another piece of Italy's sports car puzzle inadvertently fell into place in the late 1920s when racing driver Enzo Ferrari formed the *Scuderia Ferrari*. This "Stable of Ferrari" was based approximately 100 miles south of Milan in Modena, a town described by then youthful resident and future coachbuilder extraordinaire Sergio Scaglietti as "primarily countryside, with just a few foundries as the only industrial base."

Then in his early 30s, Ferrari was the youngest son of a well-to-do metal shop owner residing several miles outside Modena in Carpi. Although Enzo saw his first motor race at age 10 on the outskirts of Bologna, it would be several years before the automobile would play a major role in his life.

In his early teens, Ferrari wanted to become a tenor or sports writer. By age 16, he was freelancing for the newspapers *La Provincia di Modena* and *La Gazzetta dello Sport*.

In 1917, two years after his father and brother died from illness, Ferrari was drafted into the military. After returning home with an illness that left him hospitalized, he headed to Turin to find work. Turned down by Fiat, Ferrari found a job at a small firm in Bologna that stripped trucks for their chassis, which were then used for cars.

One of the company's customers was the Italo-Argentina coachworks, based in Milan. When in the thriving city, Ferrari often visited the Vittorio Emanuele bar, an established hangout for racing drivers and others connected with the automotive world. Here, he met Ugo Sivocci, a former bicycle racer who worked for CMN, a short-lived Milanese auto maker.

In 1919, Sivocci hired Ferrari as a test driver. An uncertain but ambitious, persuasive young man, Ferrari managed to convince CMN's management to let him race their cars. He did this over the next several months, then joined Alfa Romeo in 1920. The Targa Florio was his first race with Alfa, where he finished second.

Alfa Romeo's RLSS (Super Sport) debuted in 1925 and is distinguished by its V-shaped radiator. Here, one is seen in 1927 as it participates in Italy's Mille Miglia. Although an OM won that first edition of the famed 1,000-mile race, Alfa Romeo dominated it and numerous other venues over the next 10 years.

Alfa Romeo's victory parade greatly increased when the company joined forces with Ugo Zagato's Carrozzeria Zagato. Thanks to his background in aircraft construction, the Milan-based coachbuilder was noted for lightweight construction techniques. One of the most famous Alfa-Zagato models was the 1750 GS; seen here is the car that won the 1930 Mille Miglia.

Although Ferrari enjoyed intermittent competition success in the 1920s, for much of the decade he was an instrumental force behind the scenes, contributing to Alfa's success in other ways. In addition to luring both Bazzi and Jano from Fiat, Ferrari was the instigator of one of the company's earliest performance models, the 20/30 ES Sport.

As the decade came to a close, Ferrari realized his future was not behind the wheel. "I found myself overwhelmed by an almost morbid desire to do something for the motor car, for this creature I was passionately fond of," he noted in his memoirs. "So although I was doing well enough to justify pursuing a driving career, I had my sights set on wider, more ambitious horizons."

And thus was born the Scuderia Ferrari in autumn 1929. One night at a dinner party with Alfredo and Augusto Caniato, enthusiast fiber merchants from Ferrara, the three decided to start a company composed of driver-owners—the firm would prepare the cars and offer proper technical support to its racing owners.

As the men toasted their idea, like much of Italy they were joyfully oblivious to the economic and political turmoil that lay just ahead. Nor could they even remotely fathom that one day Enzo Ferrari would become the most visible man in the sports car world.

Convergence

2

1930-1939

Alfa Romeo began the 1930s as it had ended the 1920s: dominating Italy's sports car and competition scene. In 1930 a Zagato-bodied Alfa 1750 won the Mille Miglia, the first of Alfa's eight victories that decade at the 1,000-mile classic.

Portello also faired well at other races, a testament to its commitment to competition back in 1911. Besides being victorious at Le Mans from 1931 to 1934, Alfas reigned supreme at Sicily's grueling Targa Florio from 1930 to 1935 and had similar results at Pescara, both in grand prix and sports car races.

Yet the company was hardly racking up the victories alone. From that first toast in 1929, Enzo Ferrari's Scuderia Ferrari had access to sports racers such as Zagato-bodied 6C 1500s and 1750s.

So why would Alfa Romeo willingly offer its newest machinery to someone outside the firm? Not only did Ferrari have the Alfa franchise for the Emilia region, "(They) never saw the Scuderia 'as a competitor,'" Ferrari noted in his memoirs. "I always used to keep (them) informed about my own experiments with the cars and about what our competitors were doing. In this way the Scuderia became a small detachment of ultra-loyal Alfa clients who shared a common passion for racing, as well as engineering and financial interests."

The benefits of the arrangement were quickly obvious. According to historian Luigi Orsini's profile of the Scuderia Ferrari in *Automobile Quarterly*, Ferrari entered 22 races in 1930, the Scuderia scoring eight victories. "Enzo Ferrari had become a celebrity, something of a sensation," Orsini noted, "more so certainly as an organizer than he ever was as a racing driver."

The strength of this relationship—and a testament to how far the man had come in 10 years—was seen in early 1933 when Alfa announced its withdrawal from single-seater racing: Enzo persuaded them to let *him* continue using their formidable P3. Not only did the Scuderia Ferrari win the Grand Prix at Pescara that year, but it also came in first overall at the

This Touring-built 8C 2900 Alfa Romeo represented the epitome of elegance and style in the late 1930s and showed the versatility of applying a racing chassis to sports car design. So timeless is its appeal that six decades later several American hot rodders were using the rear-wheel styling motif. *Automobile Quarterly Publications*

Mille Miglia in an 8C 2300, leading a barrage of Alfas that swept the top 10 spots.

As victory begot victory, it was natural that Alfa would apply the lessons learned in competition to its street cars. But racing success wasn't the only strong influence on the company's offerings. Now, all of Italy's manufacturers were grasping the importance of a car's appearance.

Catalyzing this trend was the *concours d'elegance*. Although these "contests of beauty" existed during the previous decade, in the 1930s they were actively promoted by Mussolini's Fascist government. As Italian consumers caught on to the benefits of style, they "began to demand cars that would establish the difference between themselves and others who were fortunate enough to possess a private means of transport," author Luciano Greggio points out in *Bertone*. "[D]emand for the custom built special, with all that the term implies in terms of perceived social status and social climbing, was beginning to make itself felt."

Often held at elegant resorts such as Lake Como's luxurious Villa d'Este, helping to propel the concours to prominence was the fashion industry. Clothing designers would debut apparel and provide models, all done to complement the car being shown.

Although concourses were becoming a serious social happening—a fashion show and an exhibition of art and industrial style all rolled into one—they truly came of age in 1931 with the

debut of Carrozzeria Touring's groundbreaking Flying Star. One of the most breathtaking designs of the decade, industry outsiders would have been surprised to learn the man behind the look was originally trained as a lawyer. Yet to those who knew him, Felice Bianchi Anderloni was destined to become involved with the automobile.

The third of Emilio and Linda Anderloni's five children, Felice was born in Rome on April 28, 1882. Although his father was a railway engineer, "my grandmother pushed him to study law," says Felice's son Carlo. "Despite this, since his teens, he was always interested in cars."

Undoubtedly fueling the fire was his three sisters marrying the founders of Isotta-Fraschini, Cesare Isotta, and Vicenzo and Antonio Fraschini. In 1904 the company hired Felice as a test driver. He eventually became chief of the experimental department, where he worked closely with Bindo Maserati. From 1921 to 1924, Felice successfully raced Isotta's Tipo 8, often while wearing an elegant suit and bow tie.

In 1925, Anderloni and lawyer Gaetano Ponzoni bought an ailing Milanese coachbuilder, Carrozzeria Falco. The following year they changed the name to Touring, as "it was a word that was easily pronounced all over the world," Carlo says.

Having connections throughout the industry, Anderloni immediately had a number of clients such as Isotta-Fraschini,

Alfa Romeo, Fiat, and Lancia. And though Touring won several prizes on the concours circuit, its shapes were like most everyone else's, pleasant but conventional.

The Flying Star changed all that. Drawn in January 1931, it was based on a design originally intended for an OM two years earlier. Breaking cover at the Genoa-Nervi Concours on an Isotta Fraschini 8A chassis, that stunning body reeked of elegance, wealth, and speed, thanks to its sweptback windscreens, brilliant exterior accents, and cut-down doors.

Although the Isotta Flying Star would win a prize at Genoa, and another would star at the Milan Motor Show in mid-April, the best was yet to come. That September, a third Flying Star on an Alfa 1750 GS chassis debuted at the prestigious Villa d' Este concours d'elegance.

Done for Josette Pozzo of Genoa, Anderloni's styling master stroke on the Alfa was breaking up the running board, causing the front and rear sections to interweave just in front of the door. On the smaller 1750 chassis, this gave the design even more grace, propelling it to win the coveted "Golden Cup," the concours' top prize, over the more regal Isotta.

Now, Alfa was no longer the domain of Zagato. For the balance of the decade, sporty Alfa Romeos emanated from Touring's Milan-based works. Standouts included the 1932 and 1933 Mille Miglia–winning 8C 2300 that featured a 142-horsepower, 2.3-liter supercharged eight-cylinder engine.

Even more spectacular was one of the most beautiful cars ever made, a Touring-bodied 8C 2900 B. This immortal Alfa model had a 2.9-liter supercharged eight-cylinder engine that produced 180 horsepower. Capable of 115 miles per hour, it was based on the 8C 2900 A that swept the top three spots in the 1936 Mille Miglia.

Touring's tour de force appeared in 1937. Having spats over the rear wheels that featured strakes, the 8C 2900 B had the motif along the side that first appeared on the Flying Stars. Touring also produced some effective, sporty designs on Lancia's Astura chassis.

Although Touring's open and closed coachwork would become even more fluid as the decade came to a close, one Turinese carrozzeria would give Anderloni and Company a run for its money as Italy's design leader. In early 1930, Battista "Pinin" Farina decided to start his own firm by leaving his brother Giovanni's well-established Carrozzeria Farina.

Then 37, Pinin was the 10th of 11 children. He started working for Giovanni at age 11, eventually becoming head of design. In 1920, Pinin traveled to America to study the country's advanced construction techniques, methods that were put to good use when he was spurred on to start his own company by his friend Vincenzo Lancia.

Like Anderloni, Pinin was blessed with innate talent and an eye that could exploit it. Described as "very curious" by his son Sergio, Farina was a self-taught man who learned English from listening to music. More important, the younger Pininfarina notes

his father was "a very good technician who had good intuition of aerodynamics. He was a master of forms, with very good taste and a great sense of balance."

All these elements crystallized in the winter of 1934. "In my own work during those months I was thinking about the shape of the wind," Pinin recalled in his autobiography, *Born with the Automobile*. "In the mountains I used to see how the wind sculpted the snow at the edges of the road, digging out different shapes, curved in some places and sharp where it was broken. The wind even shaped the trees. I wanted to 'copy' those lines for my designs."

Like Anderloni and Touring in Milan, Pinin Farina embarked on a mission to make ever more efficient shapes. Sports car chassis were often used, the results of testing applied to the next version.

In 1935, Pinin showed two Alfa Romeo 6C 2300 Pescara Coupe Aerodinamicos. Both had a lovely harmony of lines, enclosed rear wheels, and a long hood and sloping fastback. Their general proportions and sweptback radiator and windscreen later appeared on other Pinin Farina designs such as a one-off Lancia Astura roadster.

The following year, Pinin truly came into his own when he debuted a new Alfa 6C 2300 Pescara and a Lancia Astura cabriolet at the Milan Motor Show. The Alfa's molded forms, headlamps concealed in the body for additional streamlining, and smooth mudguards front and rear, caused the press to dub Pinin "a futurist."

Yet the styling of those two cars looked tame once his Lancia Aprilia Berlinetta Aerodinamica (aerodynamic fastback) broke cover later that year. With a startling teardrop shape approved by Vincenzo Lancia several months before his death, "I was aiming for essentiality," Pinin noted in his memoirs, observing that he had learned "what you take off counts more than what you add on."

In the mid-1930s, Battista "Pinin" Farina was at the forefront of Italy's aerodynamic movement. This 1935 Alfa 6C 2300 Pescara Coupe demonstrates the maturing of the berlinetta (fastback) look and the elimination of the running boards.

Pinin Farina was continually pushing aerodynamic forms. This 1936 Alfa 6C 2300 Pescara coupe was made in aluminum and is novel in its streamlining of the headlights. A third headlight is mounted in the radiator grille.

Pinin Farina's avant garde Lancia Aprilia Berlinetta Aerodinamica broke cover in 1936 and was the first of several aerodynamic specials the coachbuilder made on the chassis over the next two years. "I was aiming for essentiality (with that car)," Pinin reflected years later.

With a rakish nose and windscreen, faired-in windows, hidden wheels and long, tapered rear, the experimental Lancia cleared 100 miles per hour, no mean feat for a car with a 47-horsepower engine. "I had drawn the Aprilia's shape to be like the section of an airplane wing," Pinin observed. "For the first time I was at ease in designing a big, curving windscreen."

That confidence showed in future Pinin Farina designs. In 1937 two fabulous Lancia Austura Berlina Aerodinamicas were built. Other cars demonstrating lessons learned from that radical

Aprilia were a sporty Fiat 6C 1500 roadster, another Aprilia berlinetta that won its class at the 1938 Mille Miglia, and a sensational 8C 2900 Cabriolet Aerodinamico that won first prize at the 1939 Turin Concours d' elegance.

Although Touring and Pinin Farina were clearly the trendsetters, they weren't acting alone. Other coachbuilders such as Bertone, Ghia, Boneschi, and Viotti and the influential independent stylist Mario Revelli also experimented with wind-cheating forms. Wanting to play into Italy's obsession with aerodynamics throughout the 1930s (the 1934 Milan Motor Show was dedicated to the subject) and tap into the public's increasing interest in sports and custom-built cars, coachbuilders started prospecting dealers to sell their wares alongside mass production automobiles.

One of the first to do so was Turin's Carrozzeria Bertone. Founded in 1912 by Giovanni Bertone, in 1934 he was joined by his 20-year-old son, Nuccio. As the younger Bertone had spent several years working in the company after school, he was soon criss-crossing Italy, visiting dealers, while his father watched over the business.

Although Nuccio was able to secure several orders, the firm that truly brought the sports car to the masses was Fiat. From

1930 to 1932, it offered the cheeky 514S and CA. Having a 1,438-cc inline four-cylinder engine, the 514 featured a classic two-seat roadster body. It was capable of clearing 65 miles per hour, and more than 500 514s were built. Several were tuned for additional horsepower by Siata, a small Turinese firm founded in 1926 by racing driver Giorgio Ambrosini.

Fiat's next sports car was the 508S Balilla Sport. It debuted at the Villa d'Este Concours in 1932, featuring a rugged 30-horsepower 995-cc four-cylinder engine. Designed at Carrozzeria Ghia, its lovely styling is normally attributed to the prolific free-lancer Mario Revelli.

In 1934, Fiat offered the Balilla Sport with 36 horsepower. Able to top 70 miles per hour, several were given aerodynamic berlinetta bodies and raced at the Mille Miglia in 1935. Sadly, a version of this car was never offered for sale to the public.

In 1935, Fiat supplemented the Balilla with the 1500. With a 1,493-cc inline six-cylinder engine and sporty suspension system, the 1500 platform soon became a favorite of the coachbuilders. Pinin Farina experimented with the chassis, offering an extremely well-proportioned, one-off, two-seat roadster in 1937. Ghia and Revelli teamed up again in 1938 for an aerodynamic berlinetta.

Helping to convince Fiat's stodgy, numbers-minded management to make sports cars were politically adroit engineers such as Dante Giacosa. Born on January 3, 1905, Giacosa's interest in things automotive began at a very young age. "I was quite curious," he recalled, "and liked to make things with my hands. There was a civil engineer living in our house who was designing a car, and I followed his progress closely. When it did not work that well, he went back to designing houses."

Still, the seeds were planted, and Giacosa graduated in 1927 with an engineering degree. After being hired by Fiat subsidiary SPA in 1928, he transferred to Fiat's Lingotto factory the following year. By the mid-1930s, he was a rapidly rising star in the company's engineering ranks.

While experimenting on the production 508 and 1500, Giacosa uncovered a latent love of aerodynamics. He made a van that, to everyone's surprise, was faster than the car upon which it was based. "This meant the van's aerodynamics were superior," the engineer recalls with a gleam in his eye. "The only difference between the two was the shape of the rear."

From these experiments came the 508 C MM. After trying several 1:5 scale models in the Turin Politechnic college's wind tunnel, a prototype coupe was built by Carrozzeria Savio in 1937. One would race in the 1938 Mille Miglia, where it would win its class.

Often Giacosa enthusiastically tested his own creations. While his team constructed the aerodynamic 508 C, "(engineer Antonio) Fessia and I spent our days off trying out the (1500) 8B," Giacosa wrote in his autobiography, *Forty Years of Design with Fiat*. "Its six-cylinder engine and the sporting qualities it got from its independent suspension made us eager to drive it flat out along the road that—in those days—was practically deserted.

This spectacular one-off 1938 Alfa Romeo 8C 2900 cabriolet is also the work of Pinin Farina. It won first prize at the 1939 Turin Concours d'Elegance and exhibits a wonderful blend of aerodynamics and elegance.

The model that brought sports cars within the reach of the average Italian was Fiat's 508 Balilla. First seen at the 1932 Villa d'Este Concours d'Elegance, its well-balanced lines are normally attributed to influential freelancer Mario Revelli and was built at Turin-based Carrozzeria Ghia. *Automobile Quarterly Publications*

Fiat's slippery 508 C MM reflects engineer Dante Giacosa's fascination with aerodynamics. Using a standard 1937 42-horsepower 508 as its base, "The only available way to increase the speed was to refine the shape of the coachwork," the engineer observed years later.

We were speed mad, not the least worried by the immense flurry of dust rising behind us."

This passion and successful experimentation would lead to Giacosa's role in one of the postwar era's most influential sports cars.

While Italy's manufacturers and coachbuilders offered ever-more interesting sports and production cars, the country's roads were often deserted for good reasons. Wall Street's crash in 1929 had an adverse effect on the economy and automotive industry. With banking institutions collapsing and automotive sales falling dramatically, established names such as OM went under, while Isotta-Fraschini had to be bought out by airplane manufacturing magnate Count Giovanni Caproni.

Even all-conquering Alfa Romeo was not immune. In 1933 the company's ownership was transferred from the failed Banca Nazionale di Sconto to the government-backed IRI (Institute of Industrial Reconstruction). In December of that year, Ugo Gobbato, one of Europe's leading industrial management experts, was put in charge of the company.

To combat economic collapse, Italy's Fascist government instituted a number of reforms and started an intensive program of public works. Making the situation more tenuous was Europe's contentious political landscape. "Only a blind man would not have seen the huge clouds which were growing on the horizon," Pinin

noted in his autobiography when referring to the mid-1930s. "The political speeches on the radio sounded like fanfares too.

"One day a friend had something curious to say to me, recalling that some time earlier I had bodied some armor-plated cars. 'Pinin,' he said, 'I fear that you will be promoted to tank constructor.'

"I touched wood, then he went on, 'Everyone takes their own precautions, fear makes you do strange things. When people prepare armor for going out in the street, it is a bad sign.'

"It was to be many years before we got rid of that fear. . . .'"

In 1935, Italy went to war with Ethiopia. Based on a conflict dating back to 1896, the campaign lasted six months, Mussolini's forces returning home victorious. Strangely, the resulting brief economic downturn would have a tremendous impact on Italy's postwar sports car boom, and the city of Modena in particular.

One piece of the puzzle was Maserati. Founded nine years earlier by the four Maserati brothers, the small firm made a name producing racing cars. In 1930 a single-seat 26M won the Real Premio in Rome, the model's success propelling Maserati to display cars the following year at the Milan Motor Show. With coachwork by Castagna and Zagato, these sports racers were clearly aimed at private buyers.

Such joy was short-lived for Italy's fledgling Alfa Romeo competitor. In March 1932, Alfieri Maserati passed away during surgery. Then 44, he was highly regarded in the motoring industry and Bologna, the company's hometown. Two days after his death there was a huge funeral procession, people filling the streets to mourn his passing.

Ernesto, Bindo, and Ettore Maserati gamely soldiered on. Although production would eventually rise from 9 cars in 1930 to 17 in 1935, it was clear that Alfieri was the most gifted of the brothers. This became most apparent during the Ethiopian conflict, when Maserati's output fell in half.

In 1937 production returned to 17 cars, and the firm set a speed record with a radical, streamlined car built at Carrozzeria Viotti in Turin. Still, if the Maseratis had learned anything during the downturn of 1936, it was their lack of managerial talent and financial wherewithal to weather another storm.

To ensure their survival, in late 1937 they sold controlling interest in their company to industrialist Adolfo Orsi. The head of Gruppo Orsi, a wide-ranging industrial and agricultural consortium, Adolfo was born in Modena, some 30 miles to the north of Bologna. The oldest of five children, he was forced to leave school at a young age to help support the family when his father unexpectedly passed away.

Ambitious, smart, and keenly perceptive of people, Orsi started out with nothing, making ends meet by selling second-hand clothes and scrap metal to foundries. As business expanded, he became the largest scrap dealer in the Emilia region, causing him to send metal outside the area to be converted into iron; this would lead Orsi to start his own railway concern and construct his own foundries. Later, he would form his own agricultural company and own Fiat dealerships.

By the mid-1930s, Orsi was an immensely wealthy man, his consortium having more than 2,000 employees. In 1939, Orsi moved Maserati to Modena, locating it near his Gruppo Orsi headquarters in the center of town.

At the same time, the second piece of the puzzle that would vault Modena to postwar sports car fame occurred when Enzo Ferrari broke up with Alfa Romeo. Like Maserati, the Scuderia was directly affected by Italy's invasion of Ethiopia. When France placed sanctions on its neighbor, Frenchman Rene Dreyfus, one of the team's key drivers, felt he had no choice but to leave the organization.

"You have to understand the period to (grasp) the enormity of what Ferrari accomplished," Dreyfus related to Orsini in *Automobile Quarterly*. "There had never been anything like the team he had, never anything that big and so well organized—And the problems—the interference from the Fascists, the sensitivity of relations with Alfa, the personality problems and rivalries within the team.

"Yet despite all this, there was no doubt he was the 'Boss'— and the only Boss. If you raced for Mercedes or Auto Union or even the Alfa works team, you raced by committee—the Scuderia was his dream. He was the whole thing."

It is thus no wonder the divorce was acrimonious. The marriage likely started to unravel in 1937 when engineer Vittorio Jano resigned from his head of design position after Ugo Gobbato hired Spaniard Wilfredo Ricart as a technical consultant. Thanks to a clash of personalities, Ferrari immediately disliked the talented Ricart, the situation exacerbated by a strong difference of engineering opinion.

Ferrari was also having difficulties with Gobbato. With the well-funded onslaught of Germany's Mercedes-Benz and Auto Union teams leading to victory after victory, Alfa's managing director preferred "everything planned in advance, down to the last detail," Ferrari noted in his memoirs. Yet Enzo felt a racing car best resulted from a small group that responded quickly to a flexible management.

"Not many agreed with me and there were times Jano and I and the drivers found ourselves muttering together like conspirators in the Alfa Romeo yard," he observed. "In the end I was

Thanks to the success of the 1931 Flying Star, Touring quickly became one of Alfa Romeo's favored coachbuilders. This sporty 6C 1750 displays the company's hallmark perfect proportioning.

Touring made the handsome coachwork for this Alfa Romeo 8C 2900. A similar car won the 1938 Mille Miglia and perfectly illustrates the early roots of Italy's enviable reputation for constructing true "dual-purpose" cars: machines that could be driven on the street and compete successfully on the track.

sacked, which seemed to be the only logical solution to the situation that had developed." His cherished Scuderia was liquidated in 1939, Ferrari signing a clause stating he could not produce a car under his own name for four years.

With money and ambition burning holes in his pockets and heart, Ferrari formed a new company, Auto Avio Costruzioni. Remaining in his downtown Modena location, Ferrari quickly went to work, making a new car.

To head the project's design and development, Enzo hired 45-year-old Alberto Massimino, an experienced engineer who moved to Modena in 1938 to work with Ferrari on Alfa's Tipo 158 race car. Joining them were technicians Luigi Bazzi, Federico Giberti, and engineers Vittorio Bellentani and Gioachino Colombo.

With material shortages becoming more acute and wanting to produce a car as quickly as possible, Ferrari and his men used the Giacosa-designed Fiat 508 C as their starting point. They reinforced the chassis, but left the independent front suspension, brakes, transmission, and steering largely untouched.

For the engine, they started with its four-cylinder 1100 engine, then shrunk its bore and stroke from 68x75 millimeters to 63x60 millimeters. By casting a new block and cylinder heads to join two engines, the resulting inline eight-cylinder displaced 1,496 cc. In final form, it produced 72 horsepower at 5,500 rpm.

Ferrari turned to old Alfa ally Carrozzeria Touring to style his car. Felice Bianchi Anderloni's son Carlo, then a 23-year-old cadet in the military who would eventually succeed his father in the business, clearly remembers the elder Anderloni mentioning Enzo paying Touring a visit. "My father said he wanted something that could be recognized at a glance as a Ferrari," the younger Anderloni recalls, not realizing at the time he would hear the exact same words a decade later. "Ferrari was obviously thinking of some type of production, for he wanted his car to have a touch of luxury."

After making the first designs, the elder Anderloni turned to his "visualizers," men inside Touring like who would make his

concepts into reality. A 1:10 model was then built and tested in the wind tunnel.

The first car was then constructed and tested on the road; Anderloni says Touring often used two stretches between Milan and Bergamo, and Milan and Como. They would cover the car in felt strips, then follow the test subject in a second car, with a photographer snapping away. Once the photos were developed, they would look at the felt strips to analyze the airflow.

Two Auto Avio Costruzioni 815s (eight cylinders, 1.5 liters) were built, their official first outing was the 1940 Gran Premio Brescia della Mille Miglia. Run at the end of April, this one-time event was a substitute for the Mille Miglia, which was suspended in 1938 after an accident killed seven people. Ferrari's 815s would finish 11th and 12th in the 1,500-cc class, an admirable achievement for a car designed and constructed in four months.

Still the most impressive achievement was the 815s being built at all. Because the threat of war hung over Europe, in the late 1930s regional conflicts such as Spain's bloody civil war antagonized an already tense situation. In 1939 the battle ended in victory for Franco, "a victory shared by Mussolini and Hitler," Pinin noted in his autobiography. "Italy seemed proud of itself and acted as if it were confident of the invincibility of the regimes set up in Germany and Italy.

"But more thoughtful minds were filled with foreboding. . . . At the Paris and Brussels shows . . . [w]e no longer said 'Goodbye until next year' to our friends."

When Germany invaded Poland on September 1, 1939, the declaration of war by France and Great Britain greatly intensified the palatable atmosphere of apprehension. Italy's stunned populace blankly watched the newsreels that touted the feats of the German army. Trying to work as if there was no threat to peace, they hoped against hope that Mussolini would preserve Italy's neutrality and avoid the atrocities of armed conflict.

Yet it was clear aggression of some type was in the air. Alfa Romeo's capital increased from 30 million to 240 million lire in 1939, and munitions started taking over car production. Eventually Portello's employees would almost triple to 14,000.

Turin was much the same. With fuel, raw materials, and other commodities becoming seriously rationed, coachbuilders were mostly producing military vehicles with strict delivery deadlines.

Couple such shortages with a claustrophobic sense of fear, and Italy's earlier preoccupation with sports cars and aerodynamics was all but gone. Already an emotional people, and now blanketed by a sense of grave danger, average Italians wore their hearts on their sleeves. "I remember that in the days prior to [the 1940 Gran Premio Brescia della Mille Miglia]," Gino Rancati related in his book, *The Genesis of Ferrari*, "my dear chemistry teacher Rusconi used to say continually, 'Let's hope they don't win.' *They* were the German BMW crew who actually dominated the Alfas and won the race.

"On the following Monday, Rusconi was furious and spoke to us at great length about what was going to happen to the world."

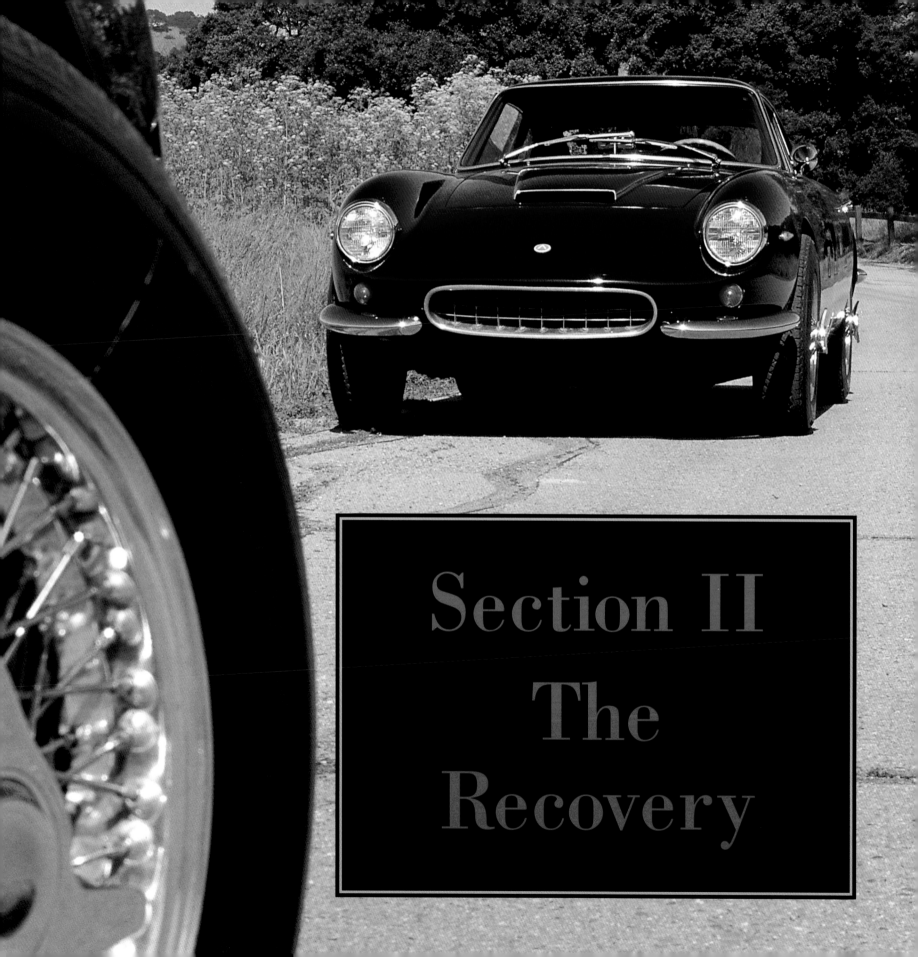

Section II
The
Recovery

Conflict, Compression, and First Steps

3

1940-1947

Professor Rusconi and his students didn't have to wait long to find out exactly what would happen. On June 10, 1940, a general order swept over Italy, ordering everyone to proceed to the public squares and courtyards of the local Fascist headquarters.

"I had to join columns of gloomy, anxious, fearful men," Dante Giacosa observed in *40 Years of Design with Fiat*. "When the booming, belligerent voice of the Duce came fiercely over the loud speakers, announcing the declaration of war, my heart skipped a beat and the crowd was shaken by perturbation. 'We'll have the French bombers over our houses tonight,' I said."

Giacosa was wrong. They came on June 11. "I was alone at home because my wife and children were in the country," the engineer continues. "I couldn't get to sleep, my mind was so troubled. Suddenly the wailing of sirens, the first air raid alarm, made me scramble out of bed and race to the window. The city was shrouded in darkness but overhead there was a brilliant web of parabolic lines, streaks of light that looked like spurts of luminous water, accompanied by a staccato, threatening rattle. . . .

"The consternation was disproportionately great, sparking off a series of flights every evening toward the hills and countryside beyond the outskirts of the town. Autos with hooded lights and whitened mudguards scuttled along the country roads to wait until the air raid was over and the all-clear sounded. At Lingotto, air raid shelters were improvised in the basement of the office block where the canteen had been. It was to be the start of a busy period of provisional decisions, frequent moves, eventful journeys, a search for new and safer shelters for food and fuel."

"After the first bombs fell in 1940 I evacuated my family to . . . the hills surrounding Turin," Battista Farina notes in *Born with the Automobile*. "I used to go in the evenings, but not always. . . . During the night bombing raids the residents [who were] still left [in the city] went down into the cellars like rats. . ."

The car that shuffled in the modern era of automotive styling was the Cisitalia 202 by Pinin Farina. The landmark model picked up where Pinin's avant garde Maserati A6 prototype left off and would become one of the most copied designs ever.

"We ran [the carrozzeria] on sawdust: that was what our furnaces and a large part of our machinery were powered by. . . . In the previous years I had managed to eliminate almost all the wooden structures from our products: now I needed half a forest to supply battalion carts and other orders which had already arrived. By the end of 1940 the carpenter's shop had become the most important sector of the factory.

"Some foreign customers who used to send Mercury, Buick and Hispano-Suiza chassis and used to visit me regularly, were never heard of again. Their place was taken by majors and colonels from the Commissary. . . ."

The conflict left no one untouched, regardless of age or socioeconomic status. Because of the frequent bombing raids on Milan some five decades ago, Carlo Felice Bianchi Anderloni's stomach still gives a little jump when he hears a plane fly over his peaceful country home.

Even the youngest were touched. Although Piero Rivolta was just four when the war ended, he easily recalls a battle waged in the backyard of his parents' country villa. He also endured mid-

night rousings, where the family was escorted to the Town Square for no other reason than maintaining terror.

Piero's industrialist father, Renzo, had numerous harrowing run-ins, including the day he was paid a surprise visit by an SS captain. After looking the elder Rivolta directly in the eye, the German officer calmly said, "I want to know everything you have in this company. If I find even one more thing than what you tell me, I will place you against a wall and kill you."

Rivolta did just that, revealing everything both in front of and behind a false wall. Once the captain was satisfied, he told Rivolta there was a spy in their midst and revealed the man's identity. After the employee was summoned, the SS captain offered to kill him. Using his fluent German, Rivolta's impassioned plea saved the man's life.

Ugo Zagato also proved adept at handling crisis situations. When informed his eldest son, Elio, was to go to Germany and fight, "My father told the officer it was not a good idea," Elio recalls. "He said, 'If he goes there, he will leave and join the resistance the instant he gets the chance. Then he will be fighting against you, not for you. I suggest you leave him here.'" Elio Zagato remained in Milan.

To the south, Modena resident Sergio Scaglietti also understood constant fear. Then in his early 20s, he had been employed in carrozzerias for almost a decade. "We were continually harassed while working," Scaglietti says. "They always threatened to take us away."

Giotto Bizzarrini was a teenager from a well-to-do family residing in the coastal city of Livorno. Without his father around for supervision and guidance, "I lived like an animal, growing up without rules," Bizzarrini says. "I went home only to eat," the family's meals normally consisting of whatever Giotto had caught that day.

Total disruption of life was everywhere. In 1941, Pinin happened to see Agnelli. "Our factory hours are set by sirens," the industrialist told the coachbuilder after noting his company had dispersed its production and engineering facilities. "As usual he was aiming at something concrete," Pinin observed, "the survival of all he had done."

Others also adapted. Carrozzeria Fissore was involved in munitions production. Giacinto Ghia saw carts for the Italian army leave through his coachworks' front door, with black-market bicycles exiting out the back door. In Milan, Carrozzeria Boneschi made anti-aircraft searchlights, Carrozzeria Touring, airplane bodies.

It was a miracle that any sports cars were built at all during the war. Yet, for a privileged few, the lure was still there.

Undoubtedly, the most sensational was an Alfa Romeo 8C 2900 B done for King Michael of Romania during 1941 and 1942. Called an "Experimental Aerodynamic Spider" by the company, its sleek coachwork earned it the nickname "The Whale" by Alfa's employees. Portello also built a small, intermittent run of 6C 2500 Sports.

In Turin, Carrozzeria Bertone received a shortened Fiat 2800 chassis from one of Italy's greatest enthusiasts, Count Giovanni Lurani. Bought in 1941, Lurani traveled to Turin to meet with Nuccio, the two men deciding on a design that, in Lurani's words, "came out looking like a development of the Touring-bodied BMW spyders that raced in 1940."

Lurani would never see the car. According to a letter the count wrote to Bertone years later, after the car was completed in 1943, it was requisitioned by the Germans, then given to their supreme commander in Italy, Albert Kesselring.

But if sports cars weren't seen on the roads, they actively existed in people's minds. For many of Italy's key players, they became a virtual safe harbor, a mental refuge against the ugliness. Nuccio Bertone recalls his father taking the family to their villa on the outskirts of Turin, where the elder Bertone would "recharge his batteries." During these episodes, father and son often discussed the "new and splendid bodies" they would produce once peace returned.

Dante Giacosa recalls similar mental escapes in Fiat. "[I]t was pleasant to let one's imagination wander off to the most disparate projects," he notes in his autobiography. "It was a practice for everyone, an excellent exercise that helped transform the younger draftsmen into proficient technical designers."

Sergio Pininfarina recalls his father often contemplating what would be made once the war concluded, a general observation seconded by Filippo Sapino, the current managing director of Carrozzeria Ghia. When queried about what his elder colleagues did during the conflict, he replied, "They often considered what they would make after the war."

By 1943, Mussolini's grip on Italy was slipping. In Turin in March, a large group of workers went on strike, refusing to move airplane engine production machinery from one location to another.

The unrest accelerated rapidly. On July 24, *Il Duce* was deposed by the Fascist party and placed under arrest. Succeeding Mussolini was Pietro Badoglio, the commander-in-chief during Italy's conquest of Ethiopia in 1935–1936. The news spread like wildfire, mobs of unruly people looking for vengeance on anyone associated—or thought to be associated—with Mussolini's regime.

The following night, thousands of American and British troops landed on the southern shores of Sicily. Taking the Italian and German troops by surprise, less than a month later the island was under allied control.

The southern tip of Italy was invaded on September 3, 1943. Nine days later, Mussolini was rescued by German troops on Hitler's order, and a new Fascist government that worked even more closely with Germany was set up to rule northern Italy.

Bombing raids now intensified, and companies such as Zagato, Ghia, and Carrozzeria Boneschi were destroyed in the process. To the south, the allies closed in on Rome in December, though it wouldn't be until June 1944 before the city was liberated. Modena was freed in the ensuing months, Sergio Scaglietti recalling, "we rejoiced when the allies arrived. It was one big party."

This 6C is identical to the one on the opposite page. The darkened headlights reduced the chance of night flying bombers seeing the car.

Fighting intensified as the troops moved north. During the war's heaviest bombing raid on Milan, Alfa's factory in Portello was destroyed on October 20, 1944.

In April 1945 the allied forces crossed the Po River. Working closely with Italian partisans, Genoa, Milan, and Venice all fell within a matter of days. On the 25th, the Comitato di Liberazione Nazionale resistance organization and the Comitato Militare called for a general strike and insurrection, the groups temporarily seizing control of Fiat. Two days later, Mussolini was captured by anti-Fascist partisans and executed.

Germany issued its unconditional surrender on May 7, Italy's battered citizens breathing a collective sigh of relief—the conflict was indeed over. With rubble everywhere one looked, their cities lay in ruin, the vast majority of their industrial base decimated. Yet, the country was once again theirs; that alone was cause to rejoice.

The process of rebuilding was about to begin.

First Steps to Recovery

Much of the war's devastation was unseen. Numerous returning soldiers drifted aimlessly, looking for a direction or purpose in life. Others, such as ordinary civilians, suddenly found themselves the subject of witch-hunts and persecution.

Engineer Gioachino Colombo exemplified this latter group perfectly. Born in 1903 on the outskirts of Milan, his career started at the young age of 14 when he became a draftsman at a mechanical technology school.

After working on diesel engines and steam turbines, he joined Alfa Romeo in 1924, where he soon found himself working with engineer Vittorio Jano on the P2 race car. Four years later, Colombo became head of Alfa's technical department.

His career blossomed in the 1930s, his name becoming associated with famed Alfas such as the 1750s, 2300s, 2900s, and radical 256 berlinettas with Touring coachwork. He also worked closely with Enzo Ferrari in Modena on the Alfetta 158 single-seater.

Despite his steady rise, Colombo had his detractors. "Like many brilliant people, he was not so easy," said longtime friend Carlo Felice Bianchi Anderloni. "Though we got along well, our type of camaraderie wasn't universal. Some remember him fondly, as a good friend, others not."

That not getting along well with everybody may have come to haunt him after the war. During the conflict, "Colombo was a major figure in the Fascist party," historian Griff Borgeson noted in *Le Grandi Automobili*. "[W]hen the war ended . . . he was regarded as a pariah."

This proved especially problematic when the Resistance gained power at Alfa. In the immediate days following the war, Italy concentrated on road cars, not unnecessary frivolities such as racing machinery. Now an outcast and of little use, Colombo was first assigned to Alfa's diesel division, and then he was laid off altogether. "There was no unemployment compensation in my case," the engineer noted in his book, *The Origins of the Ferrari Legend*. "[I]t was a real blow to my financial situation, which was far from rosy."

Although he felt his suspension was caused by "political misunderstandings" and would thus be "temporary," Colombo harbored a sense of uselessness. Then 42 years old, the forced inactivity caused the quietly ambitious man to fret he was losing the best years of his life as a designer.

A simple phone call changed all that. In July 1945, Enzo Ferrari beckoned him to come to Modena. "For me, it was something which could obliterate in one stroke those five years of war, bombardments and sufferings, and all the upsets of evacuation," the engineer observed years later.

That Ferrari was alive and kicking was no surprise. Like a cat with nine lives, when Mussolini declared war, Ferrari began producing oil-driven grinding machines and machine tools, then war materiels; both would be profitable endeavors.

In 1942 the Fascist government issued an order for Italy's industries to decentralize. Ferrari responded by looking at the Modena suburb of Formigine, then Maranello, where he already owned a small parcel of land. On December 16, he purchased two hectares and a farm from Dante and Augustina Colombini.

According to then-Ferrari employee Girolamo Gardini, Auto Avio Costuzioni moved to Maranello on July 26, 1943. By September, the company was once again producing machine tools. Over the next two years, its workforce rose from 40 to 140.

Although the facility was bombed twice, the second wave badly damaging the company, these proved to be temporary setbacks. "I was not unprepared for the end of the war," Ferrari notes in his memoirs, his undying passion for cars and competition evident by the two 815s illustrated at the top of his sales brochures.

Bertone built this one-off on a shortened Fiat 2800 for Count Giovanni Lurani in the early 1940s. Nuccio Bertone had completely forgotten the episode until he received a letter from Lurani. Because it was too dangerous for the count to travel from Milan to Turin to pick up the car, the Germans requisitioned it.

It was a given that Colombo would immediately accept Ferrari's offer. Besides their collaboration at Alfa before the war, "Ferrari had a lot of charisma, even back then," Sergio Scaglietti points out, referring to the days he repaired Alfa bodies for the Scuderia. "He was never nasty with the people working with him."

As Colombo and traveling partner Enrico Nardi found out that sweltering July, venturing outside Milan only highlighted the country's state of disrepair. With roads in craters, and many bridges crossing the Po River in ruins, ferries were commonly used. "After long hours of waiting under the broiling sun of the summer, your turn finally came," Colombo writes. "[O]n to the barge you drove, balancing precariously on the runway of the landing bridge."

Yet the trip was worth it. Within minutes of seeing his friend, Colombo says Ferrari asked him how he would make a 1,500-cc engine. "Maserati has a first class eight-cylinder engine, the English have the ERA six-cylinder job, and Alfa have their own eight-C," the engineer replied, anticipating the question. "In my view, you should make a 12-cylinder."

Ferrari grinned. "My Dear Colombo," he responded, "you read my thoughts."

And so began, in a most simple way, a chain of events that would radically alter the sports car universe and catapult Ferrari to international stardom as the world's most famous automaker.

Colombo returned to Milan, his mind filled with ideas. After designing the V-12's cylinder heads, he set to work on the balance of the car, using the bedroom of his temporary lodgings for drafting. Assisting him was Angelo Nasi, an Alfa employee who headed its industrial vehicle chassis design team and Luciano Fochi, a young freelance designer.

Colombo worked feverishly on Ferrari's car until Alfa's management learned of his activities. None too pleased by this development, in November 1945 he was rehired to run its Sports Vehicle division.

Colombo recommended Ferrari replace him with Guiseppe Busso, a talented technician who also came from Alfa. Although Busso and several high-profile engineers would continue Colombo's work, it would be another 18 months before Ferrari's car would run under its own power.

Elsewhere in Modena, Maserati was much better situated to begin producing cars. With the financial might and diversity of the Gruppo Orsi empire behind it, Maserati's automotive activities never completely died during the conflict.

In the second half of 1940, Adolfo Orsi actively courted Dr. Ferdinand Porsche, using famed racing driver Tazio Nuvolari as the go-between. The flirtation ended when increased hostilities made it all-too-obvious a German engineer would be more of a hindrance than a help, regardless of credentials.

With gas supplies severely restricted, Maserati produced batteries and made electric trucks and vans. Its engineers also constructed a new running chassis. In 1943 they fitted a six-cylinder engine with a supercharger.

Although a rolling chassis was tested on the empty streets outside Modena in 1945, it wouldn't be until the following year that Maserati's first true postwar road car was completed. Having a cigar-shaped body with mudguards, the A6 1500 prototype was powered by a 1,488-cc inline six-cylinder engine. With a single overhead camshaft, two valves per cylinder, and a compression ratio of just 7.25:1 (all the better to survive the low-grade gas then available), final power output was 65 horsepower at 4,700 rpm.

Like the engine, the A6's suspension derived from Maserati's first postwar racer, the 6CS/46. Both used a tubular chassis, the frame that would become de rigueur for Modena's high-performance constructors.

Their coachwork was a different matter. While the 6CS/46 had a crude, hand-formed open cockpit body, the A6's design would fittingly be done by Battista Pinin Farina.

When the war ended, "the first thing to be done was to clear away the rubble and face up to the reconstruction," Pinin noted in his autobiography. "Except in very rare cases, recriminations and purges proved to be a waste of time, [for] democracy had other things to get on with: houses, bridges, railways and roads to [get] back in order. Every street number became a building site, people came up with new trades and new occupations for themselves."

Within months, Pinin was actively designing and producing cars for Alfa Romeo and Lancia. The following year, the man's indomitable spirit flashed when he decided to display his wares at the Paris Auto Show.

"But aren't Italians banned?" his 21-year-old son, Sergio, asked. "You'll see," his father replied.

After the two completed the journey, Pinin was able to park his Lancia Aprilia and Alfa 2500 across from the exhibition's entrance at the Grand Palais. With onlookers continually gawking at the "outlaw" machines, over the ensuing days the two cars showed up in more than one newspaper, the stories not always entirely complimentary.

It was worth the effort. On the last day, the show's secretary approached Pinin saying, "You have earned yourself a central stand next year."

"It felt to me as though the war—which not only [meant] air-raids, artillery fire and bread rations—was over that day," Farina writes. Sensing that hostilities had festered "right up until then, I should not have had any greater success if I had been given one of the front row of stands in the Grand Palais for our cars."

Despite a fire that decimated the coachbuilder's factory on December 23, 1946, Maserati and Pinin Farina would star at 1947's Geneva Show in March when they unveiled their A6 1500 prototype. Loosely based on a scale model Pinin sent to the Orsis in 1940–1941, the avant-garde berlinetta's form and proportions were made all the cleaner by lack of ornamentation and hidden headlights.

A last-minute arrival at the show, "The Maserati represents in many ways a complete break with the previous practice of the

Modena factory," England's *The Motor* magazine summarized in their Geneva coverage. After describing the A6's mechanicals in detail, they noted, "The striking yet practical coupe had an excellent front end, [while] the [rear] shows a sensible realization that a short tail is fully consistent with a reduction in drag." They also lauded the car's "excellent balance."

Autocar, England's other weekly, concurred completely. Calling it "a little beauty," Pinin's Maserati "represents Italian style at its most advanced—[t]he smoothness of the exterior finish argues well for low air resistance, and it is not too great a strain on credibility that the maximum speed claimed is 100 mph."

While another A6 prototype with a more conventional front end would follow, production versions were heavier and more luxurious. Made by Pinin Farina in coupe, spyder, and 2+2 form, 61 were built over four years.

That manufacturers such as Maserati and coachbuilders like Pinin Farina actively sought each other was no surprise at this time; they needed each other more than ever.

In late 1945 and early 1946, many companies had to close due to the lack of raw material such as steel, tin, and glass. Alfa Romeo, Fiat, and Lancia found themselves "carrying on with reduced staffs and very small output, practically under government control, in order to avoid unemployment," *Autocar* reported in February 1946.

Coachbuilders scoured the countryside and remaining city garages in an effort to find new business. "We concentrated on repairing and reconstructing vehicles of any type, with the sole intent of helping life get back to normal," Nuccio Bertone notes in Luciano Greggio's tome *Bertone*. "Those who had managed to hang on to some pre-war chassis timidly began preparing utility-type car bodies. [S]ome ventured to create bold designs based on old patched up Fiat 1500 and 2800 chassis, or even on the odd Lancia Aprilia chassis, which was rarer still and consequently highly desirable."

Although foreign orders would help jump start Italy's production, persisting fuel and tire shortages hampered further expansion. Raw materials remained rare commodities during the winter of 1946, while the coal and electricity crisis of early 1947 was followed by another tire shortage, causing six-wheeled trucks to be delivered without spare wheels and sometimes just five tires. Cars in factories moved about on wooden tires or just the wheel rims.

As the trying times continued, the relationship between the manufacturers and coachbuilders began to change, particularly in Turin. According to author Greggio, the prewar era had an unwritten rule that, for the most part, a manufacturer's head engineer dictated a car's mechanicals and aesthetics, the belief being everything had to originate from the same source.

But the immediate postwar era's closer interaction between principals, and an abundance of inexpensive skilled labor, quietly brought the sides together. With Italy's cars firmly rooted in the prewar era, the quickest way to offer a variety of new models was changing the coachwork.

Thanks to the country's unsurpassed zeal for sporting machinery, much of this enterprise went to the construction of spyders, berlinettas, and outright racers. In addition to being great attention-getters, "The Italian view seems to be that cars and roads exist for the purpose of getting people from one place to another in the least possible time," America's *Road & Track* magazine would observe in the late 1940s. Calling the nation a "motorist's paradise," they noted "speed, per se, is not frowned upon by the authorities."

That mindset saw a new type of constructor come to the fore: the tuner. While established players such as Siata and Stanguellini had been around from the prewar days, others like Nardi and Conrero soon dotted the scene. To complement their continual experiments with carburetors, camshafts, heads, and other mechanical components, coachbuilders like Colli and Rocco Motto delivered a wide variety of sleek—and often crudely hand-formed—examples of wind-cheating shapes. Gentlemen racers also constructed their own highly modified competition Fiats, using their own mechanics and the local carrozzeria.

Italy's municipalities and central government played a role in encouraging this nascent market segment, as well. In the second half of 1946, cities such as Milan, Turin, and Genoa hosted races in the streets. The following year, the country initiated a national championship, highlighted by the return of its greatest race, the Mille Miglia. Machines competing for that inaugural championship were derived from the production Touring category; subsequent years saw the sports car class adopt international standards.

Not surprisingly, many of these races were won by Alfa Romeo. Since the war, the company had undergone a series of traumatic events. After chief engineer Wilfredo Ricart's contract expired early in 1945, he promptly returned to his native Spain.

Following Milan's liberation that April, Ugo Gobbato—the man who skillfully prevented many of Alfa's employees from being deported—was accused of collaboration. Although he was quickly cleared, Gobbato was gunned down in front of the factory on April 28.

Succeeding him was engineer Pasquale Gallo, a former general manager of the company. With Alfa's initial manufacture of street cars sporadic at best, Gallo kept the workers employed by producing window frames, shutters, and cheap wood-burning ovens.

In the summer of 1946, things had improved enough for the company to return to its roots. With a small flow of 6C 2500 Sports leaving the factory, competition activities started again. "[Racing was] seen as a necessary backing for a publicity campaign," engineer Colombo noted. A Touring-bodied 8C 2900 won 1947's Mille Miglia, and several single-seater Alfetta 158s that had been dismantled to better hide them during the hostilities were reassembled. They were soon winning events on the international scene.

Although Alfa often competed against Maserati and new constructor Enzo Ferrari, surprisingly the public was most captivated by Cisitalia, an upstart firm based in Turin.

Standing for Compagnia Industriale Sportivo Italiana, Cisitalia could have easily served as the prototypical example for the many constructors that would appear during Italy's "boom" years: One indomitable spirit would literally will the company to life. In Cisitalia's case, that man was Piero Dusio.

Born in 1899, it would be hard to imagine a better figurehead. Dusio was the quintessential Italian sportsman. Handsome, athletic, and witty, he possessed a Midas touch. A fabric salesman at age 20, within 10 years he owned a prospering textile factory. Later, he would successfully branch out to manufacture machine tools and bicycles.

As Dusio's income grew exponentially, he indulged himself by purchasing Turin's soccer team and a number of sports cars. He raced Maseratis at age 30, and found himself competing successfully in the Mille Miglia and on the grand prix circuit. In 1938 he founded his own racing team and filled it with top-notch talent.

An optimist of the first order, Dusio survived the war with a gleam in his eye. "With times what they were, if it had not been for him our brigade might have appeared to be a confraternity of the beaten," Pinin observed in his autobiography.

Dusio dreamed of building his own car and had no desire to wait for the war's conclusion to pursue that passion. In October 1944 he approached Fiat engineer Dante Giacosa through one of his right-hand men, a Mr. Casalis. "He was a clever talker," Giacosa recalled in his autobiography. "[W]ith a touch of flattery, Casalis implied that no one was better qualified than myself to help Dusio achieve his aim."

This 1947 Maserati A6 by Pinin Farina's long hood and aerodynamic rear foreshadowed the shape of things to come. The interior was as luxurious as the exterior was austere. It had corded velvet upholstery, a wood dash, and a plexiglass sunroof.

33

Giacosa agreed to meet the industrialist after getting the okay from Fiat's management. "[Dusio] plied me with arguments to demonstrate the merits of his project," the engineer went on, "putting them across with the irresistible charge of enthusiasm that was so typical of the man: smiling, likeable, full of drive, always going straight to the point.

"To clinch matters he threw in an invitation to make use of part of his villa. Since I had been bombed out of my home in 1942, I accepted eagerly, though I was haunted by doubts about the success of the enterprise."

Now ensconced in a large villa complete with air raid shelter, caretaker, and servant, further enhancing the project was Dusio telling the engineer to make the type of car *he* liked. "In America during that period," Giacosa says, "there was dirt track racing. I thought to make something like those, using Fiat components. He liked the idea, envisioning a series where his racer-friends would compete in identical cars."

After completing his daily work at Fiat, Giacosa burned the midnight oil during evenings and on weekends. "Because Dusio owned a company that made bicycles," the engineer notes, "for the ease of manufacture I felt we should do a tube frame, as his workmen were familiar with that construction technique."

On September 3, 1946, Italy learned firsthand of its newest constructor when seven single-seat Cisitalia D46s lined up at Turin's "Coppa Brezzi" race. Fittingly, they would dominate, high-lighted by famed driver Tazio Nuvolari flashing by the start-finish line holding the broken hinged-steering wheel *outside* the car and Dusio's taking the checkered flag.

The following year, Cisitalias would star on the endurance circuit. At the Mille Miglia, the company entered five 202 MMs, both in coupe and spyder form. With flowing aerodynamic coachwork designed by Giacosa and his successor at Cisitalia, fellow engineer Giovanni Savonuzzi, the cars were powered by a 60-horsepower, four-cylinder, 1,100-cc Fiat engine. They overwhelmed their class, and finished second, third, and fourth overall, behind a considerably more powerful Alfa Romeo.

While these types of achievements were indeed admirable, the model that truly brought Cisitalia and Italy international stardom was a road-going 202 by Pinin Farina. As Giacosa toiled away in early 1945 on the D46, Dusio approached his friend Pinin, informing him of his desire to make a proper sporting GT.

"I told [him] when the time was ripe I would work with him," Pinin wrote. "I thought [the project] was brilliant and exciting. We often got together to exchange notes, suggestions, and sketches either in his house, or in [our factories]."

The resulting landmark model's clean, uncluttered form exhibited magnificent balance. It also marked the first time a front-engined car's hood was lower than its fenders.

With the wooden body buck finished by July 1947, Pinin's 202 first broke cover on September 28 at the Villa d'Este Concours d'Elegance, then made its international debut at the Paris Auto Show. Called "a beautifully finished and streamlined coupe"

by *Autocar*, so exact were its proportions that *Motor* noted its "very neat coachwork creates the illusion of a much larger vehicle."

That was just the beginning. In March 1948 importer Max Hoffman parked the first 202 to hit America's shores in front of his New York Park Avenue showroom. Crowds quickly overwhelmed the sidewalk, spilling out into the streets.

Shock waves rippled across the country. Three months later, California-based *Road & Track* magazine featured a photo of a 202 parked next to a Buick; the contrast could not have been more startling. "[We] suggest some American manufacturer obtain the rights to build the Cisitalia coupe in this country," its editors pleaded in their column.

Falling upon deaf ears in Detroit, 18 months later they published an open letter to shipbuilding magnate Henry Kaiser, then America's leading independent auto manufacturer. Noting that its readers had replied to the earlier editorial "with a storm of approval," *Road & Track* stated, "The Cisitalia is unsurpassed for sheer beauty, safer at 100 mph than domestic cars are at 70, and is a true sports car. Your organization, Mr. Kaiser, is in an advantageous position to build [it]. Be bold [and] give America a *real* automobile—make your new model a copy of the famous Cisitalia."

Had Mr. Kaiser followed up on *Road & Track's* suggestion, it probably would have gone for naught. Like many Italians who would follow in his footsteps, Dusio's unbridled enthusiasm proved to be his firm's undoing. In the summer of 1947, he told *Autocar* he planned to build 1,000 to 1,500 202s a year, a figure far beyond the number of sports and GTs Alfa was constructing at the time.

Worse, the industrialist felt it was "possible to make motor racing pay," a concept the magazine noted "would be considered just naive in [England]." According to the *Cisitalia Catalogue Raisonne* (Automobilia), the success of his D46 single-seaters caused Dusio to become enamored with grand prix racing. When Savonuzzi's subsequent warning that "grand prix cars have a big drawback: they either come in first or are a complete failure," fell upon deaf ears, the engineer recommended German designers for such a project, as they had dominated grand prix racing in the late 1930s.

Althrough mutual friends, Dusio got in touch with the Porsche family, leading to a contract signing in February 1947. "[That] commission was of great significance to us," Dr. Ferry Porsche observed in his autobiography, *Cars Are My Life*. Not only did it pay for his father's release from a French prison, "it meant that we once again had a future in the automobile industry. We planned a midengined car with a [supercharged] boxer 12-cylinder engine and four-wheel drive. It was a very advanced design [which came from] our wealth of experience with the Auto Union racing car."

The episode also served as the genesis for Porsche's 356. "On the journey back from Turin," the doctor noted, "I became increasingly convinced of the viability of an idea we had before the war, namely the construction of a sports car based on Volkswagen components. Our visit to Dusio rekindled my enthusiasm

for the [concept], since we could very easily do with Volkswagen components what he was doing with Fiat parts."

Cisitalia's radical Porsche-designed 360 grand prix racer took three-plus years to make. Because its development and construction so far exceeded projected costs, the resulting cash crunch caused Cisitalia's striking employees to take over the firm's premises. While the local court would allow work on the 360 to continue, the handwriting was on the wall: Dusio could not support the effort.

Only one 360 would be built, and it never raced in Italy. In 1951, Dusio moved to Argentina, leaving his son Carlo to oversee the Turin factory. Ever the optimist, the elder Dusio hoped to open another Cisitalia factory there with outside backing. Alas, it was not to be.

Back in Turin, the Cisitalias were more rooted in reality—production berlinettas, spyders, and 2+2s couldn't save the firm. The company floundered through the early fifties, then faded altogether.

Yet the mold had been cast: Pinin Farina's 202 represented a turning point. So pure was its look, so great was its influence, that four years after the model's introduction one was placed on permanent exhibit in New York's Museum of Modern Art. Subsequently dubbed a "rolling sculpture" and the star of the museum's "Eight Automobiles" exhibit, the show's catalogue noted, "The Cisitalia's body is slipped over its chassis like a dust jacket over a book."

The Italian sports car movement had begun.

Shortly after the war, Alfa Romeo used a magnificent brochure to promote its products. The 6C 2500 illustrated here features Touring's 4/5-seat berlinetta coachwork. The chassis was equipped with central x-bracing for additional stiffness. All 6C 2500s were powered by 2.5-liter, 6-cylinder engines.
John Ling Collection

35

Release

1948 - 1952

With Cisitalia and Pinin Farina defining Italy's closed sports cars movement, it was fitting that Ferrari and Touring would do the same for its spyders. After Gioachino Colombo's return to Alfa, in early 1946 Guiseppe Busso became head of Ferrari's technical department. Then 33, Busso was hired by Fiat in 1937, moving to Alfa two years later. Working in the department of special duties, he struck up a strong friendship with engineer Satta, the man who would succeed Gobbato.

While at Ferrari, "I had to be ruthless in order to pull the 125 through its childhood illnesses, which were neither few, nor insignificant," Busso notes in *Ferrari Tipo 166*. Giving the technician, his team of young apprentices, and experienced workshop manager Luigi Bazzi continual headaches were the V-12's ignition, bearings, cylinder head gaskets, a lack of high-grade raw materials, and poorly machined components from suppliers. Still, through persistence and determination, the team first bench tested the engine on September 26, 1946.

Within weeks, Ferrari was making international headlines. "Not even damage and the threat of communism have stopped Italian enthusiasm for cars of the super-sports type," England's *Autocar* noted that December. "News is now at hand of an entirely new make, the Ferrari Type 125. Its specification is in many ways unusual and gives promise of outstanding performance. There will be three models built on a chassis of similar proportions, called Sports, Competition, and Grand Prix, respectively."

On March 12, 1947, a Ferrari 125 chassis sans coachwork moved under its own power for the first time. Like Maserati's A6, the chassis was tubular, its suspension being leaf springs and shock absorbers. Depending on the state of tune, the 1,496-cc V-12 would produce between 72 and 118 horsepower.

Ferrari's first cars had rudimentary coachwork and reflected the company's sporting pretensions. Pictured is the third Ferrari built, a 1947 166 SC. Regarding the V-12, "Our intention was simply to make a conventional engine, but one of exceptional quality," Ferrari observed years later.

The 166 MM Barchetta, "the car that gave Ferrari a face," says the man who made it, Carrozzeria Touring's Carlo Felice Bianchi Anderloni. After Ferrari 166 MMs won numerous races, the word *barchetta* was often used to describe a minimalist sports car in which performance was the model's emphasis.

Maserati's production A6 debuted at the 1948 Geneva Motor Show. Coachbuilder Pinin Farina toned down the coachwork on the production cars, making the design more acceptable to a mass audience. A hit in the marketplace, the A6 was made as both a coupe and convertible.

Ferrari's competition debut came on May 11 in Piacenza. Franco Cortese's 125 did not finish the race. Two weeks later in Rome, the same driver would score the first of the marque's countless competition victories.

By early 1948, intense development had increased the V-12's dimensions to 1,995 cc. Now called the 166, the 125- to 140-horsepower model went on a tear, winning that year's Targa Florio, Mille Miglia, and numerous other races.

Although his machines frequently occupied the winner's circle, Ferrari was a troubled man. He knew his company lacked an identity, thanks to its cars' wide variety of coachwork. To solve the problem, he contacted Felice Bianchi Anderloni in Milan.

Like Ferrari, Anderloni's Carrozzeria Touring had seen its production dramatically shift during the war. After making a sleek spyder prototype for Germany's BMW in 1941, automotive work came to a halt, save the occasional experimental electric vehicle. Now fire trucks and mobile radio stations emanated from the works, as did sections of airplane bodies and bicycles.

Immediately after the war, Touring made a sprinkling of Alfa Romeos, Fiats, and Lancias. In 1947 the company inked a deal with England's Bristol and worked closely with Isotta-Franschini on its stillborn 8C Monterosa.

Shortly after calling Felice, Ferrari was stunned to learn his friend became ill and died following a trip to Rome, thrusting Carlo Anderloni into the position of design director; then 32, Felice's son had been working full time in Touring since 1943. Still, "it was not a very easy position to be in," Carlo confides. "We have a saying in Italy that it is best to present a good face in a bad situation, and that is what I tried to do."

But all was not lost: Carlo had actively involved himself in automotive design from his youngest days, when he often gazed out the family's upstairs apartment window to absorb his father's creations, forms, proportions, and details. And thanks to surviving partner Gaetano Ponzoni, the administrative side of Touring was in good hands.

Although Ferrari made it clear he had complete faith in Carlo's abilities, Anderloni felt the weight on his shoulders. "That was my first work," he states, "and it was vitally important because all the people understood that Touring meant my father. I *knew* many were quietly wondering, 'What will happen now? Can the son follow in his father's footsteps?'

"I thus engaged myself to design something outstanding. I knew that if I missed that goal, in all likelihood everything was finished."

He was given a blank sheet of paper. "Ferrari wanted to be recognized as a true motorcar constructor," Anderloni says. "He wanted a distinctive, uniform appearance, so that when someone saw one of his cars, they said, 'That is a Ferrari.'"

After several conversations with returning Ferrari engineer Gioachino Colombo, Anderloni used the 166's mechanicals for his inspiration. Noting that "the engine and chassis were new," he felt it imperative "that this car should not be like something already seen. I wanted to give it a fresh appearance: not something extravagant, but something technical, representing what lay beneath the skin."

With the scale drawings done in early July 1948, Touring's 166 MM [Mille Miglia] spyder debuted in September at the Turin Auto Show on Ferrari's stand, the company's first ever at any show. Gracing Touring's stand was a 166 MM berlinetta.

While overall reaction was positive, the response from Italy's most prominent automotive journalist was quite different. "Giovanni Canestrini approached me at the show and said, 'I am quite shocked,'" Anderloni recalls. "'That is not a car!' he blurted out. 'It is a little boat, a barchetta.'"

The name stuck. When four Ferrari 'Barchettas' lined up at the start of 1949's Mille Miglia, Anderloni knew Ferrari was smiling: The world saw he was now a manufacturer, not making cars one or two at a time, but in series.

The Barchettas demonstrated much more than that. Besides dominating the Mille Miglia that year, they were also victorious at the Targa Florio, Le Mans, and Spa in Belgium.

Also, Ferrari's competition Barchettas were almost identical to the handful of lusso (luxury) models bought by wealthy sportsmen. Not only did this help promote the idea that Italian sports cars (and Ferraris in particular) could be driven to the track, compete successfully, and then drive home, Touring's Ferrari had groundbreaking styling. In addition to giving Ferrari the "face" he desired, the Barchetta's shape inspired numerous other sports cars, AC's Ace (and Cobra), and American Briggs Cunningham's C-1 roadster, to name just three.

As Ferrari's efforts gathered steam, Maserati was encountering growing pains. When Gruppo Orsi bought the company in 1937, Ettore, Bindo, and Ernesto Maserati signed a 10-year clause that bound them to the firm.

In the years immediately following the war, a rift was forming between Adolfo Orsi and the Maserati brothers. According to Maserati by Luigi Orsini, this likely started in 1940 when Orsi reorganized the company's technical department and flirted with hiring Ferdinand Porsche. Because the brothers were now "just" employees subject to someone else's decisions, their feathers were further ruffled when ex-Ferrari men Alberto Massimino and Vittorio Bellentani were hired.

Additionally, "Ettore, Ernesto and Bindo never really focused on money," said Ermanno Cozza, a longtime Maserati employee who was friends with the brothers. Instead, "they were always thinking of new things, wanting to develop new ideas."

Siata's diminutive Amica used a Fiat 500 engine with a Siata-designed head; final power output was 20 horsepower. That was enough to push the Bertone-designed car to more than 65 miles per hour.

The Siata Daina was a more sporting and luxurious proposition than the Amica. It used Fiat 1400 mechanicals and Siata's proprietary frame. The 1,395-cc engine was tuned to deliver 65 horsepower. Stabilimenti Farina typically did the Daina's coachwork.

In May 1947 the Maserati brothers left the company that bore their name and returned to Bologna. Few Maserati employees followed; the majority—including longtimers such as former race driver Guerino Bertocchi, his brother Gino, and racing mechanic Luigi Parenti—remained in Modena.

In December 1947, Bindo, Ernesto, and Ettore formed OSCA (Officine Specializzate Costruzione Automobili). The concern's first model, a cycle-fendered MT4 with a 1,092-cc four-cylinder engine, debuted nine months later at a race in Pescara.

NARDI "ND" 750 cc. car = 4 cylinder

4 cylinder, in line
Bore : 63.48 mm.
Stroke : 59.00 mm.
Capacity : 747.41 c.c.
Brake horse-power : 42.6 at 5500 R.P.M.
Overhead valves
Electrical equipment : 12 Volt
4 Gear ratios and reverse (2nd, 3rd, and top
synchronised)
Tubular chassis of welded construction
Independent front suspension
Rear suspension with floating axle and 1/4
elliptic leaf springs
Hydraulic brakes
Tyres : 4.00 x 15" on Rudge detachable wire wheels
Wheelbase : 1900 mm.
Seating accomodation for two
Chassis weight : 322 kgs. (710 lbs.)
Weight with "barchetta" body : abt. 400 kgs. (880 lbs.)
Weight with "Coupé" body : abt. 450 kgs. (1000 lbs)
Fuel consumption : 8.0 lt. p. 100 Km. (29.5 m. p. g. US)
Top speed of the "Competition" version : 160 K. p. h. (100 m. p. h.)
Top speed of the "Sport" version : 140 K. p. h. (87 m. p. h.)

NARDI E C
ND
TORINO

NARDI & C.
VIA PAOLO BRACCINI 86
TELEF. 31.558 - 383.869
T O R I N O (I t a l y)
★
A R N O L T
CORPORATION
W A R S A W
(INDIANA) U. S. A.

Enrico Nardi was a test driver who gained a great deal of notoriety tuning Lancias. In the early 1950s, he branched out into making his own sports and touring cars, often using the name "ND." In the late 1950s, he achieved his greatest fame by supplying steering wheels to Ferrari and numerous other high-performance makes.

Although Maserati's winning ways in competition went unaffected (the 1948 season's highlight was Guiseppe Farina's victory at Monaco's first postwar Grand Prix), the company's sports/GT production had been practically nonexistent. When the Communists nearly seized power in Italy after the war, the Modena area became a political hotbed. "The local Communists erroneously viewed Orsi as a Fascist," says ex-company employee Romolo Tavoni. "Maserati thus became plagued with strikes by Communist sympathizers."

Yet Orsi was able to weather the storm. "The Communist threat continued through most of 1948," Carlo Anderloni stated. "After they were defeated, everyone felt a tremendous release. We were all happy and wanted to amuse ourselves. This created a great desire to work, which made the concept of work itself very exciting."

Maserati was able to capitalize on this "release." Although poverty remained prevalent, Italy was starting to take its first, small steps away from the horrors of war. Cities were being reconstructed, and craftsmen such as Sergio Scaglietti were in constant demand, fixing bridges and roadways. Others, like aspiring entrepreneur Ferruccio Lamborghini, were forming businesses to meet other needs—tractors in this case.

Established industrialists were also capitalizing on the rush to rebuild. In Milan, Ferdinando Innocenti and Renzo Rivolta seized upon Italy's demand for inexpensive transportation and began building motorscooters to replace people's bicycles. Not only did these companies' snowballing prosperity allow Italians to take modest, comfortable steps in treating themselves to

Siata was also coming into its own. Standing for Societa Italiana Auto Trasformazione Accessori, Giorgio Ambrosini's Turin-based firm started manufacturing high-performance accessories in the 1920s. The following decade, it became much closer to Fiat when it began producing the Gran Sport, a Balilla-based sports car.

After the war, Siata sold more than 100,000 small engines that clipped on to a bicycle's frame. Manufactured from 1945 to 1949, the product's success allowed Ambrosini to return to automobile production.

Siata's first model was the Tipo TC. Having modified Topolino mechanicals and a proprietary tube frame, the TC featured a supercharged Fiat engine and a sporting roadster body.

Siata's next model, the Amica, aimed for a larger audience. Also using a proprietary frame, its coachwork was quite different than the minimalist TC. With attractive coupe and spyder bodies by Bertone, the sales slogan of "the little car with great luxury" said it all.

In 1950, Siata introduced the Daina. An even faster Siata, the 1400 Gran Sport, appeared the following year.

Nardi and Company and Abarth were two other specialist constructors/tuners of note. The former, founded by ex-Scuderia Ferrari test driver Enrico Nardi and Roman Renato Danese, was originally known as Nardi e Danese. Also based in Turin, Nardi

The machine that signaled Carlo Abarth's entry into the world of Italian sports car manufacturers was the 205-A. This particular 205-A competed in the 1950 Mille Miglia as a long tail berlinetta. Its Vignale coachwork was altered the following year, the result being the beautiful form shown here. It would subsequently win several concours d'elegance.

Fiat's entry into the berlinetta sweepstakes was the handsome 1100 S. Capable of almost 100 miles per hour, "The noise inside was deafening but that did not worry us," engineer Dante Giacosa notes in his autobiography. "Italian motorists in 1947 were not particularly fussy about noise." John Ling Collection

something new, the firms themselves gave many of those displaced by the war a sense of purpose, offering them stability and a place to hang their hat and grow.

When Maserati displayed the production version of Pinin Farina's A6 1500 at 1948's Turin Auto Show, the company was in the right place at the right time. After making just three A6s in 1947, production tripled in 1948 and exceeded 20 in 1949 and 1950.

Such an increase was reflective of the automotive industry as a whole. In 1948, Italy produced more than 44,000 cars, nearly a 100 percent increase over 1947's figure. Production jumped another 20,000 in 1949, with 17,000 being exported. Fiat set an all-time record that year, manufacturing 86,000 cars and commercial vehicles.

It was thus no surprise that the majority of the country's sports cars were Fiat-based. Because the company offered several models with a variety of engines, the specialist constructors and tuners flourished as people started spending money.

Modena-based Stanguellini was at the movement's forefront. Originally founded as an engineering firm in 1879, in the early 1900s Celso Stanguellini's company became a Fiat dealer. By the 1930s, its main business was modifying Fiats (calling them Stanguellinis in the process) and Fiat engines.

That activity grew after the war, one customer being coachbuilder Nuccio Bertone. Then in his mid-30s, unbeknownst to his parents Nuccio would sneak off during the weekends, compete, and show up for work the following Monday. This affiliation led to Stanguellini producing a handful of lightweight, Bertone-bodied spyders and berlinettas.

As Alfa Romeo 6C 2500 production increased, the chassis became a favorite of Italy's coachbuilders. This one-off was done by Pinin Farina in 1948 and was a forerunner to the 1951 Nash Healey.

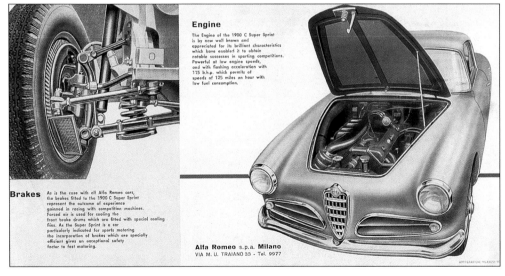

Brakes As is the case with all Alfa Romeo cars, the brakes fitted to the 1900 C Super Sprint represent the outcome of experience gained in racing with competition machines. Forced air is used for cooling the front brake drums which are fitted with special cooling fins. As the Super Sprint is a car particularly indicated for sports motoring the incorporation of brakes which are specially efficient gives an exceptional safety factor to fast motoring.

Engine The Engine of the 1900 C Super Sprint is by now well known and appreciated for its brilliant characteristics which have enabled it to obtain notable successes in sporting competitions. Powerful at low engine speeds, and with flashing acceleration with 115 b.h.p. which permits of speeds of 125 miles an hour with low fuel consumption.

Alfa Romeo s.p.a. Milano
VIA M. U. TRAIANO 33 - Tel. 9977

The last of Alfa's 1900 C Super Sprints was this handsome coupe. Designed by Touring, it first appeared in 1956 and was built in limited quantities.

diverged from other firms by primarily using Alfa Romeo and BMW mechanicals.

Abarth was the brainchild of Carlo Abarth. Born in 1908, by the late 1920s the soft-spoken Abarth was successfully competing with motorcycles of his own construction. During the war, he stayed in Yugoslavia, then emigrated back to Italy in 1945.

Thanks to his friendship with Tazio Nuvolari and Ferdinand Porsche, in 1947 Abarth joined Cisitalia. As the company's financial difficulties worsened, in 1949 he founded Abarth and Company with Armando Scagliarini. In its first year, the fledgling firm continued to have a close association with Carlo's former employer, Abarth's first car being the Abarth Cisitalia 1100.

In 1950, Abarth began building his own competition offerings and became a prolific tuner of Fiats and other cars. The following year, the company debuted the 205-A. This ravishing low-roof Vignale berlinetta was the first in a long and incredibly diverse line of Abarth sports cars.

As could be expected, Fiat was not oblivious to this active, visible market segment. In 1947 it introduced its own "go fast" model, the 1100 S. Sporting an aerodynamic berlinetta body, its engine was considerably more powerful (51 horsepower versus 32) than the standard 1100 sedan, thanks to a higher compression ratio, different camshaft, and Weber carburetion.

According to Dante Giacosa, the 1100 S was a direct descendant of the prewar 508 C MM. Now back at Fiat full-time after his stint with Cisitalia, the engineer feels the model marked something of a turning point for the company. With its postwar management undecided on what to produce, "the project for the 1100 S helped galvanize the atmosphere," Giacosa writes in his autobiography. "Fiat could not keep out of [1947's] Mille Miglia. . . . It was decided to go all out to build a coupe capable of putting up a good show in the race, but also adapted to use as a tourer by a sporting clientele."

First appearing in May 1947, a handful of 1100 Ss were delivered to dealers and preferred private buyers. At the Mille Miglia, the cars finished fifth through eighth overall and second through fourth the following year.

As the effects of 1948's political release spread across Italian society and automotive industry, clients capable of purchasing more sophisticated and luxurious sports cars were able to get them in the early 1950s. Although Alfa produced a number of 6C 2500s in the second half of the 1940s (the Freccia d'Oro (Golden Arrow) and Touring's beautiful Villa d'Este being the most sporting), Portello's management recognized it needed to change its core fundamentals to survive and prosper.

Prior to the war, even in the best of times, Alfa's annual production consistently measured in the low hundreds, exceeding 500 just once. With Satta looking at large production, the company focused on making an all-new four-cylinder model. To help in its development, in September 1947 the engineer called his friend in Modena, Guiseppe Busso.

The timing could not have been better. Much to Busso's chagrin, Gioachino Colombo had returned to Ferrari. "His opinion

America's *Car and Driver* magazine says the car that introduced the famed "GT" letters to the world was Lancia's B20 GT. One of the best balanced cars of the early 1950s, its Pinin Farina coachwork is a continuation of the berlinetta theme first seen on 1947's Cisitalia 202.

Alfa Romeo introduced the 1900 Sprint in 1951. Although the chassis was a coachbuilder favorite, Carrozzeria Touring made the majority. The last of the series was the 1900 Super Sprint (pictured). First seen in 1954, its body was almost identical to the 1900 Sprint. Alfa Romeo produced an 8-page, English-language brochure to assist American and United Kingdom distributors.

Fiat's 8V startled the automotive world in 1952, with the resulting avalanche of positive press catching the firm off guard. "Since it wasn't a big project in the commercial part of the company," engineer Dante Giacosa notes, "we really didn't know what to expect."

Fiat's 8V was truly a hand-built car. The chassis was made at Siata, then sent to Fiat's experimental division (eloquently called "Carrozzeria Speciale") to be clothed with its Savonuzzi and Giacosa-designed aerodynamic, sheet-metal body.

of what I had designed was, 'It is all wrong, and this is what I think of it,'" Busso noted in *Ferrari Tipo 166*. "Fortunately, on the same day I had to swallow the bitter pill of this judgement, I received Satta's invitation to go to Alfa. And suddenly it was so."

The result of Busso's, Satta's, and Alfa's engineering departments' efforts was the 1900. First breaking cover as a sedan at the Turin Auto Show in May 1950, "[T]his new Alfa Romeo . . . promises to be a most important addition to the range produced by the Italian industry," England's *Autocar* observed. "[I]t has acceleration, speed and handling qualities fully in keeping with Alfa tradition."

The 1900's 1,884-cc four-cylinder engine followed Alfa's practice of twincam heads and a cast-iron block. Suspension up front was wishbones and coil springs, while the rear saw a cost-saving rigid axle, coil springs, and radius arms.

In 1951 the debut of the 1900 C "Sprint" clearly demonstrated that Alfa had not lost touch with its sporting roots. By shortening the sedan's wheelbase 5 inches, the resulting chassis and more powerful engine offered an ideal platform for a proper sports GT.

With coachwork by Carrozzeria Touring, Anderloni and his designers used their concours-winning 2500 Villa d'Este as the Sprint's starting point. The resulting 1900 effectively used styling cues from the more exclusive model, including haunches over the rear wheels, the roof's greenhouse, and elliptical door handles.

Other coachbuilders were soon showing their wares on the chassis. Pinin Farina first exhibited a simple but attractive 1900 C cabriolet, which was produced in small numbers. A one-off berlinetta for the King of Egypt and a limited production run of well-balanced 1900 coupes followed.

Others trying their hand on the 1900 C chassis included a handsome coupe by Castagna (seven were made), several Supergioiello (super-jewel) coupes by Carrozzeria Ghia, and an unsuccessful 2+2 by Carrozzeria Colli. The most extravagant 1900 was undoubtedly the Astral, a two-seat cabriolet by Carrozzeria Boneschi.

Interestingly, Lancia seemed to match Alfa, blow for blow. Also in the beginning throes of a renaissance, the company's first postwar model was most important, for the firm began the 1950s in dire financial straits. Having produced military transport vehicles during the war, management felt it should continue with truck production when fighting stopped. The strategy backfired in 1948 when a massive sale of the Allies' war surplus left Lancia with large amounts of unsold inventory.

Their backs now to the wall, Gianni Lancia and crew proved up to the task. Ex-Alfa/Scuderia Ferrari engineer Vittorio Jano, technical director Guiseppe Vaccarino, and patent and planning head Francesco di Virgilio began working on an advanced V-6 engine, a chassis that featured independent front suspension and a novel rear-mounted clutch and gearbox unit.

The result was Lancia's innovative Aurelia B10 sedan, which also debuted in 1950 at Turin. Called by *Autocar* "one of the most interesting cars evolved in postwar Europe," the Aurelia would serve as the basis for an all-new GT, the Aurelia B20. In his autobiography, Pinin wrote that Gianni Lancia and Vittorio Jano let him know of their desire by simply saying, "We are preparing a chassis for you to produce something like the Mona Lisa, a masterpiece."

"Speed had entered into people's lives," Pinin reflected of the era, and the effort. "Style had to be the soul of construction now. I worked [on] the B20 virtually in a state of trance, with a pleasing tingling in my hands."

Pinin Farina's Lancia debuted at Turin in 1951. Featuring the coachbuilder's hallmark simplicity and balance, and a larger, more powerful version of Lancia's sophisticated V-6, the fastback Aurelia was described by *Autocar* as "one of the most important exhibits of the show."

From day one, Gianni Lancia and Company were extremely confident of the B20's capabilities. Entering four in the grueling Mille Miglia, amazingly one finished second overall; two months later, another would finish 12th at Le Mans. "Without any hulla-baloo, a quiet touring car has broken the tradition of the Mille Miglia," Italy's press noted after its classic race. "The technology of the normal car has turned over a new page, showing a car's practical performance can achieve exceptional heights."

As Lancia B20 and Alfa 1900 production ramped up, there was another release, one totally unrelated to politics and the Communist defeat. Although automotive development ceased during World War II, people's minds remained active as ever. Both Sergio Pinin Farina and Nuccio Bertone pointed out

that their fathers constantly thought of what they would make, once hostilities ended.

It was much the same on the engineering side. Dante Giacosa speaks for many when he observed his staff's imagination often "wandered off to the most disparate projects." These episodes, he said, "helped transform younger draftsmen into proficient designers."

When peace took hold, the creative juices soon ran free. "It was like a giant, compressed spring," said Filippo Sapino, Carrozzeria Ghia's managing director. "When the war ended, that spring released."

Sergio Pininfarina concurred: "Because people went a long time without walking, they took big steps, not little ones."

Fiat's startling 8V perfectly exemplified this effusive release. Debuting at Geneva in March 1952, "No motor show is complete without its surprise," *The Motor* noted in its coverage of the event, "and the surprise in this case was sent along at the eleventh hour from Turin. Prophets have long since read in the stars the prospect of new FIAT cars [b]ut the last thing which had been expected was a truly streamlined 2-seater saloon."

According to Dante Giacosa, the model was an outgrowth of a large sedan, aimed at the American market. When that V-8-powered

project remained stillborn, the engineer noted, "the idea of mounting the engine in a sports car for a small production run was attractive and aroused the keenest interest among the design engineers."

And so was born the 8V. Designing the chassis from a blank piece of paper, "the idea was to have it very strong and rigid, with a suspension that was independent front and rear," Giacosa continued. "Because the suspension we envisioned needed a great degree of chassis stiffness, we ruled out a tubular frame. We ended up choosing Siata to make it and many of the mechanical components, as they were used to working on these type[s] of cars."

For the 8V's shape, Giacosa used the 1100 S as the starting point, then turned to Fabio Luigi Rapi to design the car. Then in his late 40s, Rapi was a gifted engineer whose resumé included aircraft construction and recent stints with Zagato and Isotta-Fraschini. The two engineers were soon spending many hours at the wind tunnel, refining the scale model's form.

Like the chassis, the sophisticated all-alloy engine also started from a blank sheet of paper. Displacing just under 2 liters, it had an unusually narrow 70-degree V. "Since it was our first V-8, we had to learn as we went along," Giacosa said. "Early on, I was relying a lot on my lengthy experience with

military vehicles, for they typically used larger engines. But because the V-8's construction was so much lighter, I had to adapt to that mentality."

Prior to production, Fiat test driver Carlo Salamano put the 8V through its paces. "He often went up into the mountains, where he showed no fear," Giacosa smiled. "He was such an incredible driver that a number of the directors would go to watch him test. He would come down the mountain, drifting around corners, the brakes glowing red."

Once production commenced on a special assembly line in Fiat's Lingotto factory, the effects of imaginations running free became obvious. All one had to do was look at the international auto salons and the racetrack: The 8V quickly became a favorite of racers and Italy's coachbuilders.

Outside those 8Vs with Fiat coachwork (using the exotic name "Carrozzeria Speciale"), Zagato bodied the most; spearheading the effort was Ugo's son Elio. Then in his early 30s, Elio actively raced his company's products and would win five Italian championships in Zagato 8Vs. "It was my favorite car," he remembers, "for its chassis was fabulous. It was the first car with fully independent suspension, and I saw the advantage of that."

With Fiat encouraging all carrozzerias to use the chassis, the resulting coachwork was prolific and diverse. Starring at numerous international auto shows, for several years the 8V continued to appear in automotive magazines around the world. With Zagato, Vignale, Ghia, and Pinin Farina exhibiting their wares, these wild-looking machines often had outrageous names such as "Supersonic" and "Demon Rouge."

The mechanicals backed up those exotic designs, for the 120-mile-per-hour 8V may have been the best balanced car of its day. For example, *Autocar* concluded its road test by noting, "[F]or the enthusiast requiring a fast 2-litre car, it would be difficult to find one which would provide better performance and be more of a delight to drive."

Surprisingly, the magazine was wrong. With Italy's "Boom" just around the corner, over the following years the English weekly—and countless other publications around the world—would utter even more effusive praise, again and again.

Vignale's beautiful one-off Spider shows America's influence on Italian design in the car's Corvette-inspired wraparound windshield and small tail fins.

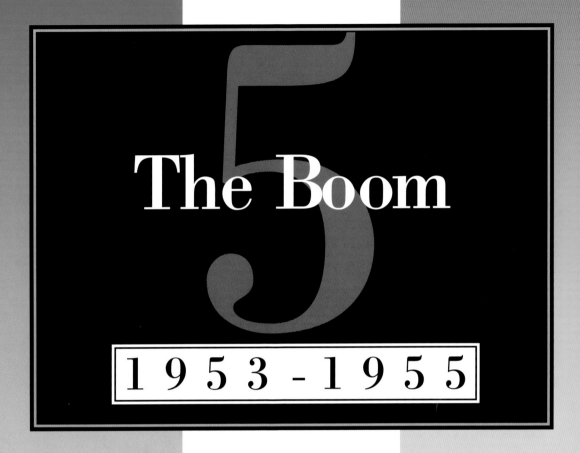

The Boom

1953 - 1955

I taly's coachbuilders were flourishing as the Boom began in 1953. "After the war, most of the key people were in their early 40s to early 50s," Turin-based designer Tom Tjaarda reflected. "This allowed them to present mature forms, shapes without childish ideas."

Also playing an important role in the explosion of show cars, and limited production *fouri serie,* were collaborators such as the model makers. "They often came from the furniture industry," Tjaarda continued, "so they were used to working with wood. They easily translated what the stylists wanted into three-dimensional forms. It was a very synergistic relationship, everyone working well together."

The 1953 Turin Show clearly reflected the coachbuilder's incredible diversity. "[While] the overall first impression is a preponderance of Italian cars," *Autocar's* commentary noted, "[o]n closer examination it is found that many of the stands bearing Italian names are [only] featuring Alfa Romeos, Fiats or Lancias, with special bodies so distinctive in appearance that they give the impression of [having] separate identities."

"The Italian influence leads the automotive design world," *Road & Track* observed the following year. "It remains consistent, commanding, spirited, and graceful."

Turin and Milan were not alone in their leadership roles. One hundred miles to the south, Modena was well on its way to becoming the undisputed king of the sports car universe, compliments of a hidden (though equally influential) revolution.

Maserati's A6G/54 was a coachbuilder's favorite, with Allemano, Frua, and Zagato all making a number of bodies for the chassis. "Sometimes," Maserati engineer Giulio Alfieri reflects on this prolific period of design, "the body was studied by its constructor and would arrive completely finished. Other times, we would try to transfer our opinion to the body builder." Shown here is a 1956 Maserati A62000 Zagato with an Alfa 1750 Zagato in the background.

From 1950 to 1954 the most prolific coachbuilder for Ferrari was Vignale. His cars included this one-off 340MM berlinetta that won the 1951 Mille Miglia.

In the years immediately following World War II, "there was a big fallout in Italy's aircraft industry," said Giordano Casarini, one of Modena's leading managers who started with Ferrari. "There were numerous talented people—both engineers and craftsmen—who were incredibly skilled. Since fighter planes were no longer needed, all of a sudden they found themselves unemployed."

Osmosis made sure they did not stay that way for long. Central Italy's sports and racing car constructors were a small world, one with an effective grapevine. Once they learned that labor from companies such as Bologna's airplane manufacturer Reggiane

was available, the constructors, fabricators, and engineers began actively courting each other.

The result was a massive infusion of aircraft technology into the industry in the late 1940s/early 1950s. "For example," Casarini says, "Walter Salvarani designed propeller gears at Reggiane. At Ferrari, he used these principles when designing gearboxes." Casting technology, and the use of lightweight materials and construction techniques, also saw similar advances.

An ideal working environment ensured the transfusion happened quickly. "Modena had a free, independent atmosphere," Sergio Pininfarina observed. "While Turin also had a large supply of

craftsmen, the Modenese could easily take the initiative, for they were not obliged to follow the Fiat regulation, the Fiat permissions."

Further, the Italian workforce harbored a strong sense of duty, particularly in the transportation industry. Not only were they passionate about the product they manufactured, "the desires we had, that the managers had, everyone had, were the same as those of the owner," an assembly line worker notes when recalling the Boom years. "We had great pride in what we made."

People thus willingly sacrificed for the good of the company and industry. Because sports, racing, and GT car production was not a particularly cash-rich endeavor, each employee felt their hard work made a tremendous difference to the firm's welfare. This, in turn, ensured the industry would remain healthy. Overtime was never considered a sacrifice, so burning the midnight oil became a widely accepted practice, particularly in the days and weeks before an auto salon or key race.

Firms like Ferrari and Pinin Farina had another, powerful asset: a father-figure owner. When Pinin or Ferrari arrived at work, they frequently walked the production lines, spending time with their employees. Not only did they know all of their names, they knew the names of their wives and children, thus imbuing a sense of extended family into the workplace.

As the memories of nightly bombing raids and the corresponding migrations into the countryside faded away, a sense of euphoria swept across Italy, particularly in the industrious northern regions. International capital flowed into the country, thanks to the numerous exports and external capital investment.

From 1953 on, Italians from all walks of life became comfortable showing their newfound affluence. Now filled with hope, industriousness, and prosperity, automotive sales skyrocketed, clearing 140,000 for the first time ever in 1953. Sports car production, and the desire for ever-increasing speed, also boomed.

That year, Maserati introduced the A6GCS; overseeing its design and development was the prolific Gioachino Colombo, who had joined the firm in 1952. Primarily produced as a sports racer, the company's newest featured a potent 1,985-cc twincam six-cylinder engine, tubular chassis, independent front suspension, and rigid rear axle. While most were delivered as a handsome, minimalist Fantuzzi barchetta, a handful had Frua, Vignale, and Pinin Farina coachwork.

For the sportsman more interested in tearing up the streets, the Maserati A6G/54 debuted at the Paris Auto Show in late 1954. While its chassis and suspension shared much with the A6GCS, the A6G's engine was detuned to make it a better proposition for daily driving. Allemano and Frua made a handful of elegant coupes, berlinettas, and spyders on the chassis.

The most sporting A6G/54s were those made by Zagato. A true dual-purpose car, these beautifully balanced, lightweight berlinettas often competed in Italy's championship racing series.

Ferrari also came of age during the Boom. Not only was its production continually increasing, its unparalleled success in international competition made it the marque of choice for Italy's coachbuilders.

From 1950 to 1954, the most prolific user of Ferrari chassis was Alfredo Vignale. Born in Turin in 1913, he became an apprentice panel beater at age 11. In 1931, Vignale joined Carrozzeria Farina, staying with the firm until 1946 when he set up his own concern with his two brothers and a partner.

Although Alfredo was a capable designer himself, his company was at its best when he teamed up with Giovanni Michelotti. Then in his early 30s, Michelotti's career also started at Carrozzeria Farina. A true student of design and the coachbuilding craft, in 1949 Giovanni branched out on his own as a freelance designer.

Although he worked with Ghia, Bertone, and others, Michelotti and Vignale were a marriage made in sports car heaven. Ferrari historian Marcel Massini has catalogued more than 150 different Ferraris the prolific duo designed and produced, often using a race car chassis.

Yet the Michelotti-Vignale dominance of Ferrari factory–sanctioned designs proved to be temporary, once Enzo and Pinin finally

Vignale was also quite adept with beautiful spiders and barchettas such as this 250MM. Like many of the period's race cars these machines could easily be used on the street.

After Ferrari and Pinin Farina joined forces in 1952, the Turin coachbuilder quickly became Ferrari's *carrozzeria* of choice. The first production car by the two was the 250 Europa (pictured). Depending on the source quoted, 15 to 20 of these 130-mile-per-hour machines were made during 1953 and 1954.

One of the most spectacular Ferraris ever was this 375 MM by Pinin Farina. Built in 1954 on a racing chassis, the coachbuilder first presented the car at the Paris Auto Show, where famed film producer Roberto Rossellini purchased it for his wife, actress Ingrid Bergman.

sat down and talked business. "My father was very intuitive," Sergio Pininfarina recounted, "for he believed Ferrari would one day become the most important name in Italy, much like Alfa Romeo prior to the war.

"This made him want to go to Ferrari. At the same time, Mr. Ferrari wanted to work with Pinin Farina because, in his mind, he thought Pinin Farina was the best."

Although the two had known each other since the early 1920s, they continued to admire each other's work from afar. The reason was simple: "They were both prima donnas," Sergio smiles. "Ferrari was a man of very strong character, and my father was much the same. Mr. Ferrari was NOT coming to Farina, and my father was NOT going to Modena. So they met half way in Tartan, something like Gorbachev and Reagan agreeing to meet in Iceland."

Attending the luncheon were Battista and Sergio Farina, Ferrari, and Ferrari's sales manager, Girolamo Gardini. "Everything became extremely easy once they sat down at the table," Pininfarina said. "It was 'I will give you one chassis, you make one car.'

"They never spoke about any type of price. Both were very enthusiastic, for each thought 'This will be great.'"

On the ride back to Turin, Sergio got quite a start when his father turned to him and said, "You will take care of the Ferrari account." Once the initial surprise passed, "I was in paradise," Pininfarina recalled. "My father was a very good strategist, and this was very intelligent. It was his way of showing confidence in me, while being able to check on what I was doing."

The collaboration started slowly, with Pinin Farina making three 212 Inters in 1952. One was a cabriolet that was purchased by famed film producer Roberto Rossellini as a wedding present for Ingrid Bergman. A handful of 342 and 375 Americas, 250 Europas and Europa GTs, and several competition cars followed.

Like Vignale and Michelotti, Pinin Farina also made a number of memorable Ferrari one-offs. In 1954 at the Paris Auto Show, the coachbuilder debuted a 375 MM that was one of the most spectacular designs of all time. Featuring covered headlights, a mile-long hood, and trend-setting buttresses, it would be bought by Roberto Rossellini. A highlight of 1955 was a beautiful 375 Plus for Belgium's King Leopold.

When Ferrari and Pinin Farina had their meeting in Tortona, Alfa Romeo was actively planning its new car, the reasonably priced, sporty Giulietta sedan. Finmeccanica funded Alfa's initial foray into the world of mass production by floating a bond issue. To ensure the public quickly gobbled up the offering, the government holding company came up with a clever marketing scheme: 50 Giuliettas would be given away to bond holders.

Unfortunately for Alfa, the car's development lagged considerably. By fall 1953, nervous contest winners were asking for their cars, the response being a wall of corporate silence. The

The car that marked the turning point for Italy's sports car producers and coachbuilders was Alfa Romeo's Giulietta Sprint (foreground). First shown in 1954, "if Alfa Romeo knew how many Giulietta Sprints would be sold," coachbuilder Nuccio Bertone reflected years later, "they would have never turned to us to produce it."

press smelled a scandal of astronomical proportions and started having a field day.

With lions now at the gate, something needed to be done, and in a hurry. Knowing a coachbuilder could have a car ready for the rapidly approaching 1954 Turin Show introduction date, Alfa's management contacted Carrozzeria Bertone.

The choice could not have been better, for the firm was clearly a star on the rise. Since hanging up his racing helmet in 1952, Nuccio Bertone's first order of business was finding new clients. Within months, he had inked a deal with American Stanley "Wacky" Arnolt for a limited production run of Bertone-bodied, English MG TDs. The resulting Arnolt-MG would lead to another car, the Arnolt-Bristol.

Nuccio quickly took on additional duties. While not a stylist per se, Bertone possessed an outstanding eye for properly assessing talent. Using his own personal good taste as his anchor, over the ensuing decades he would guide numerous designers to international stardom.

Nuccio's first protege was Franco Scaglione. Born in Florence in 1917, Scaglione's youthful interest in mechanics had him major in engineering in college. When the war cut his studies short, following its conclusion he turned his attention to design. Nuccio hired him in early 1952.

Scaglione was truly an artist with sheet metal. One of the most creative and flamboyant of all stylists, his first design at Bertone was a highly original Fiat-Abarth berlinetta. It debuted at Turin in 1952, *Road & Track* calling it "one of the most radical designs of the year."

The following year, Carrozzeria Bertone vaulted into the world's automotive spotlight when its astonishing BAT 5 stunned Turin's press and public alike. Standing for "Berlinetta Aerodinamica Tecnica #5" (the first four BAT designs remained stillborn), Bertone and Scaglione's goal

The Giulietta Spider was designed and built by Pinin Farina and was also a tremendous marketplace hit. Both the Giulietta Sprint and Spider were succeeded by the larger displacement (1,600-cc vs. 1,300-cc) but nearly identical-appearing Giulia Sprint and Spider in 1962. The Giulia Spider remained in production into 1966.

Lancia's Aurelia B24 Spider and Convertible were launched in 1955. The more luxurious Convertible (pictured) had a longer wheelbase and wider track and outsold its sportier cousin by a two to one margin. The two models remained in production into 1958.

was to create an aerodynamic shape that dramatically reduced drag and turbulence.

The BAT's form did that, and more. Constructed on a fully functioning Alfa 1900 chassis and capable of touching 125 miles per hour, "The car seemed very stable at high speeds," journalist-racing driver Paul Frère observed in *Auto Italiana*, "tending to straighten up automatically after cornering at sustained speeds."

Now eager and confident, Bertone warmly welcomed Alfa Romeo's approach in the fall of 1953. Acting as lead man for Alfa was Rudolf Hruska, the advisor to Finmeccanica.

Then in his late 30s, Hruska received his degree in mechanical engineering from the University of Vienna, then went to work with Professor Porsche in the late 1930s. After the war, he was a key participant on Cisitalia's mid-engined type 360 race car.

Hruska became friends with Bertone when Nuccio competed against Cisitalia with his Stanguellini. While touring the Bertone works in 1952, Nuccio says the Viennese engineer paused when seeing the Arnolt MGs. "Why are you concentrating on the export market?" Hruska asked. "I'm only doing what is not possible to do here," Bertone responded.

"But we could do something like this at Alfa," the engineer replied.

It is thus no wonder the company turned to Bertone to solve the Giulietta crisis. Although Alfa management wanted to produce just 50 cars, Bertone says Hruska felt the idea of a Giulietta sports/GT would be a winner, and maintained that production should be at least 1,000 units. Bertone bit the bullet, then teamed up with Scaglione and designer Mario Felice

Boano (whose carrozzeria would make a one-off Alfa for Argentine president Juan Peron) to give the existing Giulietta design a proper massage.

The final product broke cover at Turin in April 1954. Called the Giulietta Sprint, it was the hit of the show. With a 65-horsepower, 1,290-cc, twincam four-cylinder engine, four-speed gearbox, independent front suspension, and handsome wind-cheating body, Alfa listed its top speed at 100 miles per hour.

The Giulietta Sprint's performance backed up its well-balanced looks. "The road holding and comfort of this amazing little car is streets ahead of anything offered to the public," *Road & Track* enthused in November 1954. "[We have] little doubt [Alfa] will find a large number of small car enthusiasts quite happy to pay about $3,250 for this delightful motor car."

They were right; almost 25,000 would be sold over the following 10 years. Dubbed "the pioneer of small-displacement GT cars" by the same publication in 1964, not only did the Giulietta Sprint transform Alfa Romeo's production, it did the same for Bertone and the entire coachbuilding industry. Now a carrozzeria could look beyond the typical *fouri serie* production run, one in the tens to low hundreds in volume, each hand-built car minutely different from the one before and after it.

Giulietta Sprint production quickly hit 32 a day, the mountain of incoming cash allowing Bertone to dramatically expand his works. Within a decade, Nuccio's firm would challenge Pinin Farina as Turin's most notable coachbuilder.

Shortly after the Giulietta Sprint went on sale, American importer Max Hoffman began pressuring Alfa for a spyder version.

Although Bertone proposed a swoopy Scaglione design, the production Giulietta Spyder was the work of Pinin Farina.

The model first appeared at the Paris Auto Show in 1955. Having the same drivetrain and a shortened Giulietta Sprint platform, it was called the exhibit's prettiest car by England's *Motor* magazine.

Within months, Alfa's newest was beguiling consumers and magazines alike. After lauding its roadholding, ride, braking, and engine, "without a doubt," *Road & Track* stated in its April 1956 road test, "[this] is the most fascinating small sports car we have ever driven. With an engine of only 78.7 inches of cubic displacement, it provides a performance which approaches the modern American behemoth so closely that one wonders if [Detroit's] claims of 300 horsepower are not closer to an honest 150."

Like the Giulietta Sprint with Bertone, the Giulietta Spyder served as a turning point for Pinin Farina. "At the end of 1954, I had built five cars and Alfa wanted 2,000," Pinin wrote in *Born with the Automobile*. "[A]s agile as gazelles, [t]hey were highly enjoyable mass-produced cars [that were] assured a place in history."

During the same period, Pinin Farina also made a beautiful spyder for Lancia, the Aurelia B24. Breaking cover at 1955's Brussels Auto Show and called a "superbly styled two seater with a claimed maximum of 115 mph" by *Autocar*, it featured the B20's underpinnings, smooth V-6 engine, and a wonderfully proportioned body, highlighted by an American-style wraparound windshield.

"If you pride yourself on being a connoisseur of fine craftsmanship, you don't have to look much further than the Aurelia Spyder," America's *Motor Trend* noted. "What the Lancia is," the magazine's Walt Woron wrote, "is a car that handles as well as the best I have driven: Ferrari, Mercedes 300 SL, Siata."

That specialist constructors like Siata were mentioned in the same breath as Ferrari and Mercedes demonstrates the prominent role they played in establishing and perpetuating Italy's sports car mystique.

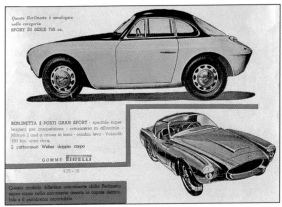

Thanks to its close association with Fiat, Siata offered something none of its direct competitors could touch: a model with a V-8 engine. After showing a handful of interesting, V-8 powered one-offs at various auto shows, the car that truly brought the firm international acclaim was its 208S spyder.

Introduced in 1952, this dual-purpose Siata proved to be a popular and successful racer in America. *Road & Track*'s November 1953 test lauded the smoothness of the engine, the car's "phenomenal" cornering prowess, and its "very comfortable" ride. "Inevitably," they concluded, "this car will be compared to a Ferrari and scores considerably in reliability, durability, quietness, smoothness, and accessibility."

Moretti—another name with prewar links—was also finding an audience in the early to mid-1950s. Originally founded in 1927 by ex-motorcycle racer Giovanni Moretti, after the war the firm made the Cita, a small, curiously styled coupe powered by a 350-cc engine. In 1950 it began building a convertible with a 600-cc powerplant.

Hudson's Italia demonstrates that anything could economically be created in Italy. "At the end of a dinner, I did a little drawing on a napkin," Carrozzeria Touring's Carlo Anderloni recalls. "Several months later, we signed a contract, and Hudson sent us disassembled chassis to make the cars." Touring would produce 25 from 1953-55.

Moretti's first true sports car burst on to the scene three years later. Called the Gran Sport and offered as a diminutive berlinetta or barchetta, it was powered by a Moretti-massaged, 750-cc twincam engine.

In 1954 a Gran Sport Berlinetta was on the cover of *Road & Track*. Having nimble road manners and capable of touching 100 miles per hour, the magazine dubbed it "a baby Ferrari."

Other flourishing specialist constructors included Stanguellini and OSCA. Throughout the decade and on into the 1960s, Stanguellini would build numerous Formula 2 and Formula Jr. single-seaters, and a handful of beautiful, two-seat dual-purpose sports cars. Called the 750 and 1100 Bialbero (twincam), and having beautiful, sleek open coachwork, the latter machines competed all over the world and finished in the top 20 at Le Mans in the late 1950s.

As prolific as Stanguellini, Moretti, and Siata were during the Boom, the segment's benchmark was undoubtedly OSCA. After splitting with Gruppo Orsi, the Maserati brothers began producing the Mt4 in 1948. By the 1950s, the model had evolved enough so that Zagato, Michelotti, and Vignale made several with berlinetta bodies.

The most famous Mt4s were those done by local coachbuilder Morelli. Having an attractive, lightweight aluminum barchetta body on OSCA's proprietary tube frame, the heart of every Mt4 was its gem of a four-cylinder engine. Designed and constructed in-house, over the years it grew from 1,100 cc and 60 horsepower to 1,490 cc and 110 horsepower.

America proved to be Siata, Stanguellini, Moretti, and OSCA's most active foreign market, thanks in great part to the country's blossoming sports car movement. In addition to good press coverage, each make had a distributor in that faraway land, their clients actively (and often successfully) campaigning the cars.

Florida's endurance race at Sebring highlighted the specialist boom perfectly. In 1954, an OSCA made headlines around the world when it won the 12-hour contest outright, beating Ferraris, Lancias, Jaguars, and Porsches in the process.

Given their marketplace and competition successes, surprisingly the specialist constructors' days were numbered. Within a matter of years, most would be replaced by an entirely new group of manufacturers, firms financed beyond the specialist constructors' wildest dreams.

Section III
Prosperity

Capitani d'Industria

1956 - 1960

O ne specialist constructor who would survive and prosper through the 1950s and 1960s was Carlo Abarth. After displaying his beautiful, Vignale-bodied 205-A in 1951, the company went on a tear. For 1952's Turin Show, Abarth teamed with Bertone and Scaglione, preparing the engine, chassis, and suspension for the coachbuilder's avant-garde Fiat 1400 that so captivated *Road & Track*. A director of Packard bought it on sight at the show and sent it back to America.

Garnering even greater publicity were three Lancia B20 Aurelia GTs that Abarth modified for Mexico's grueling four-day, 1,800-mile endurance race, the Carrera Panamerica. Thanks to Carlo's tweaks on the engine, suspension, brakes, and exhaust, one finished fourth overall, behind two competition Mercedes and a Ferrari. A series of hopped-up, Lancia Aurelia B20 *Elaboraziones* followed.

In 1953, Abarth began his long and fruitful collaboration with Fiat and France's Simca with two attractively styled coupes by Ghia. He also teamed with Ferrari to make a lightweight 166 that would win Italy's 2,000-cc championship.

The company's most memorable car from the first half of the 1950s was the radical 207-A Spyder Corsa. The last in a series of front-engined, Fiat-based specials, its wild Boano coachwork captivated magazines around the world.

Yet, Abarth's true profit center and reputation-builder was its unequaled success in manufacturing performance components. Thanks to constant growing demand for Abarth's multi-carburetor manifolds, free-flow exhaust systems, and other items, Carlo's workforce mushroomed from 12 to more than 100 in just four years.

When the company waved its magic wand over Fiat's humble 600, the results were astounding. "Driven fast and hard over our local stretch of abominable roads with a high quota of potholes, ruts and rills, the little Abarth-Fiat was a good

Bertone's desire to build an even faster Alfa Giulietta resulted in the Sprint Speciale. First shown in 1957, the Giulietta Sprint Speciale went on sale in 1959, its avant garde styling drawing much from Bertone's wild Alfa Romeo BATs of the mid-1950s.

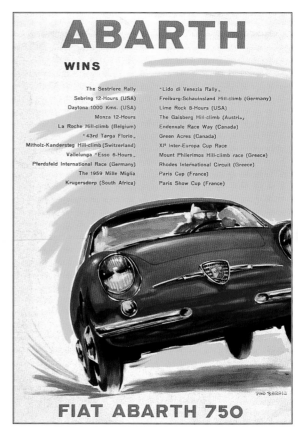

The car that brought Abarth international fame was its "giant killer," the Fiat-Abarth 750 Zagato. First seen in 1956, "as often happened with our products," Elio Zagato says, "the inspiration for the car's shape came from an airplane wing. We also carefully studied driver compartment visibility, and the form-fitting bucket seats." *John Ling Collection*

Holy Toledo are the two words that best describe Abarth's 1955 207-A. It is hard to believe a Fiat 1100 chassis lurks underneath the spectacular aluminum Boano coachwork. One competed at that year's 12 Hours of Sebring, where it was disqualified for refueling outside the pits.

deal more comfortable than the family's Detroit-built sedan, and transmitted none of the shudder that racked the big car," America's *Speed Age* observed.

Even more startling was the difference in acceleration. With the 0 to 60 time versus the standard Fiat dropping from 54 to 15 seconds, the magazine noted the Abarth-prepared 600 was quicker than 10 other imported (and larger displacement) cars it had tested during the previous months.

Such dramatic improvements did not go unnoticed in Turin. "Not many years ago, Siata acted as an unofficial external experimental department of Fiat," America's *Sports Car Illustrated* observed in the late 1950s. "[Now], Abarth seems to be standing in the benevolent gaze of the Agnellis."

In 1955, Abarth teamed with Zagato to create a Fiat that served as the small-displacement benchmark for the next several

years. That the two firms would be perfect tag team partners was a given their raison d'etre was too similar for the relationship to fail.

Like Abarth, Zagato had prospered during Italy and Europe's so-called "economic miracle." Because Ugo Zagato's factory was razed during the war, in 1946 he had a new facility erected on the outskirts of Milan. In addition to designing and making a radical, rear-engined Isotta-Fraschini prototype with engineer Fabio Luigi Rapi, in 1947 Zagato began producing the innovative Panoramica, a small GT on Fiat 500 and 1100 chassis with glass that extended well into the roof. Other cars using the Panoramica concept were Ferrari, Maserati, Lancia, and Alfa.

Zagato also returned to competition with a vengeance. When its Fiat 750 Testadoro (Golden head) proved so successful on the racetrack, several foreign magazines thought Zagato was a constructor rather than a coachbuilder.

The highest performing Giuliettas were those made by Zagato. The rare machines used a chassis that was identical to Bertone's Sprint Speciale. The Giulietta SZ (Sprint Zagato) that was first seen in 1959 had a stubby, aerodynamic body. In 1961 this aesthetically pleasing long tail version (called the Coda Trunca) broke cover and was the ideal dual-purpose car.

As the 1950s began, Ugo's son Elio started managing the firm. Working closely with his father, the company expanded and moved upmarket. Besides the Fiat 8V and Maserati A6 2000, Zagato introduced the Alfa Romeo 1900 SSZ in 1953. Undoubtedly the sportiest of the production 1900s, these true dual-purpose cars were equally at home on the street or the track.

The model also served as the genesis for one of Zagato's most distinctive styling elements, the double bubble roof. "I had a client I wanted to sell one to, but he was too tall," Elio Zagato recalled. "So instead of remaking the car or enlarging the roof, I tried a 'bubble' over the driver and passenger seats. When it was done, I like the way it looked. The design made the roof a lot more rigid, allowing us to use thinner gauge metal, making the car lighter."

With Zagato cars racking up class win after class win, "[The coachbuilder] has established [itself] as a true wizard of lightweight design," Bernard Cahier observed in Road & Track's June 1957 issue. "No one can help but admire greatly the men who, with small means, have proved capable year after year of making a faster car out of anything brought to them."

When the coachbuilder turned its attention to Fiat's 600, "I was at 1955's Turin Show, half hidden by our Fiat 8V, Siata 1250, and of course, the Fiat," Elio Zagato recalled. "I saw Carlo Abarth looking at our cars, so I took the opportunity to introduce myself. The meeting was very short: just enough time to show him our little coupe and have his comment that, with its original, unmodified engine, it would not have a big future."

That simple observation planted the seed. With Abarth being "the most practical way" to make something truly competitive, Elio arranged a follow-up meeting late that summer. "I

FIAT 1200

roadster

The **Fiat 1200 roadster** accentuates the brilliant qualities of the Fiat 1200 Full-Light Saloon: higher speed (**about 145 km = 90 miles per hour**) and the advantage of using it preferably in the open position, with the hood down. This is of canvas on a steel frame and when down is completely hidden inside the car panelling.

Fiat's attractive successor to its awkwardly styled 1955 Transformabile convertible was the 1200 Roadster. Introduced at the 1959 Geneva Show, it was soon supplemented by the larger displacement 1500 Roadster. The most potent of the series was the 1600S that used an OSCA-derived twincam engine.

If any car sums up elegance and style in the late 1950s, it has to be Ferrari's Series I 250 Cabriolet by Pinin Farina. Masterfully proportioned with magnificent details such as the sweep up just behind the seats, approximately 40 were made between 1957 and 1959. Ferrari's famed 250 Spider California was similar in appearance, but weighed less and had a more powerful engine.

OSCA's dual-purpose 1600 GT often battled Alfa Romeos in the early 1960s. Zagato was the most popular coachbuilder, as its berlinettas often raced; this particular example competed at Sebring. Milan's Carrozzeria Boneschi made two 1600s and called them the Swift. After Zagato, Carrozzeria Fissore was the most popular coachbuilder, offering both a coupe and spider.

absolutely need your engine," Zagato told the engineer. "Together, no one will beat us."

"You drive well and show a lot of courage," Abarth replied. "I think we can reach an agreement."

The resulting Fiat-Abarth 750 Zagato was truly an extraordinary little automobile. Where the standard Fiat-Abarth 750 did 80 miles per hour, the Zagato would touch 100.

Even more impressive were its all-around road manners. *Autocar*'s editors found the steering "wonderfully light and precise at all times," its "surprisingly soft and comfortable" suspension going around corners "much faster than most drivers would dare to discover."

"In brief," they concluded, "the Abarth is a gem which not only gives the driver an enormous amount of fun and pleasure, but is extremely safe and comfortable, [having] performance that belies its size, though not its shape."

In America, the land of gargantuan cars and roads, the reaction was much the same. *Sports Car Illustrated* found it "hung onto the road like the proverbial painted center line." *Motor Trend* called it a "miniature Maserati," noting its body was "a sample of Italian coachwork at its best—[n]ot since driving the

Moretti coupe have [we] seen so many people gawk in admiration as we drove by." More remarkable was the spacious interior: a 6-footer easily had room for himself *and* his luggage!

That Italy's manufacturers and coachbuilders made their products more commodious and habitable in the second half of the 1950s was a reflection of the times. Throughout the decade, and in particular, from 1953 on, the era of prosperity saw a large—and constantly increasing—demand for luxury. On top of this, a new phenomenon—the desire for a second car—just started making itself felt for large portions of Italy and Europe's populace.

With fun and glamour rapidly becoming the "in" things, Italians seemed to have a handle on the latter better than anyone else. It is thus no surprise that for those who could afford it, the car of choice was the gran turismo, or GT.

In basic terms, a gran turismo is an automobile that gets its occupants from Point A to Point B as quickly as the driver can go. But unlike many of the era's sports cars, a GT's occupants arrived at their final destination feeling as refreshed as when they started the trip, regardless of length. "When a knowledgeable European driver wants to get places in a hurry," *Sports Car Illustrated* succinctly summed in 1959, "he uses a GT-type machine."

All one had to do was look at Italy's *Capitani d'Industrie* to understand why the market was booming. When the "economic miracle" took hold, these "captains of industry" were the driving force behind Italy's rebirth. Operating in an environment free of restraints, "they practically established Italy's postwar industrial style," says Piero Rivolta, son of one of the Milan area's most noted capitani. "Not only did they find the money, products, and people, they also had to beat the competition."

Much more motivated these men than just profits; they harbored a great interest in all facets of their business. In addition to shouldering capital risk, they were intimately involved in creating, producing, marketing, and the selling of their goods or services.

They also recognized the importance of their employees. "Many capitani were like good fathers," Rivolta observes. "They took care of the people working for them," a trait that instilled great loyalty to the firm and its owner.

In truth, Rivolta's father, Renzo, serves as the ideal case study. He first manufactured refrigerators after the war, then gutted his Isothermos factory to produce motorscooters. When the market asked for greater luxury, Iso's scooters became motorbikes. He then made the Isetta bubblecar, eventually selling its production rights to BMW and several other foreign entities.

As Rivolta's net worth expanded exponentially, he never forgot the people who got him there: his employees. More than once he underwrote the purchase of a key worker's home, taking a small amount from their paycheck until the interest-free loan was paid in full. He also gave his secretary a new car as a thank you for her commitment and dedication.

As the economic miracle continued largely unabated (crises such as 1956's Suez Canal conflict were minor aberrations), Rivolta, numerous other Italian (and European) capitani and their

managers, bought new GTs. Yet these machines were much more than a "reward" purchase, something to tastefully display their success. With Italy's autostrada system coming of age, and air service throughout Europe spotty at best, the gran turismo became the transportation mode of choice, the perfect way to travel hundreds of miles in comfort and refinement.

As more people bought GTs, market segments began to blur. "A few years ago it would have been unthinkable to group together under one heading sports and Grand Touring cars," Road & Track observed. "However, the GT car has become much faster and many sports cars have acquired some creature comforts, so the sharp distinction is no longer there."

"Practically every European manufacturer is building a high-performance version of its production car," photojournalist Jesse Alexander observed in an article appropriately titled "GT Cars Are Here to Stay." "This was never more evident than at the 1958 Turin Show when Italy's staid 'Big One'—Fiat—jumped onto the GT bandwagon with a 1 1/2-liter coupe."

Called the 1500 GT, most startling was its use of an OSCA engine. So how did Italy's largest manufacturer turn to one of its smallest for a proper, sporting powerplant?

"The story began on July 11, 1957, when I welcomed Ernesto Maserati to [Fiat's] Mirafiori [facility] for the first time," Dante Giacosa observed in his autobiography. "[He] was serious and unassuming in manner, a great expert in racing engines [who] awakened my interest and liking.

"We soon agreed to propose mounting an OSCA 1500 cc engine on the 1200 with coachwork by Pinin Farina. After getting the go ahead from the presidential office we carried out tests and modified the engine to fit our requirements." Debuting on the coachbuilder's stand at Turin, *Sports Car Illustrated* called it the hit of the show.

That 1.5-liter prototype was the first in a number of new Fiat sports cars. During the summer of 1959, the company introduced the 1500 Spyder, the production version of its collaboration with OSCA. Called by *Road & Track* "a quality machine that is very pleasant to drive," the 1500 had been preceded four months earlier by the tamer, Fiat-engined 1200 cabriolet.

Zagato also teamed up with Lancia to make the highest performing version of its luxurious Flaminia. First shown in 1959, its sleek berlinetta look drew heavily on the earlier Lancia Appia Zagato. Zagato's most potent Flaminia was the 148-horsepower, 130-mile-per-hour Supersport that was introduced in 1964.

The 250 GT that Ferrari introduced in 1958 marked a turning point for the company. Unlike the previous collaborations with Pinin Farina, this model's body was uniform for the most part throughout its production run, being devoid of the custom coachwork and small aesthetic differences seen on the previous 250 series. The 250 GT was a tremendous success, with Ferrari producing 350 from 1958 to 1960.

In 1962 the 1500 was succeeded by the faster, OSCA-derived 1600S. Fiat would sell more than 15,000 of its roadsters in a four-year period, and coachbuilders often used the platform to exhibit their wares.

Alfa Romeo was also on a roll; the Giulietta Sprint's runaway success prompted the company to further explore the gran turismo concept. Using that best-seller as a base, in 1957 the company again teamed up with Bertone to create the Giulietta Sprint Speciale. Using the Giulietta Spyder's shorter chassis, "[It] was a long, low streamlined coupe of rare beauty," *Motor Trend* commented on its 1957 Turin Show introduction, "one that brought enthusiasts jostling like bees around a honey pot."

Road & Track found the Speciale's additional length and weight were offset by the model's unusual, wind-cheating shape. Despite having the same 1.3-liter engine as the Giulietta Sprint, it would touch 120 miles per hour. "Taken as a road car," the magazine observed, "the Speciale is ideal: fast, safe, [and] economical insofar as gas mileage is concerned."

Zagato made an even quicker Giulietta, the SZ. Its development began in 1957, with the production version going on sale in 1959. Lighter than the Speciale, *Road & Track* noted the Zagato was one second quicker to 60 miles per hour and four seconds faster to 100. "Whereas the Bertone coupe has unmistakable understeer and feels a bit heavy in some corners," the magazine observed, "the Zagato strikes a good compromise between the ability to keep straight on bumpy roads and a very unusual degree of controllability.

"If your car must have race-winning potential in addition to the features required for fast touring," *R&T* concluded, "the Zagato is the obvious choice. If fast touring is your only aim, then the steel-bodied Veloce or Speciale models, very little slower but less expensive, seem preferable."

This observation highlights another reason for Italy's leadership role in sports cars and GTs: Its manufacturers excelled in rudimentary "platform engineering," using the same basic under-pinnings and drivetrain to provide widely disparate personalities in different models.

The coachbuilders played a pivotal role in the process. "The manufacturers expected us to present our own version of a specified model, one that typically reflected the personality of the carrozzeria," Touring's Carlo Anderloni said. "With each coachbuilder offering a different type of body, it gave diverse results. Usually, Zagato was the most sporty, while Pininfarina was classical. We were a combination of sporting and luxury."

Lancia's Flaminia illustrates this perfectly. Having rebounded from another financial crisis in the mid-1950s, now at the helm of the company was Carlo Presenti. "He would say, 'You are the coachbuilder,'" Anderloni recalled. "'You know how the car should be presented.'"

When the company introduced its range of sporty Flaminia GTs at the 1958 Turin Show, their underpinnings and drivetrain came from the Flaminia sedan. Per Presenti's philosophy, Pinin Farina coachwork graced an attractive 119 horsepower, 107-mile-per-hour 2+2 coupe, while Touring was responsible for the 112-mile-per-hour GT and Convertible. Ugo, Elio, and Company designed and built the fastest Flaminia: the lightweight, 120-mile-per-hour Sport Zagato.

Lancia's newest models were considerably more luxurious than its Appias (which also had a variety of coachwork) and Alfa Romeo's Giulietta, Giulietta Speciale, and SZ. "Driving the Lancia Zagato was a rare pleasure," *Road & Track* commented in its May 1960 test. "[It] is a gran turismo car in the strictest sense, which means that it will probably never win any races but . . . provide its owners with many miles of pleasurable driving. The interior fittings are posh enough for anyone and the car should be unexcelled for high speed, long distance touring in comfort."

Touring's Flaminia GT also found fans in America. "Slide into the shapely leather seat, swing shut the close-fitting aluminum door, fire up the unique V6, and discover how elegant earthbound motion can become," Car & Driver magazine enthused.

With the gran turismo market booming, Fiat's dance partner, OSCA, also wanted in on the action. In 1960 it introduced a model suitable for the street, the 1600 GT. Having a 1,568-cc four-cylinder engine that would produce 95 to 145 horsepower, Zagato, Touring, Fissore, and Boneschi produced a wide variety of bodies on the chassis.

As the mass producers rolled out one new model after another, the leaders of the sports and GT universe remained Ferrari and Maserati. Recognizing that well-heeled customers wanted—indeed, expected—something more sophisticated than a racing car wearing a new suit, compliments of a leading carrozzeria, Ferrari responded with its first "mass-produced" car, the 250 GT.

The model reflected the synergy of the Ferrari-Pinin Farina relationship. "Right from the first job we did together," Pinin wrote, "I realized we complemented each other, not so much in the mechanical or design sense." Rather, "it was the creation of a car, [t]he result [being] as precise as two hands clasping."

"What I wanted for my cars was character, and I found it with the help of Giovanni Battista Pininfarina," Ferrari noted in his memoirs. "I always admired Pinin for what he was able to make of his work and his life, and for the taste he injected into both. He launched a distinctive style [and] transformed the car into a high fashion statement. Pinin was a great artist."

While their mutual admiration was truly genuine, the first few years were anything but easy for the young man in the relationship's hot seat, Sergio Pininfarina. When he was first put in charge of the account, "everybody was happy except Mr. Ferrari, for he wanted to work with my father," Pininfarina smiled as he said that. "You must remember I was 25 years old, and if you see the pictures of me at that time, I looked like I was 18, just a boy.

"So my first three to five years were terrible. Everything was wrong. Whatever I did was never enough—the body was too heavy, or it cost too much."

Still, young Sergio's earnestness and dedication would pay off. After what undoubtedly seemed an eternity, "Mr. Ferrari began to appreciate my sense of good will and commitment to the work," Pininfarina continued. "I was a very serious young man, a committed engineer, very reliable, fastidious and precise.

"So Ferrari started to say, 'He is reliable.' Then he began saying, 'He is a good engineer.' Then, at the end, I became like a second son. In the last years of his life, he was like a father for me, a very sweet man."

The "marriage" came of age in the second half of the 1950s. In addition to designing and making a number of competition cars, one-offs, and *fouri serie* models, the Pinin Farina–designed 250 GT was a handsome, understated two-seat coupe. Powered by Ferrari's 3-liter, 240-horsepower V-12 that was based on Gioachino Colombo's original 1,500-cc V-12, the production 250 evolved from a short series of Pinin Farina design exercises in 1957 and 1958.

When the prototype was unveiled in June 1958, "Farina's new Ferrari Gran Turismo coupe delighted everyone at its first public presentation," Bernard Cahier noted in *Road & Track*. "Its distinguished and racy looks sold out the first planned series of 200 cars well in advance."

Once journalists spent time behind the wheel, it was clear that production would stretch beyond that initial batch of 200. "The main impression this car gives is outstanding silence and smoothness," John Bolster wrote in England's *Autosport*. "I would describe this Ferrari as a superb luxury car, combining great performance with extreme refinement to an almost unapproachable degree."

America's publications concurred completely. *Sports Car Graphic* magazine voted it 1960's "Sportscar of the Year," while *Road & Track* felt it was "the ultimate in driving."

Pinin Farina and Ferrari also produced two open-air 250s during the same period. While the 250 Cabriolet was a luxurious, fast touring car, the more sporting 250 Spyder California was destined to become an all-time classic.

According to Ferrari sales manager Girolamo Gardini, the man behind this memorable model was Ferrari's impresario in California, Johnny Von Neumann. Wanting an open-air car that would appeal to sunny southern California's wealthy clientele, the California's striking yet aggressive looks were based on a series of Pinin Farina–designed 250 competition coupes, and three, unique 250 GT spyders the coachbuilder made in 1957.

The Ferrari legend was further enhanced by the 250 SWB. Although ex-Ferrari engineer Giotto Bizzarrini would later reflect "they had the ride of a Wild West wagon," the 250 SWB was the ideal dual-purpose car, capable of driving to any race, winning it, and then driving home. A 250 SWB placed fourth at Le Mans in 1960, while another was third the following year.

While many Californias had steel bodies and lived rather sedate lives, ambling along the Italian coast near Portofino or zipping up Beverly Hills' Sunset Boulevard, one equipped with a more powerful competition engine and lightweight aluminum body finished fifth overall at Le Mans in 1959.

Another Ferrari-Pinin Farina masterpiece from the period was the 250 SWB, or Short Wheelbase Berlinetta. Debuting at the Paris Auto Show in October 1959, it was based on a competition Ferrari 250 GT that placed fourth overall at Le Mans, just ahead of that special Spyder California. The SWB's taut shape featured perfect proportions, aggressive "haunches" for rear fenders, and a sloping fastback.

"Without equivocation," *Sports Car Illustrated* noted in its lengthy report on the model, "[the 250 SWB] is powered by the greatest automotive engine in the world today." This was just one of many reasons they called it "the finest genuine sports car we have ever driven."

A key figure in the Spyder California/SWB story was coachbuilder Sergio Scaglietti. Born in Modena in 1920, at age 15 he joined his brother at a local carrozzeria when his father unexpectedly passed away. In the late 1930s, Sergio followed the elder Scaglietti when he opened a new coachbuilding firm across the street from the Scuderia Ferrari. Following the war, the Scaglietti brothers were constantly kept busy, repairing cars, bridges, and boats.

Sergio went out on his own in the early 1950s. A good study of the coachbuilding craft during his formative years in the trade, he put those lessons to good use when he started repairing, then designing and building, competition Ferraris. As the decade progressed, Scaglietti-bodied cars began winning world championships.

What is most remarkable is Scaglietti never drew a single design. Instead, the simple, modest man says, "Everything was done by the eyes alone." When pressed for keys to his success,

"aerodynamics were important," he observes, "for we understood the more aerodynamic a car was, the more beautiful it became."

He also notes he tried to "follow the style of Ferrari. My main inspiration was Pinin Farina, for their lines were very elegant, sober and timeless."

After helping Ferrari win the 1957 and 1958 world championships with the 250 Testa Rossa, in 1959 Scaglietti began constructing the Spyder California and 250 SWB. Sergio Pininfarina fondly recalls collaborating with the master craftsman from Modena: "He was a man with no tradition or culture. When you looked at the shoes, the way he spoke, he was very much a countryman.

"On the contrary, I was young, refined, and educated, like a young lord. So here was this 'young lord' and the 'beast'—we were very good friends and had a very nice feeling. I must say Scaglietti was very kind to me, and we worked very well together."

Although Ferrari concentrated on its 250 models, the company also made the 410 SA (Superamerica). The perfect Ferrari for the prominent *Capitano d'Industria* who desired something truly special, each one of these pricey, jewel-like GTs was custom-built for the owner. Featuring a 4.9-liter, 340-horsepower V-12, the model debuted early in 1956 at the Brussels Show.

The 410 SA that truly set the tone for the series was the second one constructed, Pinin Farina's seminal showcar, Superfast I. Introduced at the 1956 Paris Auto Show, "[this] is one of the most beautiful cars in the world," *Road & Track* noted in 1957. "Its performance [is] so fantastic as to be almost beyond all comprehension [for it] can spin its driving wheels in 3rd gear at 100 mph."

Maserati also benefited greatly from the economic miracle; but while Ferrari's expansion during the 1950s was unabated, Adolfo Orsi's company traveled a much more difficult road to production prosperity.

One of the mid-1950s most spectacular cars was Pinin Farina's Superfast I. This dream car Ferrari debuted at the Paris Auto Show in 1956 and introduced a number of future Ferrari and Pinin Farina design hallmarks: the greenhouse; proportioning; shape of the nose; and two-tone paint that seemed to split the car in half.

In early 1958, the racing world was stunned to learn the firm was withdrawing from competition after winning the 1957 Formula 1 championship, the European Hillclimb championship, and narrowly missing the endurance championship. Magazines around the world quickly launched into numerous theories on why the famous name was withdrawing, most focusing on a sudden rule change in F1 and the associated cost of designing, engineering, and producing new cars.

Such reasoning only scratched the surface. Where crosstown rival Ferrari was strictly an automotive concern, the Gruppo Orsi empire stretched into numerous other endeavors. "During World War II, Maserati began producing milling machines," said Adolfo Orsi's grandson, who is also named Adolfo. "Their sales were instrumental in supporting the company's racing efforts in the 1950s."

That highly profitable endeavor nearly proved to be the firm's undoing. "Mr. Orsi was friendly with the Peron government in Argentina, and was selling very large quantities of lathes and milling machines there," said engineer Aurelio Bertocchi, son of famed Maserati test driver Guerino Bertocchi. "When Peron was deposed, Orsi was left with a lot of outstanding credits."

Despite the withdrawal from competition, Orsi still faced a massive cash flow crunch. In April 1958 he was forced to declare the equivalent of America's Chapter 11 bankruptcy.

Yet, there was light at the end of the tunnel. "At the time all of this was happening, we had just started the 3500 GT program," Bertocchi continued. "So we concentrated all our efforts in that area, rather than racing." It would prove to be a wise decision, one that would see Maserati vault ahead of Ferrari in terms of production.

Leading the design and development of the company's offerings was Giulio Alfieri. Then in his mid-30s, the brilliant engineer was born in neighboring Parma in 1924. The son of an accountant and elementary school teacher, "my family had a very rigid, structured life," he says. "It was very important that I studied, read, and learned."

Those traits remained with him throughout his career. After graduating with an engineering degree from Milan's prestigious Polytechnic College, he first started working for a ship builder in Genoa, where he studied steam engines and gas turbines.

Yet, Alfieri always harbored a strong desire to work on cars. "The reason was simple," he said. "For me, the engine was not something static, a block of steel or aluminum. It was something with life."

A chance meeting with Adolfo Orsi changed everything. Hired by Maserati in 1953, within three years he was the company's chief engineer. Now able to indulge to his heart's content, "every day I always looked forward to waking up and going to work," the engineer beamed.

And so began a 20-year stint that saw a number of new and memorable GT cars emanate from the Maserati works, the first being the 3500 GT. Its 3.5-liter, 220-horsepower six-cylinder engine

derived directly from Maserati's lengthy competition experience. An independent front suspension and rigid axle, leaf springs, and shocks at the rear augmented the car's tubular chassis.

Unlike its previous offerings, Maserati wanted the 3500 to be a true production model, made in large numbers. After looking at proposals from several coachbuilders, the firm settled on Carrozzeria Touring to design and construct the 3500's body.

"They needed something sporty but luxurious, a GT that could be used every day," Carlo Anderloni said. "They wanted an understated car, one that didn't scream 'I have arrived.' It had to say you were important, but not a star; that you were serious."

The resulting 3500 GT's sober, attractive lines clearly reflected this design brief. Debuting at the 1957 Geneva Show, "Maserati [has] entered into direct competition with Ferrari in the American market with their Gran Turismo saloon," *Autocar* observed. "Bodywork by Touring of Milan is most elegantly executed, and the car has a claimed maximum of 145 mph."

All in Maserati comprehended the model's importance. "We made a prototype and started our testing, making it ready for production," Alfieri said. Then the crisis hit. Before the Orsis made any announcement to its employees, "you could tell there was something in the air, so we figured it out indirectly," Alfieri continued. "We began to produce the cars very fast, pushing them out, perhaps before they were fully developed. It was necessary to demonstrate that Maserati was alive."

Alfieri needn't have worried. "The buyer of a Maserati pays a lot for the privilege of ownership," *Road & Track* wrote in the

Maserati's first production car was the 3500 GT. The car was a collaboration between Maserati and Carrozzeria Touring, "That was a happy period for them," ex-Maserati chief engineer Giulio Alfieri reflected. "Their 'superleggera' [superlight] construction of thin tubes and aluminum bodies was the technique of the moment. Their quality, and the lines which were soft and serious, reflected Maserati's philosophy."
John Ling Collection

maserati3500gt

The first Maserati 5000 GT was the result of a phone call from the Shah of Persia in late 1958. Carlo Anderloni of Touring referenced Persian architecture to come up with its ornate front end. "It wasn't bad for an important car," Alfieri said. "It is obvious this was a car that was not connected with a quantity production." Maserati would build just three of the Touring-bodied Shah of Persia 5000 GTs.

first road test of a 3500, "but he gets a lot in return." The marketplace agreed, causing the company to have its best year ever in 1958. Sales would almost double the following year and easily clear 300 in 1960.

Wisely, the firm didn't rest on its laurels. "Maserati continues to increase the sales of the their 3500 GT, particularly in America," *Autocar* noted in 1959. "The appeal of this very fast and desirable car will be widened by [English] Girling disc brakes, used on a foreign car for the first time."

Like Ferrari and its 250, Maserati augmented the 3500 coupe with a spyder. Although Touring and Frua presented open-air prototypes, the production 3500 spyder was designed and built by Vignale. Going on sale in 1960, *Road & Track* called the model "a Modenese masterpiece for the touring enthusiast."

After Adolfo Orsi paid off his debts by selling a large portion of his estate, Maserati capped off its spectacular rebound with the perfect model for Italy's *Capitano d'Industria* period, the 5000 GT. Given the exclusive nature of the product, most fittingly the colorful saga started with a phone call from the Shah of Iran.

"I was in Turin at the time," Alfieri recalled of that fateful November in 1958, "and my family had received a number of calls from the Iranian embassy in Rome. Mr. Orsi had also been contacted, for they wanted to meet the two of us in Livorno the following day."

The two men dutifully traveled to the coastal city, where the Shah and his entourage joined them. After a brief exchange of pleasantries, "he pulled out a sales sheet on the 450 S," Alfieri said, referencing Maseratis powerful endurance racer that narrowly missed 1957's championship. "He then said, 'I want a car, using this as the basis. I would like something special I can use on the street.'"

Powering the Shah's car was Maserati's 400-horsepower, 4.5-liter V-8, the 5000 GT chassis being a modified and reinforced version of the 3500's tubular frame. On why he did not use the 450S chassis as a starting point, "in a successful gran turismo," Alfieri responds, "you have to pay attention to the occupants, and accessibility of the engine. In a racing car, you have nothing."

Like the 3500 GT, Anderloni and Touring clothed the first 5000. Its public debut was the 1959 Turin Auto Show, Maserati appropriately calling the model the "Shah of Persia."

"Touring presented the powerful new 5-liter Maserati V-8," *Road & Track* summed up in their coverage of the show. "This car should be a very strong competitor for the 5-liter Ferrari, if they ever really compete against each other. The 5-liter Maserati has very good lines, but we didn't care for the overworked front grille

A number of prominent clients purchased 5000 GTs from Maserati and had the chassis sent to their favorite coachbuilder for a distinctive one-off; carrozzerias used included Monterosa (one of two made, pictured), Michelotti, Frua, and Allemano.

American Gary Laughlin was the man behind the Scaglietti Corvette. "When I tried to get a replacement crankshaft for my Ferrari Testa Rossa, I was told it would be $1,500," Laughlin said. "A Corvette crank was around $50. As I always admired Scaglietti's work, I approached him to make the bodies." After the coachbuilder got the okay from Enzo Ferrari, he would build three of the machines in the late 1950s.

and hood, which spoiled the appearance of this otherwise fine piece of machinery."

As always, there was a method behind Anderloni's approach to styling. "While the 3500 was supposed to be understated," the designer said, "this car was a different school of thought: Our objective was to show the person inside was of wealth and importance. The design also had to reflect the Shah's culture. We referenced examples of Persian architecture and found it was quite ornate, heavily embellished."

Others trying their hand on the 5000 GT included Pinin Farina, Bertone, Ghia, Michelotti, Monterosa, and Frua. "These cars were special commissions, very personal and tailored," Alfieri noted. "We were giving them to customers, who then went to their 'couture' to do, much like a suit."

As these flamboyant, custom-made Maseratis reflected the individual tastes and desires of their owners, Alfieri said they were not suitable for production. "Traffic-stopping was not Maserati's target," the engineer succinctly summed up. The company thus settled on the Indianapolis, an understated design by Allemano, for small series production.

Maserati's 5000 GT was undoubtedly the world's fastest production car in the late 1950s/early 1960s. When test driver Geurino Bertocchi gave journalist Peter Coltrin a ride in an Allemano-bodied 5000, "[he] shifted into 5th at 6,000 rpm, the speedometer showing 150 mph," Coltrin reported in *Car & Driver*. "[With] the rate of acceleration seemingly not falling off much, he went on up to an indicated 170 mph."

When Maserati built the last 5000 GT, it represented much more than the ultimate expression in speed and exclusivity.

Although these sporting cars were the essence of prestige, glamour, and style, customers now demanded quality and refinement, which were commodities such custom-built models sorely lacked. Quietly, and without fanfare, the fouri serie era had come to an end.

Yet, the marketplace's changing demands were not the only reason the event went overlooked. As Maserati began developing Allemano's Indianapolis, the industry's key player was undergoing an upheaval that would shake the company to its core, and radically alter the sports and GT landscape forever.

Ferrari's 400 Superamerica was based upon Pinin Farina's "Superfast II" showcar that debuted in 1960. These custom built machines used a 340 horsepower V12 that gave the model a top speed of around 160 mph. Pictured here is "Superfast IV," which was made in 1962. Its shape is an evolution of Superfast II's fluid form.

The Ferrari Factor

1961-1965

The announcement was completely unexpected. In November 1961, Enzo Ferrari acknowledged that eight of his directors—including chief engineer Carlo Chiti, experimental department head Giotto Bizzarrini, sales manager Girolamo Gardini, and racing team manager Romolo Tavoni—were no longer working for the company. The news spread through Italy like wildfire. It soon became known as the "Walkout" or "Purge" and proved to be the first in a series of events that would dramatically alter Italy's sports, gran turismo, and competition landscape.

According to those involved, at the eye of the storm was sales manager Gardini. Born on October 7, 1923, this only child of a Modenese grain shop owner had a modest upbringing, a characteristic that remained with him throughout his life. "He has always been very much in the shade," a family member noted, "and that was the way he wanted it."

After joining Ferrari at Auto Avio Costruzioni in August 1942, in 1950 Gardini became Ferrari's sales manager. Quiet, polite, and reserved, he was the perfect man for the position and helped vault the firm to stardom. "You never should go chasing the client," he said when recalling his sales philosophy. "You should wait for them to come to you." He did this with considerable effect, playing Italy's burgeoning sports/racing/GT market, and its wealthy clientele, like a fiddle.

As his power inside Ferrari grew, Gardini kept his cards close to his vest, often causing rumors to swirl around him in the process. Still, he remained a principled man, one to whom loyalty to Ferrari meant everything. It is thus no wonder he had a number of allies inside Maranello.

The spectacular ATS 2500 GT of 1963 was the direct result of the management upheaval that hit Ferrari two years earlier. The engineer behind its advanced V-8 engine, tubular chassis, and independent suspension was Carlo Chiti. "He was really the heart and soul of the company," said former ATS technician Giorgio Molinari. "He tried everything possible to keep the company alive."

The handsomely styled ASA 1000 GT also had its roots tied to Ferrari, for its 995-cc four-cylinder engine was originally designed and developed by the company in 1959. "Pininfarina was quite surprised when Bertone was given the commission to design and build the body," said former Ferrari sales manager Girolamo Gardini. The definitive version of the 1000 GT (pictured) was first shown at 1961's Turin Auto Show.

One such person was engineer Giotto Bizzarrini. The son of a wealthy landowner in Livorno, Bizzarrini was three years Gardini's junior and of completely different temperament. Due to the trauma he suffered during the war, he would sometimes explode at the drop of a hat.

After graduating from the University of Pisa with an engineering degree, Alfa Romeo hired him as a test driver in 1954. He soon gained quite a reputation by offering solutions to problems encountered while testing. After catching Ferrari's attention, Enzo hired him in early 1957.

Thanks to Bizzarrini, another Gardini ally came to Maranello several months later. Then 24, Carlo Chiti also started as an engineer at Alfa Romeo. "Imagine my surprise when Bizzarrini took me in to see Ferrari, who was already approaching legendary status by that time," Chiti recalled.

Surprisingly, he turned the approach down, finding "the duties too vague for me to feel comfortable." But Ferrari was not dissuaded, and he snared the large, gregarious engineer on his second attempt.

All Walkout participants interviewed say Ferrari's wife, Laura, was a meddlesome thorn in their sides when the 1960s began. As Chiti relayed to this author and gave even greater detail to Oscar Orefici in his book *Carlo Chiti: Sinfonia Ruggente*, "She was a woman completely devoid of any diplomatic sense . . . [and] had none of the characteristics needed to live alongside a man of the stature of her husband." He also noted that "[Ferrari] allowed her to get away with a great deal . . . just because she was the mother of his son Dino."

Mrs. Ferrari started attending races, much to the dismay of team manager Tavoni and her other "handlers." In addition to trying to influence the company's finances and direction, particularly disruptive to everyone around her was her erratic behavior.

According to Chiti and Bizzarrini, the flashpoint occurred when Mrs. Ferrari had a physical altercation with Girolamo Gardini. As one who respected personal space and demanded the same, the intensely focused sales manager quickly headed to the restaurant where Ferrari was dining.

The two had an explosive confrontation, which basically boiled down to Gardini laying down an ultimatum: Get your wife under control, for if you don't, either she goes, or I go.

Ferrari's response was simple: "You are gone."

And so started The Walkout. When asked what caused it some 30 years later, Gardini remained his ever respectful and very private self: He politely declined to answer fully, only saying on two different occasions that "it was not about business reasons."

Those at the upper echelons of Ferrari were stunned by the news. Bizzarrini, Chiti, and Romolo Tavoni say all the managers decided to unite in an effort to have Ferrari rehire Gardini. But Ferrari said no and fired everybody.

In truth, the timing couldn't have been better for the Ferrari renegades to be swept aside, for Europe's economic miracle had been in full swing for almost a decade. With the building, and contemplated building, of sports cars and gran turismos nearing its zenith, everyone wanted in on the act.

Thus, a new breed of sports car manufacturer was just waiting to be born: the industrialist-backed constructor. When Ferrari's Walkout participants suddenly became available, the final hurtle to market entry—proper engineering talent to make the sophisticated, refined product the market demanded—disappeared.

Within a matter of weeks, Italy's newest firm was born. Called ATS (Automobili Turismo Sport), the first shareholder was hard-charging Giorgio Billi, a classic Italian *capitano d'industria* who prospered greatly in the 1950s by designing, patenting, and manufacturing machines that made pantyhose. Next was Jaime Ortiz Patino, the heir to a Bolivian tin fortune. Last was Count Giovanni Volpi, a young member of one of Italy's most wealthy families whose Scuderia Serenissima primarily raced Ferraris, often with great success.

Almost immediately, there was a conflict of egos. Because of Volpi's tremendous financial strength and notoriety in the competition world, Chiti and Gardini say self-made man Billi was jealous and tried to upstage the 24-year-old count at every turn.

To a lesser degree, tension also existed on the engineering level, for Chiti felt they should use a V-8 engine, while Bizzarrini pushed for a V-12. "In other words," Volpi recalls, "right away the intrigue started."

After several months of roadblocks, the Count decided he had had enough "intrigue." "Though Billi owned half the company," Volpi says, "he needed me, otherwise they would not have called me. So when he came to me one day and said, 'You buy us, or we buy you,' I said, 'Buy me, and goodbye.'"

Gardini and Bizzarrini quickly followed the Count, to whom they were loyal. Billi would eventually buy out Ortiz-Patino, as well.

As successful as Billi was, he did not have the financial wherewithal to shoulder the entire effort. In addition to erecting a large factory outside Bologna, he had to underwrite the design, development, and construction of a Formula 1 team *and* a street-going GT.

The team's first year in F1 spoke volumes on how thin the effort was spread. Even with former world champion Phil Hill at the wheel, in 1963 ATS finished only one race and did not score a point.

Surprisingly, the firm's streetcar, the 2500 GT, was the exact opposite. As Italy's first midengine production offering, it was more sophisticated than anything Ferrari, Maserati, or anyone else was building at the time. With striking coachwork by Franco Scaglione, the 2500 GT's all-aluminum V-8 was longitudinally mounted in a rigid tube frame. Its suspension was independent front and rear, and it had disc brakes at each corner.

The beautiful ATS debuted at 1963's Geneva Auto Show to great fanfare. "Leave it to the Italians to provide the fireworks," Henry Manney noted in *Road & Track*. "[The] central-engined GT coupe with handsome coachwork by Allemano . . . is a real startler [that] I hope goes into production."

According to Chiti, the 2500 GT did more than just wow the press, for ATS received a flood of orders. "Unfortunately," he laments, "we put ourselves in the spotlight with a product that wasn't yet perfected."

Despite enthusiastic reviews from the press, the ASA 1000 GT floundered in the marketplace. In an attempt to boost sales, the company introduced a 1000 GT Spider in 1963. This was followed by the 411, and the racy, six-cylinder Roll Bar (pictured). Lack of sales forced ASA to close it doors in 1967.

One of the reasons ASA's lineup had a difficult time was Fiat's 2300 S. Introduced at the same time as the ASA, the 2300's coachwork was the work of Carrozzeria Ghia. While the Fiat was not as sporty as the newcomer was, it boasted a higher top speed, superior acceleration, and name recognition.

The Alfa 2600 Bertone coupe and Touring Spider debuted in 1962. These elegant, 125-mile-per-hour touring machines had lusty 2.6-liter in-line six-cylinder engines. Seen here is the most sporting of the 2600 range, the SZ (Sprint Zagato). Production started in 1965, two years after the prototype's debut. Just 105 SZs were built over a three-year period.

The world would find out how good the car was too late. In *Road & Track's* September 1964 cover story, author Griff Borgeson noted the 2500's braking was "a revelation," its acceleration "tremendous." After seeing 150 miles per hour on the autostrada and cornering at "racing speeds," "Thanks to the absolute perfection of the car's performance in every way, I have never felt safer in a car at high speed nor have I been more impressed," Borgeson concluded.

When ATS went under several months later, Volpi, Gardini, and their hired engineering gun, ex-Ferrari/Maserati man Alberto Massimino, were hard at work on their own midengined sports GT, the Serenissima 8V. Using a larger V-8 similar to the ATS engine, several Serenissima prototypes would be made through the 1960s but never enter production.

A third new GT grew directly from Ferrari during the period. But unlike ATS, ASA (Autocostruzioni SA) had the blessing of Enzo himself.

Its origins can be traced back to December 1959 when Ferrari tantalized the automotive world by displaying an 850-cc four-cylinder engine. Using heads quite similar to those found on his V-12s, Ferrari quoted the type 854's horsepower between 64 and 82, depending on the state of tune.

Following a successful series of bench tests, one engine was installed in a slightly modified Fiat 1200. Subsequently dubbed the "Ferrarina" (little Ferrari) by the press, the car's most startling design element was the machine gun logo on the grille.

That styling touch remained a mystery for years until author Graham Gauld uncovered its significance in a conversation with Ugo Beretta, president of the Italian gun manufacturing concern.

In the late 1940s the company flirted with building a small car, the BBC. As the project remained stillborn, Ferrari telephoned Piero Beretta to see if he had any interest in backing his baby GT.

"A meeting was arranged in Maranello and my uncle and I visited Mr. Ferrari to see the Ferrarina prototype," Ugo Beretta recalled in Gauld's delightful book, *Modena Racing Memories*. "When we looked at the car, we saw Mr. Ferrari had put a badge on the grille, which had an etching of one of our machine guns."

Although the Barillas passed on underwriting the project, the press continually reported production was imminent. Inside the factory, sales manager Gardini recalls the Ferrarina being a nuisance, a product completely out of character with the company's elite image. Yet, with "The Old Man" firmly behind it, it would not die.

Ferrari hit pay dirt in 1961. That July, Italy's *Quattroroute* magazine scooped everyone by reporting the car would be backed and constructed by Milan's De Nora family. The owners of a large chemical manufacturing concern, the ASA effort was headed by prominent Ferrari client Oronzio De Nora and his son Niccolo.

The company's production prototype was a far cry from Ferrari's original dowdy Ferrarina. It debuted at the 1961 Turin Show, where it caused a sensation. Underneath its svelte Bertone coachwork was a tubular chassis, independent front suspension, and 998-cc four-cylinder engine, quoted at producing 95 horsepower.

Called an "excellent example of elegance combined with compactness" by *Motor*, "The [Show's] only headliner was to be found on the Bertone stand," *Road & Track* observed. "This was the baby Ferrari, . . . its clean shape proclaiming it to be the newest style of businessman's express."

The venture was like many Italian sports/GT concerns of the era—great camaraderie existed inside the company. "We were all friends," French Grand Prix winner and ASA test driver Giancarlo Baghetti observed in *Ferrarissima*. "We spent our evenings and vacations together, talking of ASA, of course. When testing began on the car, our enthusiasm became indescribable. We immediately realized this was an exceptional automobile, extremely advanced [compared] to what the market then had to offer."

The final production version debuted one year later at Turin. Sporting a nearly identical body, "the Ferrari-designed Mille will shortly go into production at ASA's works," *Car and Driver* noted in February 1962. "It is expensive for a small car, but may prove worth it."

Bernard Cahier certainly thought so in *Sports Car Graphic's* January 1963 issue. Recording a top speed of 112 miles per hour, he found the "brilliant little car" had "superb road handling."

England's Gregor Grant thrashed one in the hills above Monte Carlo and also adored its road manners. "The ASA is an important addition to the G.T. vehicles of the world," he wrote in *Autosport*. "It is intended to meet a demand amongst connoisseurs for a small-capacity sporting car, built to the engineering standards of Ferrari."

Despite refinement and impressive performance that belied its 1-liter capacity, the car languished in the marketplace. Costing approximately 40 percent more in Italy than Alfa's larger-engined Giulia Sprint, it found few takers.

They proved to be a difficult sale in America, as well. When 32 were sent to the United States in the mid-1960s, they languished at Ferrari importer Luigi Chinetti's premises for some time.

Other ASA models such as the beautiful 1000 GT Spyder, larger displacement 411, and six-cylinder Roll Bar, could not change the company's fortunes. High-class finishes at 1965's Targa Florio didn't help, either.

"To be economically competitive," Baghetti reflected, "the small company needed to be transformed into a large firm and produce at least 10,000 cars a year." With the writing on the wall, in late 1966 ASA quietly closed its doors.

For those desiring a "half-priced" Ferrari-like GT, Fiat's 2300S was a more sensible alternative. Also debuting at 1961's

Turin Show and costing approximately the same as the 1000 GT, the attractively styled coupe was powered by a 150-horsepower, 2.3-liter, inline six-cylinder engine.

With mechanicals designed by former Ferrari chief engineer Aurelio Lampredi, not only was the 2300S quicker to 60 miles per hour than the ASA, its 120-plus-mile-per-hour top speed was higher. More important, it had the name recognition, dealer network, and financial might of Fiat behind it.

Positioned just above the ASA and Fiat was Alfa's 2600 series. Introduced at Geneva in 1962, the 2600 was developed from the 2000 series that was launched in 1958 and had a new 2.6-liter, 145-horsepower six-cylinder engine.

Like the Alfa upon which it was based, the 2600 was available as a handsome spyder by Touring or a well-balanced coupe by Bertone. *Road & Track*'s test of the spyder found it to be "stylish, moderately fast, and incredibly smooth—it puts a lot of grand in touring."

Lamborghini's 350 GT was designed and built by Carrozzeria Touring. While most 350s had large single headlamp lenses, this particular car has the four headlamp treatment that was found on the later 400 GT and 400 2+2. When he reflects on why Lamborghini's first car was one of the finest GTs of its day, "I would have to say it involved some luck," said former company chief engineer Gian Paolo Dallara. "We really didn't know any better."

One of the world's most sophisticated GTs was the Iso Rivolta GT. Built in Milan, two things separated it from its Modenese competitors: Its chassis was a pressed steel platform, and its engine was a Chevrolet Corvette 327 V-8. "When we started producing the car," former company president Piero Rivolta said, "a number were returned with blown engines. When we determined they couldn't handle sustained high rpm running, we made an extra capacity oil pan, and our own connecting rods."

In 1963, Alfa introduced a third 2600, the SZ by Zagato. With an aerodynamic body and lighter weight, it was most sporty of the series.

That same year, another new constructor entered the upper echelon of Italy's GT marketplace. But unlike ASA and ATS, Lamborghini was destined for far greater success.

The man behind the company was Ferruccio Lamborghini. Born on April 28, 1916, some 15 miles outside Bologna in Renazzo, his humble farming origins belied the strength of the man.

Another *capitano* who made his fortune outside the automotive field, he first apprenticed at a mechanical workshop in

Iso's A3/L Grifo prototype stunned the automotive world when Bertone unveiled it on their stand at the 1963 Turin Auto Show. "That car was my own personal initiative in order to get my own personal car," said coachbuilder Nuccio Bertone. "It was a very important experience for me. For a small class atelier, it was pretty incredible to achieve these kinds of high class products."

Bologna, then was assigned to the island of Rhodes in the Aegean Sea when World War II began. During his stay of duty, Lamborghini earned the reputation of a wizard mechanic.

He returned to Italy in 1946 and competed two years later in the Mille Miglia, not finishing the race because of a crash.

In 1949, Ferruccio founded Lamborghini Trattrici (Lamborghini Tractors) in Cento, a small town near his home village of Renazzo. His products quickly built up a following as they were often victors in tractor tug-of-war exhibitions in town squares.

By the mid-1950s, Lamborghini was one of Italy's largest tractor manufacturers. Having profitably mastered one field, Ferruccio was soon looking for another endeavor to tackle. A trip to America prompted him to found Lamborghini Bruciatori, a manufacturer of boilers and air conditioners. It met instant marketplace success.

With his wealth growing exponentially, by the early 1960s Lamborghini had owned a number of fast cars. In an oft-told tale, he supposedly entered the GT field after having problems with his Ferrari's clutch. When he went to the factory to complain to Enzo, he was left waiting for an inordinate amount of time. He then stormed off, vowing to build a better car.

Talk with those in the know and it becomes clear that this tale is exactly that—colorful fiction. "He actually believed he would be able to do something better than anyone else," said Franco Lini, one of Italy's top journalists who was well connected in the country's burgeoning gran turismo and competition circles. "Driving him to do this was [that] he felt he could make a profit at it."

Bob Wallace, Lamborghini's legendary test driver, agreed: "That story never happened. He thought he could make money while gaining prestige by making a name for himself."

Regardless of the impetus, by 1962 Lamborghini was actively combing Modena for engineers. When visiting Neri and Bonacini, a small firm named after two well-known engine builders, Ferruccio learned of Giotto Bizzarrini, the Walkout participant who was the brains behind Ferrari's all-conquering endurance racer, the 250 GTO.

After leaving ATS, Bizzarrini had quickly established himself as Italy's top engineering "gun for hire." In addition to developing and performing a number of disc brake conversions at his Autostar lab in his hometown of Livorno, he sorted and refined ASA's 1000 GT.

Lamborghini's approach came as a complete surprise. Yet the engineer had just the thing to present the aspiring constructor: drawings of a 1.5-liter V-12 he made in his days with ATS. In subsequent telephone conversations, "Lamborghini made it clear he did not want a competition engine," the engineer recalled. "Instead, he wanted a car like a Ferrari, something for the highway. He said he liked the idea of 12 cylinders but wanted it to be 3.5 liters."

When Bizzarrini met Lamborghini in his tractor factory in Cento, any trepidation he felt about the seriousness of the effort

was immediately put to rest. "His facility had numerous machine tools that were more modern than Ferrari's," the engineer recalled.

The tour ended in Lamborghini's office, where the two men quickly hammered out a contract. At its basis were the V-12's parameters: normal aspiration, a displacement of 3.5 liters, and a power output of 350 horsepower. Bizzarrini was given several months to complete its design and would receive 4.5 million lire for his efforts—one-third up front, the balance due upon completion.

Soon after he started to work, Bizzarrini says Lamborghini visited the blueprint shop he was using unannounced, asking to see the engineer's technical drawings. With this apparent end run raising the fiery engineer's hackles, Bizzarrini recommended Lamborghini hire Gian Paolo Dallara, an associate he knew at Ferrari, to handle future work.

Lamborghini found the young engineer at Maserati. Then 26, Dallara's career began with Ferrari in 1959 after he graduated from the Milan's Polytechnic College. But because he remained stuck behind the drawing board, rather than in the thick of things at the racetrack, he was lured to Maserati by chief engineer Giulio Alfieri in mid-1961.

Within months, Dallara knew this was also a temporary stop. After attending Sebring and Le Mans in 1962, he realized Maserati was slowly in the process of withdrawing from racing. Lamborghini's carrot, the *potential* they might tackle the track, saw the young engineer quickly jump ship.

Dallara joined Lamborghini at his partially erected factory in Sant' Agata Bolognese, approximately 15 miles south of Modena and 10 miles from Cento. Surprisingly, the venture wasn't initially welcome in the economically depressed town. "Most everyone

At the same time Bertone debuted the luxurious Grifo A3/L, Iso displayed a competition version of the car, the Grifo A3/C. The brainchild of Iso consultant Giotto Bizzarrini, "I always wanted to go racing," the engineer said. "Renzo Rivolta gave me a chassis and said, 'Here, now you can go make a racing car yourself.'" His basis for the radical machine was his masterpiece at Ferrari, the immortal 250 GTO.

When Iso started testing the Grifo A3/L, "We went to Bertone and said, 'The car is 90 percent there,'" Iso's Piero Rivolta recalled. "We told them we wanted to make something we could produce." The resulting Grifo GL was widely hailed as one of the finest GTs of its day. Here, an early production version is seen behind the Rivolta's magnificent Villa Rivolta.

was quite suspicious," said longtime Lamborghini employee and Cento resident Giuliano Pizzi. Lamborghini's charm and promise of jobs eventually won them over.

Once Bizzarrini's V-12 was successfully bench tested, Dallara went to work on making it suitable for production. He also designed a tubular chassis and independent front and rear suspension.

Lamborghini's prototype was the 350 GTV. With coachwork designed and built by Franco Scaglione, Dallara recalls the effort skating on thin ice, causing him to wait nervously at the company's partially built factory for the completed car to show up for the press introduction.

Several days later, the 350 GTV had its public debut at Turin's 1963 show. "[T]he Lamborghini seems to be trying too hard to be different, especially at the rear," David Phipps observed in *Car and Driver*. "[The GTV] is very much a prototype, and has not yet run, but Ferruccio Lamborghini makes no rash claims for it and seems well aware of the problems involved in developing high performance machinery."

This latter statement was indeed true, for during the show's last three days, Ferruccio approached Touring's Carlo Anderloni. After meeting "this unknown commodity" on Lamborghini's stand, Anderloni immediately understood the industrialist was not happy. "He made it very clear he wanted to have a *real* car quickly," the designer recalled, "something that could undergo proper testing, then be produced and sold. Because it was important not to change the look of the car too much, we decided to use the GTV as the starting point."

Carrozzeria Touring was soon a bee's nest of frenetic activity. With Lamborghini pushing them, "we were working day and night for two to four months to produce a prototype," Anderloni smiled. "It was not a problem though, for we always had the habits to work quickly during those occasions."

Back in Sant' Agata, Dallara and crew were also busy, making a production feasible tubular chassis and modified V-12 engine. The result would be a simpler frame, and an engine that produced 270 to 280 horsepower at 6,500 rpm.

Ferruccio's new car, the 350 GT, broke cover in March 1964 at Geneva. "Lamborghini made a business-like appearance with a much prettier smoothed-off coupe . . . ," *Road & Track* noted in its June 1964 issue. America's *Sports Car Graphic* also liked the new Lambo, commenting that "the new . . . Coupe [is] a much cleaner treatment than the prototype shown at Torino last fall."

Once in the hands of eager journalists, it appeared that Lamborghini's lofty ambitions of "being able to do something better than anyone else" were close to reality. When Henry Manney tried one of the first 350 GTs, he felt it was "the most desirable sports/GT I have driven." Appropriately, he titled his article in England's *CAR* magazine, "This one will give Ferrari a migraine."

America's *Car and Driver* agreed with that conclusion. Lauding the 350's 156-mile-per-hour performance, refinement, and quietness, they called it "a smooth challenger to Ferrari's title of king of the GT cars."

Although that first Lamborghini received gushing praise throughout its life, Gian Paolo Dallara says the 350 suffered a shortcoming all Modenese products had during the era. "None of us did any real type of endurance testing," the engineer reflects. "We basically had to deliver a mechanic with each car, for the amount of testing was no more than 7,000 miles, maybe a maximum of 12,000. So in many ways, the first customers were really the test drivers."

This lack of development had an effect on cooling and heating systems: "If a car was born in winter, the heating was good but not the cooling," Dallara smiled. "If it was born in the summer, it was the exact opposite."

Designer Giorgetto Giugiaro agreed completely: "At that time sports and GT cars were still an adventure. You were never sure if you would arrive at your final destination."

It is thus no wonder that another nascent constructor's key to refinement was reliability. Like Ferruccio Lamborghini, Milan industrialist Renzo Rivolta also owned a number of GTs but remained unsatisfied. "He always said he was putting money in front of his Jaguars and Maseratis," said former Iso chief technician Pierluigi Raggi, referring to the cars' temperamental manners and unreliability.

As Rivolta eyed entry into the gran turismo field, he wanted to make sure his product would not suffer the same drawback. After looking at producing his own engine, he concluded that the answer was in America with Chevrolet's Corvette V-8: Not only was it reliable, it produced as much horsepower as anything Italy had to offer.

To expedite his car's design and development, Rivolta hired Giotto Bizzarrini to assist his engineering team, headed by Raggi. Together the two made a steel platform chassis that was likely the era's most sophisticated frame.

Rivolta's first car, the 2+2 Iso Rivolta GT, debuted at 1962's Turin Auto Show to extremely favorable reaction. "With Corvette power, a light chassis with a de Dion rear end and Bertone body,

Here, one of the two production prototypes is seen at its press introduction at Monza. Piloting the Grifo A3/L for Iso was racing driver Bob Bondurant (standing behind open door).

When Iso and Bizzarrini parted ways in late 1965, the engineer kept producing the competition-minded Grifo A3 under his own name, calling it the Bizzarrini Strada or GT America. Its sleek shape and front midengine design show how he valued performance above all else. "I consider it a second-generation 250 GTO," Bizzarrini reflected. Like Iso's products, a Corvette V-8 powered the Bizzarrini Strada.

the Iso is one of the most interesting transatlantic combinations ever in automotive history," *Car and Driver* summed up.

Former racing driver Count Gianni Lurani was enthralled when he tested one in 1963 for Italy's *Autorama* magazine. Lauding its "gorgeous lines," ease of use, and superior performance and lower price, "the Iso Rivolta deserves full rights of citizenship," Lurani noted. "We believe it has all the qualities needed to become a great success in markets all over the world."

That model proved to be Rivolta's warm-up act. At the 1963 Turin extravaganza, Iso debuted the Grifo. Also designed by Bertone, the sleek berlinetta was shown in two forms: one for the road (the A3/L), another for competition (the A3/C).

The production version of the A3/L was developed at Iso by Pierluigi Raggi and his team. Called the Grifo GL, it could clear 160 miles per hour when fitted with a 365-horsepower Corvette V-8.

"Cars like the Iso were very exciting for us to work on," Nuccio Bertone reflected. Not only did the project's lack of parame-

ters instill a sense of passion, but "once it was on the market, the car gave great excitement and impact to the people. This made it really rewarding in terms of image and prestige, for we would get a lot of that from this type of car."

The coachbuilder says the Grifo went on to become a legend in its own time. Docile, refined, yet exhilarating to drive quickly, it was a masterpiece of proportioning, elegance, and beauty. *Autocar* would dub it "the ultimate in transport for the enthusiast, a kind of dream come true." *Autosport* was equally enthused, concluding "for the man who wants the ultimate in two seaters, this is the best that money can buy."

The competition Grifo was designed and produced by engineer Giotto Bizzarrini. So how did a former Ferrari engineer react to the Corvette V-8? "The first time I tried one," he said, "I was shocked. I remember telling Mr. Rivolta it was superior to Ferrari's engines, offering the same power with more immediate throttle response."

That largely explains why he used the engine after parting ways with Renzo Rivolta in late summer 1965. After campaigning Iso's competition Grifo for two years, he continued producing the low-slung model in his small Livorno factory. He first called the car the Bizzarrini Grifo, then changed the name to Bizzarrini Strada and GT America.

Essentially an endurance racer for the street and one of the wildest looking machines available, the Bizzarrini was not as refined as Iso's more thoroughly developed GT. Still, it found a loyal clientele in Italy, Germany, and America.

Another nascent manufacturer embracing an American engine was Apollo. The brainchild of Californian Milt Brown, his idea became feasible when he teamed up with Turin-based Frank Reisner and his Intermeccanica firm.

The Apollo GT was powered by 3.5- and 5-liter Buick V-8 engines and had a strong, ladder-type frame. Its original berlinetta body was designed by American Ron Plescia and then cleaned up by Reisner associate, stylist Franco Scaglione.

Apollo's production process was completely different from Iso and Bizzarrini's. Brown would manufacture the frame in his Apollo factory in Oakland, California, then ship it to Reisner in Turin. At Intermeccanica, Reisner's men would fabricate and paint the body, then install the interior. The car would then return to Oakland for the mechanical components and testing. On why he used Italy for body construction and assembly, "the labor cost just 60 cents an hour," Brown responded. "Can you imagine that?"

Although Apollo's coupes and Scaglione-designed spyders were well received in the press and marketplace alike, Brown suffered from an affliction many nascent businesses battled: lack of proper capital. Apollo survived for five years, then folded. Having the capabilities of producing something himself, Reisner's Intermeccanica firm became a successful constructor in the second half of the 1960s.

Argentinean ex-pat Alejandro De Tomaso also relied on an American engine to power his cars. Born in Buenos Aires in 1928, De Tomaso immigrated to Italy in the mid-1950s and

Apollos were another GT powered by American V-8s. "I wanted a car with a hood as long as a Jaguar E-type," said Milt Brown, the man behind the effort. Brown would make the Apollo chassis in California, then send it to Frank Reisner's Carrozzeria Intermeccanica for the coachwork and interior. The car then returned to Oakland to fit the drivetrain and suspension. In total, 88 Apollos were built from 1961 to 1966.

De Tomaso's first street car was the mid-engine Vallelunga. The prototype was a roadster, the production cars this beautiful berlinetta. Like all of De Tomaso's subsequent street models, the Vallelunga was powered by a Ford engine—a 1,500-cc four-cylinder in this case. *John Ling Collection*

1500 VALLELUNGA

Nella storia della motorizzazione
ci sono sempre state delle vetture che hanno
simbolizzato un'epoca, perchè esprimevano
il « non plus ultra » della tecnica del loro tempo.
Il Vallelunga
appartiene a questa ristrettissima élite.

Long hailed as one of the most beautiful production street Ferraris, the 250 GTL (also called the Berlinetta Lusso) was first introduced at the Paris Auto Show in 1962 and was the successor to the 250 Pininfarina Coupe that went out of production in 1960. The year-plus delay in launching the new model was caused by the success of the 250 GT 2+2.

found a job as a test driver for OSCA. While visiting the Maserati factory in 1956, he fell for a tall, statuesque American race driver, Isabelle Haskell. The two married and competed on the international circuit together for the balance of the decade.

By 1959, De Tomaso was constructing his own Formula 2 and Formula Junior cars in Modena. After unsuccessfully trying his hand in Formula 1 in the early 1960s, at 1963's Turin Show he displayed an attractive midengined roadster, the Vallelunga. Having an innovative spine chassis, it was powered by a modified 1,500-cc, four-cylinder Ford engine.

The diminutive production Vallelunga was an even more beautiful berlinetta. Like the one-off roadster, the prototype was also designed and built at Carrozzeria Fissore.

Production Vallelungas were bodied by Ghia. Called "one of the most intriguing cars to emerge from Italy in recent months" by *Autosport* in 1965, unlike many of Italy's newest constructors, De Tomaso fell short on product refinement and build quality. "We imported one of the earliest Vallelungas [to England]," Colonel Ronnie Hoare recalled in *De Tomaso Automobiles*. "[I]t was turned out in pretty deplorable condition, with no reverse gear at all."

Although less than 60 Vallelungas would be made over a four-year period, De Tomaso's next car would announce he was ready to crash the sports/GT ball and become a full-fledged constructor of note.

That Ferrari prospered in the onslaught of so many new manufacturers and models only serves to highlight the strength and depth of the company.

Within days of the Walkout, Enzo had promoted a young engineer, Mauro Forghieri. Born in Modena in 1935, Forghieri graduated from the University of Bologna in 1959 with an engineering degree. He intended to travel to California to enter its burgeoning aircraft industry, but says "a family situation caused me to remain in Italy."

First hired by Maranello in 1960, the lean, energetic engineer was filled with enthusiasm. He started in the engine department, performing calculations on the 1.5-liter F1 engine and acting as liaison between chief engineer Carlo Chiti and the engine-testing room.

When he suddenly found himself wearing the "chief engineer" hat, Forghieri says he was on the verge of leaving Ferrari for another job in Turin. "But I was one of the few engineers remaining," he recalled, "so I stayed. Mr. Ferrari made it very clear he was behind me 100 percent," giving the untested young man the confidence boost he needed.

The company didn't miss a beat. Ferrari continued its championship-winning ways in both F1 and endurance racing, all the while reeling off four consecutive Le Mans victories.

The firm also prospered on the production front. In 1960 it entered the 2+2 market with the 250 GTE. First shown at Paris that year, it went on sale in 1961. Called by *Autosport* "a wonderful combination of luxurious touring and super-sporting characteristics," they felt it was a "remarkable value for the relatively few who can afford it." Almost 1,000 of the 135-mile-per-hour model would be sold over a three-year period.

Ferrari also attacked the two-seat market, first with the 250 GTL (commonly called the Berlinetta Lusso), then the 275 GTS and GTB. The Lusso was introduced at the 1962 Paris Auto Show and featured a 240-horsepower V-12 and delicate, almost feminine coachwork with near perfect proportioning. Voted The Best Sports/GT Over $6,000 by *Car and Driver* in 1964, "it makes for grand touring in the grandest manner possible," the magazine commented.

Considerably more sporting were the 275 GTS and, in particular, the 275 GTB. This new range was introduced at Paris in 1964 and was powered by a new, 3.3-liter V-12 producing 260 to 300 horsepower, depending on carburetion and compression. The 275s were also the first production Ferraris to have a five-speed gearbox and fully independent suspension as standard equipment.

The GTS was a handsome, understated, 145-mile-per-hour spyder. "For all its creature comforts," *Car and Driver* observed in their cover story, "this is a hairy, demanding GT car that will stretch the driving skill of the most talented driver."

"On top of all the excitement," *Road & Track* concurred, "[the 275 GTS] is a genuinely luxurious car."

Ferrari introduced the more aggressive 275 GTB in 1964. In 1966 the car's V-12 engine received double overhead cams and saw power output jump from 260 to 280 horsepower to a quoted 300. This new model was called the 275 GTB/4 (pictured) and has a slightly longer nose than most of the earlier 275 GTBs. It remains an all-time classic Pininfarina design.

Yet, the Ferrari of the period was undoubtedly the 275 GTB. Having a classic berlinetta shape that was aggressive and elegant at the same time, its performance was in another league. Called "the most usable high performance GT car to come out of Maranello" by *Sports Car Graphic*, road-tester Bernard Cahier recorded 0–60 in 6 seconds, 0–100 in 14.6, and a top speed of 156 miles per hour. "Those numbers are really quite sensational," he observed, "and for comparison, a 4.2 Jaguar coupe will do 0–60 in 7.2 seconds and zero to 100 in 17.2."

Like the Berlinetta Lusso, both 275s were designed by Pininfarina, the family and company's name having become one word in 1961. But more than the name had changed in the early 1960s, for Sergio Pininfarina and his brother-in-law Carlo Renzi were now in charge of the carrozzeria.

The decision to step down was an easy one for Pinin. "I [understood] the important role which children take on in developing and continuing a man's work," he observed in his autobiography. After summoning the two to his office, he informed them of his wishes. "Wheat is harvested at the beginning of summer and not autumn. I want to experience this and other pleasures while I am still well planted in my life."

Across town, Carrozzeria Bertone had also undergone major changes. While Nuccio recognized Scaglione's great talent, the designer's follow-through on his work's development was lacking. According to author Luciano Greggio, Bertone noted "[Scaglione] was often absent without leave, and his habit of disappearing eventually irritated [him] so much that he later decided to deprive himself of the designer's services."

After letting Scaglione go in late 1959, Bertone discovered an able successor in Giorgetto Giugiaro. "One day our coach painter mentioned a young 21-year-old designer who was working at Fiat under Boano," Nuccio recalled years later. "He was very inexperienced but had an exceptional talent for drawing and painting."

That Giugiaro would have such skills was a given: His grandfather was a well-known painter of frescoes on churches and villas in the province of Cuneo. Having started the craft himself at age six, the artist mindset would never leave Giorgetto.

He moved to Turin at age 14, living with an aunt while he attended art school during the day and technical drawing classes in the evening. Recognizing the youth's talent, his art professor recommended Giugiaro to Fiat's Dante Giacosa.

Carrozzeria Ghia experimented with the berlinetta (fastback) theme on this one-off Fiat 230 S. The car used a shortened Fiat 2300 chassis and was the work of Sergio Santorelli and Filippo Sapino, who is Ghia's current managing director. Although the model would remain a one-off, it served as the basis for the design of the Ghia 450 SS, an attractive two-seat convertible that used a Plymouth chassis and drivetrain. The 450 SS was built in limited quantities in the mid-1960s.

Bertone hired him away from the massive auto manufacturer at the perfect time. "I never felt fulfilled in Fiat's styling department," Giugiaro reflected. "While I did learn the trade, I never knew what became of my drawings."

Although Giorgetto had never driven a car when he started work at the carrozzeria, that did not stop him from blossoming under Bertone's tutelage. Together, the two would become one of the biggest proponents of the berlinetta shape, causing the design to vault to the forefront of the automotive world.

The first of the Bertone-Giugiaro berlinettas was ASA's 1000 GT. Next was 1963's startling Testudo, an avant garde show car that used Chevrolet Corvair mechanicals. Then came Iso's two Grifos, the magnificent Alfa Romeo Canguro prototype and a one-off Ford Mustang, done on commission by America's *Automobile Quarterly*.

Combined with such memorable shapes as Pininfarina's 250 SWB and 275 GTB, the Zagato-designed Alfa Romeo TZ-1, and Frua's Maserati Mistral, in the first half of the 1960s the front-engined fastback GT came to represent the epitome of glamour and style.

It is thus no wonder Italy's manufacturers and coachbuilders were riding a wave that never seemed to break. With company owners, managers, and employees bursting with optimism, even the Italian government's ill-conceived new tax on cars in 1964 only slowed things down temporarily.

The Era of Prosperity would continue unabated, or so everyone thought.

Designs don't come much nicer than Bertone's one-off Iso Grifo A3/L Spider that debuted in 1964. "That car was totally the work of Bertone, for they never contacted us about stiffening the chassis," Iso chief technician Pierluigi Raggi recalled. Iso would revisit the idea of an open air Grifo in the second half of the 1960s when a Grifo Targa was put in production.

The Hot Years Begin

1966-1967

As the market for glamorous 130-plus-mile-per-hour GTs exploded, Italy's manufacturers were just as active in the affordable sports car segments. The onslaught of all new products began at the 1963 Frankfurt Auto Show when Alfa Romeo displayed the Giulia Sprint GT. The most obvious change from its Giulietta predecessors was it coachwork. This included an attractive Bertone coupe that Giugiaro said he sketched in late 1959 during his days off from military duty.

The Sprint GT's delay in coming to market was likely due to its production process. Where the Giulietta Sprint's coachwork had been built in Turin, this Alfa would be made entirely in-house at the firm's new facility in Arese, on the outskirts of Milan.

The Sprint GT's four-cylinder engine initially displaced 1,570 cc. Suspension up front was independent, while the rear had an effective live axle.

Like its sporting predecessors, the car was a hit with road testers and the marketplace. "The strongest feature of the Sprint GT is its ability to cover ground quickly without effort, and it is sometimes necessary to remind oneself that the engine capacity is only a shade over a liter and a half," *Road & Track* commented in its 1965 road test. The magazine also lauded the car's five-speed transmission, disc brakes, and interior appointments.

Alfa's decision to produce the Sprint GT itself paid off in spades. Including subsequent versions with larger and smaller engines, the model would remain in production well into the 1970s, with more than 190,000 units being sold.

It also became a formidable race car in Giulia GTA guise. Weighing approximately 400 pounds lighter than the standard Sprint GT and sporting a more powerful engine, the GTA would win the European Manufacturer's Championship three years in a row (1966 to 1968).

Ferrari's regal 365 California was the last of the custom-built cars available to general clientele. Just 14 were made in 1966 and 1967. The model was designer Tom Tjaarda's last piece of work with Pininfarina.

The successor to Alfa's Giulietta/Giulia Sprint was the Giulia Sprint GT. Its more contemporary body was also designed at Bertone and was one of the first pieces of work of the company's new styling chief, Giorgetto Giugiaro. Like the Giulietta Sprint, the Giulia Sprint GT was a smash hit in the marketplace and would remain in production into 1976, when it was called the 2000 GT Veloce.

In 1966, Alfa introduced a new Pininfarina two-seat spyder using a shortened Sprint GT chassis. Called the Duetto, the name originated in a worldwide contest sponsored by Alfa that generated more than 140,000 entries. Thanks to its starring role opposite Dustin Hoffman in the film *The Graduate*, the Duetto would go on and become a 1960s icon.

Yet it was not well received when it debuted. England's *Motor* commented the car was "not distinguished in appearance." When one showed up at *Road & Track's* office in southern California, "One [staff member] condemned it as a contrived design," the magazine noted, "[while] another said 'I think Pininfarina missed the ball this time.'"

But if its appearance didn't satisfy everyone immediately, its road manners were a different story. When *Car and Driver* compared it to five other Italian, British, and Japanese sports cars in September 1966, it recruited Shelby American's star race driver Ken Miles to help in the evaluation. The Duetto was unanimously judged superior, for not only did the editors find it the most attractive but the Alfa also had the best acceleration, lap times, top speed, and was the most comfortable. "When I get into it," Miles summed up for everyone, "I immediately feel the car is part of me, not some strange machine."

One of the Duetto's competitors in terms of price was Lancia's Fulvia. With the Flaminia line priced in the $6,500 range and the Flavia costing approximately $4,800 (for comparison, Lincoln's two-door Continental cost $5,500), Lancia launched the $3,400 model in 1965. A handsomely styled, sober coupe, it used a shortened Fulvia sedan floorpan.

Like the Aurelia GT many years earlier, the Fulvia boasted interesting mechanicals: Its engine was a 1,216-cc V-4 that powered the front wheels.

A more aggressively styled Fulvia was the Sport, a small berlinetta by Zagato. With less weight and a smoother, more aerodynamic body, its listed top speed of 105 was 6 miles per hour higher than the Fulvia Coupe.

In 1967, *Road & Track* tested a Zagato and a more powerful version of the coupe, the 1.3 Rallye. Noting the Lancias were "the best handling front wheel drive cars we have tried," the magazine lauded their brakes, supple ride, refined character, and good finish. "The Rallye coupe is . . . for anyone who wants a precision motorcar, an engineering *tour de force* for less than $4000. [T]he Zagato adds a styling *tour de force* in aluminum to the package for a price."

Like Alfa's Giulia Sprint GT and Duetto, the Fulvia would see several different versions over the years and remain in production for the better part of a decade. It also became a championship-winning car—rallying in this case.

Fiat was also attacking the sports/GT market with a vengeance. At the 1965 Geneva Show, it debuted the 850 coupe and spyder. With a 52– to 54–horsepower, rear-mounted, 843-cc, inline four-cylinder engine, like Fiat's other sports cars, the 850s derived from an another model, the mass market 850 of 1964.

"It is not hard to understand the popularity of the 850 coupe," Road & Track enthused in its 1967 road test. "Following the current rage for fastbacks, Fiat has come up with one of the handsomest, best-balanced designs we have seen on a small car." Liking the brakes, ride comfort, spacious interior, and freely revving engine, "considering the many sophisticated features it offers," the magazine concluded, "its price of $1,834 is almost too good to be true."

Motor also enjoyed the 850 coupe. Calling it a "pocket GT," the magazine felt the Fiat was "a highly individual 2+2 with low running costs, convenient size, Fiat reliability and world-wide service." On the road, it found the car's performance "adequate," the brakes "faultless," its handling "responsive."

The market responded with vigor, as Fiat would make more than 340,000 over the next eight years.

An even more sporting proposition was the 850 Spyder by Bertone. One of the stars of that Geneva Show, it had a sleek, magnificently proportioned body featuring flush headlights. It went on sale in Italy later that year, with Nuccio Bertone saying his production quickly hit 25 a day.

Within a year, orders had slipped in half. According to author Luciano Greggio, the reason was simple: Fiat never promoted the car. When informed production would soon be cut back, Nuccio was able to convince them to try the export market in America, overcoming their objections that a small displacement car would not sell.

Bertone's gut instinct was right. *Road & Track* felt the tiny Fiat was "one of the most beautiful designs ever seen on a small car," its testers commenting that "more than one owner of a small displacement British roadster cast covetous eyes on it."

They concluded the 850 Spyder was "an excellent value in terms of esthetics, finish, detail design, ride and handling, giving an exceedingly high fun-per-dollar quotient. As soundly built as it is beautiful, the Spyder gives every indication of maintaining its appeal over a long period of time."

That observation could not have been more prescient. Almost 125,000 were produced over the next several years.

Yet the 850 Spyder was not Fiat's most popular open-air sports car, for that distinction belongs to the 124 Spyder. When Fiat turned to Pininfarina for the 124's coachwork, its design was entrusted to American Tom Tjaarda. Then in his early 30s, Tom was the son of famed designer John Tjaarda, the man behind Lincoln's futuristic, aerodynamic Zephyr of the 1930s.

That the younger Tjaarda ended up in Italy was compliments of one of his University of Michigan professors. For a class thesis, "I wanted to make a scale model of [a] sports car," Tjaarda said. "But Professor Lahti instantly ruled this out, saying it was not innovative enough. I thus decided to do something that didn't exist: a sports station wagon."

When presented with the completed model, Lahti was so impressed that he immediately contacted Luigi Segre, an acquaintance at Carrozzeria Ghia who was the firm's managing director. Without so much as an interview, Tjaarda was hired.

The nascent designer arrived in Turin on August 15, 1959, and was immediately thrust on the hot seat. Without any type of formal training, Tjaarda was soon designing while studying Italian at night. His sports cars at Ghia were Innocenti's diminutive 950 Spyder and an update of Volkswagen's Karmann Ghia 1600.

He would last two years with the company. "Segre was a difficult man to work for," Tjaarda remembered. "His moods seemed to change daily—friendly one moment and dark the next."

When an opportunity developed at Pininfarina, the budding designer jumped at the chance. Here, Tjaarda truly learned the intricacies of design and coachbuilding under the tutelage of Franco Martinengo and Battista Pininfarina, gaining a sense of proportion and refinement that remains with him to this day.

Tjaarda easily recalls one episode that typified the excellence of Pinin's eye. Although he was now retired, one day "the master" came in to examine a full-scale plaster mock up of the Corvette Rondine. After eyeing Tjaarda's model for several minutes, "This is a little too fat on the sides," Pinin noted, "so why don't you take off 5 millimeters?"

When the company founder left, Tjaarda and the modelers had a brief discussion. Agreeing the model would look more lean when it was painted, they did nothing.

When Pinin examined the finished work two weeks later, he said, "I hate to inform you guys this, but the design still isn't right. We need to take off another 5 millimeters."

Coincidentally, that one-off served as the impetus for the 124 Spyder. "After 1963's Paris Auto Show, Martinengo asked me to do a 1:1 scale drawing of a sports car, using the Rondine as the basis," Tjaarda recalled. "I must admit I had a devil of a

Pininfarina's follow up to the Giulietta/Giulia Spider was the Duetto. It broke cover in 1966 and used two of Pininfarina's one-offs as the basis for its design: the 1959 Alfa 3500 Spider Super Sport and the 1961 Alfa Spider Speciale Aerodinamico. Like Bertone's Giulia Sprint GT, the model had an incredibly long life in the marketplace. On sale until 1993, the Duetto used a number of different names during its 27-year production run.

Lancia's Fulvia coupe demonstrated a completely different line of thinking when compared to the Alfa and Fiat sports coupes. It featured front-wheel drive and had styling that wouldn't be mistaken for anything else. The Fulvia remained in production into the mid-1970s and won a world rally championship in 1972.

Lancia first introduced its midrange, technically advanced Flavia sedan in 1960. It had a flat-four-cylinder engine, front-wheel drive, and disc brakes front and rear. In 1962, Lancia introduced the Flavia Coupe, Convertible, and Sport models that used shortened Flavia sedan chassis. The Flavia Sport (pictured) offered the highest performance and featured an awkwardly designed body by Zagato. With the later 1.8-liter engine, its top speed was listed at 116 miles per hour.

Fiat's rear-engine Bertone-designed 850 Spider was a tremendous hit in the all-important American market, where 90 percent of the 125,000 manufactured, were sold. Former Bertone chief stylist Giorgetto Giugiaro notes the Spider's well-proportioned looks were influenced by several elements from two previous Bertone show cars: the 1963 Chevrolet Corvair Testudo and the 1964 Alfa Romeo Canguro. The Fiat Styling Center designed the Spider's 850 Coupe stablemate.

time. What made it so difficult was the Rondine's long, flowing shape. The chassis I was using had a much smaller wheelbase and shorter overhangs."

After completing the project, Tjaarda remained with Pininfarina for several more months, his last design being Ferrari's regal 365 California. He then went to Fergat-OSI, an automotive venture funded in part by business machine maker Olivetti.

At the 1966 Turin Show, Tjaarda got the surprise of his life when he saw the 124 Spyder. "I never knew who the client was," he mused. "The production car differed from my sketches in the front end, for my original design was more pointy and streamlined. But overall, I liked what they did."

Fiat's newest used a shortened and reinforced 124 sedan platform. Having a lower ride height and stiffer springs, the front suspension was independent, and disc brakes were used on each wheel. Its in-line four-cylinder engine featured a cast-iron block and an aluminum head. The transmission was a five-speed, and claimed maximum speed was 106 miles per hour.

Like Bertone's 850 Spyder, the 124 would become a tremendous marketplace success, particularly in America. "We see the 124 Spyder as a milestone," *Car and Driver*'s road test observed. "[It marks] the beginning of the end of the hardship sports car. . . Not only is it quiet and comfortable, but everywhere you look there are features normally found in cars costing far more."

Road & Track's comparison test came to the same conclusion. When stacked up against an MGB, Porsche 914, and Triumph TR-6, the Fiat was the runaway victor.

In various guises, the 124 Spyder would remain in production for two decades. In total, almost 200,000 were sold.

Yet, its 1966 Turin Show debut was overshadowed by Fiat's Ferrari V-6-powered sports car, the Dino. The connection with Maranello made for intrigue at the highest levels. With Enzo having recently rebuffed a buyout offer from Ford Motor Company, "At the end of 1964," Dante Giacosa writes in his autobiography, "rumors were bandied about in the corridors of the [executive offices] that negotiations were going on between Enzo Ferrari and the president, but no one knew the subject."

Behind the collaboration was a rule change in Formula 2 competition: any powerplant used had to come from an automobile in which at least 500 units had been made, something impossible for Ferrari to accomplish. "A visit by [managing director Gaudenzio] Bono to Maranello made the contacts official and marked the start of full collaboration," Giacosa goes on. "Valletta, Giovanni Agnelli, and Bono thought it a good idea to accept Ferrari's proposal and made arrangements for the design of a sports car with the Dino engine."

And so was born Fiat's most prestigious model since the 8V. As the engine had been conceived for racing, "This meant redesigning [it] to reinforce the components subject to the greatest wear, avoid deformations and deterioration, and achieve an adequate degree of durability," Giacosa noted. "Tests were conducted both at Fiat and the Ferrari works, in close collaboration."

Dashboard with full instrumentation. Steering in special wood.

Easily manoeuvrable folding top. Wide rear light. Rear quarter window glasses which drop away when the top is folden down.

Rear section.

Roomy interior. Contouring bucket seats with folding backrests and rear bench for two extra passengers.

A dynamic new style

A new concept of value expressed in terms of performance, roadholding, braking capacity and driving comfort, with acceleration, speed, trim, fittings, colours, looks and styling to match. Plus easy upkeep, sturdiness and durability.

The first Fiat Dino was a spyder designed by Pininfarina. Several months later at Geneva, Bertone presented a coupe. Both cars used a 1,987-cc V-6 that produced 160 horsepower at 7,200 rpm. The Dino's pressed steel chassis had an independent suspension up front and a live axle in the rear. The gearbox was a five-speed, and brakes were discs. Given the car's exotic engine, surprisingly its price in Italy was just 10 percent above the 2300S.

Road & Track's Henry Manney was one of the few journalists that tested the exclusive model. "The Dino is a real sports car," he noted of the Spyder, "with lots of rasp from its V-6. [It also has] a lovely 5-speed gearbox (not the same as on the 124 Spider), supreme comfort for the driver, sleek Italian lines, and instruments for every contingency. Under way [it] felt . . . Ferrari-like in spite of the Fiat construction."

That Fiat launched the Dino was indicative of the role prestige and top speed played in the marketplace in the second half of the 1960s. "Everyone was focusing on performance," Piero Rivolta recalled. "Whether you went from Milan to Turin in 31 or 32 minutes had become very important."

Comprehending Rivolta's observation was Maserati. Now in the process of finishing up a corporate and product transformation that first started with the 3500, Orsi's company was just about to jump into the thick of the top speed wars.

When the Frua-designed 5000 GT broke cover in 1962, Giulio Alfieri noted it was the precursor to two new models: the V-8-powered four-door Quattroporte of 1963 and the 2+2 Mexico of 1965.

Yet Maserati's most sporting car, the Mistral, still used a six-cylinder engine. First offered as a handsome berlinetta that debuted at Turin in 1963, an equally attractive Spider broke cover

Fiat's 124 Spider spelled the beginning of the end of the British roadster. Introduced in 1966 and vastly more sophisticated than its MG and Triumph counterparts, its effective mix of an affordable price, comfort, civility, and outstanding road manners saw it win comparison test after comparison test. Like the Alfa Duetto, the 124's timeless shape helped it remain in production for two decades.

According to former Pininfarina stylist Tom Tjaarda, the car that served as the basis for the 124 Spider was the one-off Chevrolet Corvette Rondine of 1963–64; a look at the rear-end treatment clearly shows the family lineage. "I struggled with the Fiat's shape," the still active designer admitted. "Its shorter wheelbase and overhangs made for a difficult transformation."

Fiat and Ferrari joined forces to develop and manufacture the Fiat Dino Coupe and Spider. The Pininfarina-designed Spider first appeared in 1966, while the Bertone-designed Coupe debuted the following year; Ferrari V-6 engines powered both. While it has often been speculated the Sergio Pininfarina played some role in bringing Fiat and Ferrari together on this car, "I did not play any direct role in the Fiat-Ferrari agreement," the man said. Rather, "I was asked by Fiat and Ferrari to design and build the Spider."

the following year. Despite journalists such as *Autosport*'s John Bolster noted "everything about the Mistral is so right," "we knew we needed to do a new car," Alfieri said. "Lamborghini had begun production, and Ferrari had its new products. We understood we had to reply with something."

Orsi and Alfieri dipped into their bag of V-8 tricks for the answer. To compete with his Modenese competitors, the engineer increased the engine's bore and stroke and bumped the compression ratio. The result was a 4.7-liter V-8 that produced a quoted 330 horsepower at 5,500 rpm.

Maserati then turned to Giorgetto Giugiaro for the car's styling. Now at Carrozzeria Ghia after leaving Bertone in 1965, the stylist attacked the project with glee. "It was important that Ghia present something different from what I was doing at Bertone," he reflected. "My key was to make a line and windshield that had a more severe rake."

He accomplished this and more with Maserati's Ghibli. Named after a hot desert wind and also debuting at Turin in 1966, its stunning styling brought the house down. Described as "*the* esthetic hit" of the show by *Road & Track*, the Ghibli followed Maserati's tradition of a tube frame, independent suspension up front, and live axle with leaf springs and trailing arms in the rear.

Both Alfieri and Giugiaro fondly recall the day the designer chided the engineer about Maserati's star having "antiquated" underpinnings. "Why haven't you gone to an independent rear suspension?" Giugiaro asked. "Come with me," the engineer said, motioning toward the parked Ghibli.

Alfieri put on a show, delivering a hair-raising exhibition of speed. When they returned to the works, the designer was white as a sheet. "Does that answer your question?" the engineer calmly asked.

The Ghibli entered production in 1967, *Car and Driver* declaring it was "well on its way to becoming [the year's] In car." But the American publication found other things as appealing as

those striking lines. "Despite the faintly archaic exotica under the hood, this one-time race engine has been refined to the point where stop-and-go driving is no cause for worry," its testers noted. "Here is this beautiful, powerful car that has a top speed faster than the Tokyo to Osaka express, and *anybody* [anybody rich enough] can drive it."

While they estimated their test car's top speed at 145 miles per hour, Paul Frère saw 160 in the example he tried. "The acceleration times up to 120 mph (23.5 seconds) and for the standing kilometer (25.5 seconds) can be matched by a few other very high performance cars," he noted. "[But] none [are] quite as fast and as [well] appointed. This car is so luxurious and refined that its behavior is quite deceptive."

Another stunner that debuted at that memorable 1966 Turin show was De Tomaso's mid-engine Mangusta. Another masterpiece by Giugiaro and Ghia, its lines were more startling than the rakish Ghibli.

So how did the controversial Argentinean go from the four-cylinder Vallelunga to a big-league contender in one fell swoop? At least one book on De Tomaso has claimed the Mangusta was supposed to be a new, mid-engine Iso. Reportedly, Giotti Bizzarrini proposed the idea to Piero Rivolta, who had taken over Iso after his father unexpectedly died in the summer of 1966. When Rivolta passed on the idea, the chassis and project found their way to Giugiaro and De Tomaso, the result being the Mangusta.

While the story makes for good reading, it never happened. "We never considered anything like the Mangusta," Rivolta said. "I never had anything to do with Mangusta," engineer Bizzarrini seconded. "Anyone who associates my name with that car is making up history."

Surprisingly, the Mangusta's origins lie in California. According to former Shelby American designer Pete Brock, "The chassis was done for Shelby to compete in the Can Am series," a point that is backed up in *Road & Track*'s March 1966 cover story. "The frame was designed by De Tomaso and is basically an enlarged version of the Vallelunga spine chassis. Several were to be made under contract, for a car that was going to be called the King Cobra.

"But the Can Am series quickly moved on, with people using larger engines. As the chassis wasn't working too well, Shelby split from the project. Because De Tomaso had some extra chassis in his factory, that is how the car and Mangusta name (Italian for *mongoose*, an enemy of the cobra) were born."

The prototype Mangusta was powered by a Ford 289 that De Tomaso claimed produced 400-plus horsepower, thanks to its four double-throat downdraft Webers. Other mechanical highlights were its five-speed transaxle, independent front and rear suspension, and large Girling disc brakes.

Just how potent the production Mangusta was depended on the engine. While the European version was fitted with a Ford 289 V-8 De Tomaso rated at 305 horsepower (DIN), most American cars had an ordinary, 230-horsepower 302. *Road & Track*'s test of the latter yielded 0–60 in 7 seconds and a paltry 118-mile-per-hour top speed.

Their comments make it appear that some of the Vallelunga's lack of development and build quality carried over to the new De Tomaso. Noting items such as doors that only opened half way, nonadjustable seats, a heavy clutch, and difficult-to-shift five-speed, "the Mangusta is a car to which you adapt," the magazine observed.

Paul Frère's test of a 289-powered Mangusta was much more favorable. While he also encountered an extremely heavy clutch, "the rest [of the car] came as an unbelievable surprise,"

he wrote in *Motor*. "The noise I had been expecting from the engine was practically non-existent; the suspension was beautifully smooth and exceptionally well damped, and the noise on badly paved [streets] was extremely subdued."

Frère recorded 0–60 in 6.1 seconds, 0–100 in 14.1, and a top speed of 152 miles per hour. "What I thought would be a fierce and crude beast," the Le Mans–winning journalist concluded, "was

Maserati entered the front-engine berlinetta fray in 1963 with its handsome, Frua-designed Mistral. The following year, the company introduced the Mistral Spider. Both used the Maserati's famed inline six-cylinder engine. "The Mistral's greenhouse is based on the Frua-designed 5000 GT," Adolfo Orsi, grandson of the company's former owner, pointed out. *John Ling Collection.*

If any car truly defined the word *sleek* in the 1960s, it was Maserati's fantastic Ghibli. It was designed by Giorgetto Giugiaro, who had left Bertone to work at Ghia. "[W]e liked his system of thinking, for it was the best at doing this type of sports car," engineer Giulio Alfieri said. "Because the Ghibli used our V-8, we went with a dry sump oiling system. This allowed a lower body profile and a better center of gravity." This Ghibli is a later SS version with a 4.9-liter engine.

Giugiaro also worked his magic for De Tomaso on the Mangusta. Like Maserati's Ghibli, the Mangusta debuted at the star-studded 1966 Turin Auto Show and brought the house down. Its spine chassis has long been rumored to have been the work of Giotto Bizzarrini, but the engineer emphatically stated "I never had anything to do with that car." What is certain is this Giugiaro *tour de force* was one of the decade's most spectacular-looking machines. "I used the Mangusta and the Ghibli to establish a new style, one that was different from what I was doing at Bertone," the designer pointed out.

in fact a smooth and silky, but at the same time extremely potent Grand Touring car, in the truest sense of the work."

As impressive as the Ghibli, Mangusta, and others were, the era's benchmark was undoubtedly Lamborghini's midengine masterpiece, the Miura. *The* car that brought the centrally mounted engine configuration to the attention of the world's car-buying public, it also marked the beginning of the end for the front-engine berlinetta as the configuration upon which a manufacturer would show its most glamorous and exciting wares.

Contrary to what is commonly written, the Miura was not some secret, after-hours project that was sprung on an unsuspecting Ferruccio Lamborghini in an attempt to get him to go racing. "He knew about the project from Day One and actively encouraged us," said Gian Paolo Dallara, the man test driver Bob Wallace calls the father of the famous model. "Besides, if we really wanted to do some type of competition car, why we would have shown it with a wet sump engine?"

Assisting him in its design and construction were the aforementioned Bob Wallace and another 20-something engineer, Paolo Stanzani. "Basically we were making a street car that had a chassis inspired by a race car," Dallara said. "We liked Ford GT40's semi-monoque design. Since we couldn't stamp one out, we made it by hand."

The idea of exhibiting the chassis sans coachwork came from Ferruccio Lamborghini. "He was so much more than 'just' an owner," Dallara went on. "He was interested in mechanics, and it was important to him to have things that looked good. At a certain point, he said, 'We will bring it to the Turin Show.'"

That turned out to be a wise decision, for the naked chassis was headline material. "Perhaps the most interesting exhibit came from a less expected source although its existence had

been rumored—Lamborghini's rear-mounted, transverse V-12 engine sports racer," *Motor* reported.

"The prize for the big poker hand was reserved for Comm. Lamborghini, who not only showed up with a slightly shortened Touring-bodied convertible but also with a wild new transverse-engined chassis," Henry Manney noted in *Road & Track*. "Various Ferrari bods were seen drifting by in overcoats, with collars turned up to have a look at it."

One such person was Sergio Pininfarina. "When I saw that chassis with its transverse engine, I was envious," he smiles.

He had every reason to be. For the past several months, he had actively been trying to convince a truculent Enzo Ferrari to produce a midengine streetcar. "He kept insisting it was too dangerous," the coachbuilder recalled. "For racing, he felt it was fine. But for nonprofessional drivers, it was too much."

Although Ferrari would eventually relent, leading to the six-cylinder Dino design research prototype the coachbuilder debuted several weeks prior to Turin at Paris, Pininfarina recognized Lamborghini was holding a serious trump card. Should they desire, the young company was months away from having an outstanding midengine streetcar.

The precise number of *mesi* was four. When Lamborghini chose Bertone at the Turin Show to design and construct the car's body, Nuccio immediately went to work with Marcello Gandini, his new chief stylist who had replaced Giugiaro.

Born in August 1938, Gandini began drawing racing cars as a youngster. By his late teens, he was modifying the coachwork and mechanicals on a number of hillclimb specials.

His career formally started in 1960 when he was employed by a number of small manufacturers, such as Abarth. "Because it was difficult to get paid in those days, I found myself doing other jobs for additional income," Gandini says. Although his main source was interior decorating, he also worked for an advertising agency and had a nightclub in Turin until it unexpectedly burned down.

Through some mutual friends, Gandini first met Bertone in 1963. "He wanted to hire me immediately, but I wasn't that interested," the stylist said, "for he had Giugiaro. So I told him to contact me if something happened."

Two weeks after Giugiaro left Bertone in 1965, Nuccio found Gandini at Marazzi, a small carrozzeria in Milan. At the Turin Show, Lamborghini gave Bertone the proverbial "blank sheet of paper" and supplied the coachbuilder with some drawings of the chassis.

Bertone telephoned Lamborghini shortly after Christmas, informing him he was ready to present some sketches. Dallara met the two men the following day in Sant' Agata at the closed Lamborghini factory.

When Bertone unfurled Gandini's initial renderings, the impact was instantaneous. "We immediately realized this was extraordinary, something that happens once in a lifetime," Dallara smiled. "Touring had earlier presented us a 1:4 model, and while it was indeed very nice, this was far beyond 'very nice.' It was something unique, with a shape that was a complete departure from any other production car."

The finished Miura appeared less than three months later in Geneva. Called "*the* show sensation" by *Automobile Year*, Sergio Pininfarina had an equally strong reaction: "When I first saw it," he recalled, "I said, 'I wish I could do that myself.'"

Lamborghini was quickly overwhelmed by the onslaught. "Immediately," Dallara chuckled, "people tried to buy it, before it had even gone 1 meter!" When Bob Wallace and Dallara drove the car to the Monaco Grand Prix approximately two months later, the reaction was equally as strong: Everyone wanted one.

Magazine articles simply dumped gasoline on an already hot fire. "We vote [the Miura] far and away the most exciting production development since the war," England's *CAR* magazine waxed after spending time with Wallace in a production prototype. "[A]n inspired creation which will undoubtedly become a classic, [it is] fit to stand beside the most desirable possessions man has yet succeeded in manufacturing for his delectation."

The Miura completed rudimentary testing and development in a matter of months, and the first production cars left the factory in the first quarter of 1967. "Fortunately," Dallara remembered, "those customers were prepared to accept problems. Every rich and impatient man wanted to have one."

With cars leaving the factory, the clamor only intensified. "As part of a stable," *CAR* concluded in its 1,000-mile test of a production Miura, "this dramatically conceived Lamborghini can be employed for what it is—an immensely fast, modern two seater with the world's finest engine, society's highest cachet, and plenty of scope for further development. It is still really a prototype, but one which is already the undisputed master of the road."

Every other test came to the same basic conclusion. The Miuras tested by *Autocar* and *Motor* cleared 170 mile per hour, the latter accelerating to 60 in 6 seconds, 100 in 13.4, and covering the standing kilometer in 24.8.

Stateside, *Road & Track* called the Miura "the most glamorous, exciting and prestigious sports car in the world." It is thus no wonder one was referenced in a television advertisement for that most staid of American institutions, a bank.

On the flipside of the coin, *Playboy* magazine was also in on the act. In August 1967, it prominently featured the Miura alongside Maserati's Ghibli, Iso's Grifo, Ferrari's 330 GTC, a Bizzarrini Strada, and several other cars in an article entitled "THE GT . . . Motordom's New Glamour Car, The Gran Turismo," by noted journalist Ken Purdy.

With that giddy atmosphere engulfing Europe, America, and Japan, the unions' rise to power in Italy went completely unnoticed. Largely dormant since the Communist defeat in the late 1940s, issues such as inflation solidified their reemergence.

"In 1960," Maserati's Aurelio Bertocchi recalled, "the typical Italian middle class family had a small Fiat 500. Five years later, there were two people working in each family, and they had two cars minimum. Employees now wanted higher pay, rather than higher benefits. This made the risk factor in building factories, and starting new businesses, much greater." Still, banks continued to lend liberally, causing too much money to chase too few goods.

The average Italian was also becoming increasingly aware of his rights. When ever-higher expectations for the future weren't met, a feeling of discontent slowly set in.

Lamborghini's Miura was the model that brought the midengine configuration to the fore of production car design and engineering. It was first shown as a naked chassis at the Turin Show in November 1965, then reappeared in March 1966 covered with a sensational Bertone body.

"The Miura wasn't the creation of a new line," said Marcello Gandini, the man who penned its unforgettable form. "Rather, it was an arrival point of all the sports cars of the 1950s and '60s. The lines were very soft, but very animalistic." The model shown here is the last and best of the Miuras, the SV.

To get an idea of how sports cars had become big business, all one had to do was wander inside the Bertone factory in 1967 and see the production lines for Fiat's Dino and 850 Spider bodies. At this time, Italy was the undisputed master of the sports car and styling universe.

The unions keyed on this. By concentrating on issues such as school and transportation shortcomings, they were able to transfer a good portion of that agitation to the workplace, then focus it on something else.

Their primary target was typically Fiat. Because the union's leadership knew it would be difficult to accomplish anything against an organization of such immense size and power, they targeted its suppliers. "By squeezing the small guy," Marcello Gandini aptly summarized, "slowly the strikers started making inroads."

Workplace safety was now becoming another point of contention. "We joined the unions because there were no restrictions on hazardous types of work," two employees of a large coachbuilder remembered. "For example, there was the 'White Death,' which was caused by glue and its effects on a person's lungs after prolonged exposure."

The two employees recalled the situation started turning ugly in late 1965. After finishing work one day, "we came out and found a large group of women outside of the factory. At first, we didn't think anything of it, for people from factories that were close by would often go to another. But as we passed them, they started insulting us *solely because we were working*. Then they started spitting on us and beating us."

As strikes became more frequent, more than one company turned to strike busters. "We had two very large bosses that said 'If you don't work, we are going to fire you,'" an industry employee remembered. "But if we [didn't] strike, we ran the risk of being badly beaten. It really seemed as if something was boiling in Italy at this time."

As the feeling of malcontent and rebellion widened, it touched Italy and Europe's universities. Peaceful demonstrations and sit-ins started, and the quality of education dropped dramatically. Soon there were "collective exams" that, as one student of the times recalls, "you could easily pass by showing a newspaper in your pocket."

Then a wind from the Far East started sweeping across the landscape, with many students finding comfort in the teachings of Mao. Wearing androgynous clothes and using *The Red Book* as their bible, a movement against capitalism and its trappings gathered momentum on college campuses. As violence became the norm, it was necessary to have a pass to move from one part of campus to another.

This unrest did not go unnoticed by the unions. As their leadership congealed in the hands of fewer and fewer people, the colleges suddenly became fertile recruiting grounds to join the stand against big business and management. "We lost many hours of work during that period," a gran turismo assembly line worker summarized. "It really was three very hot years."

In truth, the industry hadn't seen anything yet. Those hot years would soon grow into an inferno, one that would push Italy's manufacturers—and its sports car and GT constructors, in particular—to the brink of extinction.

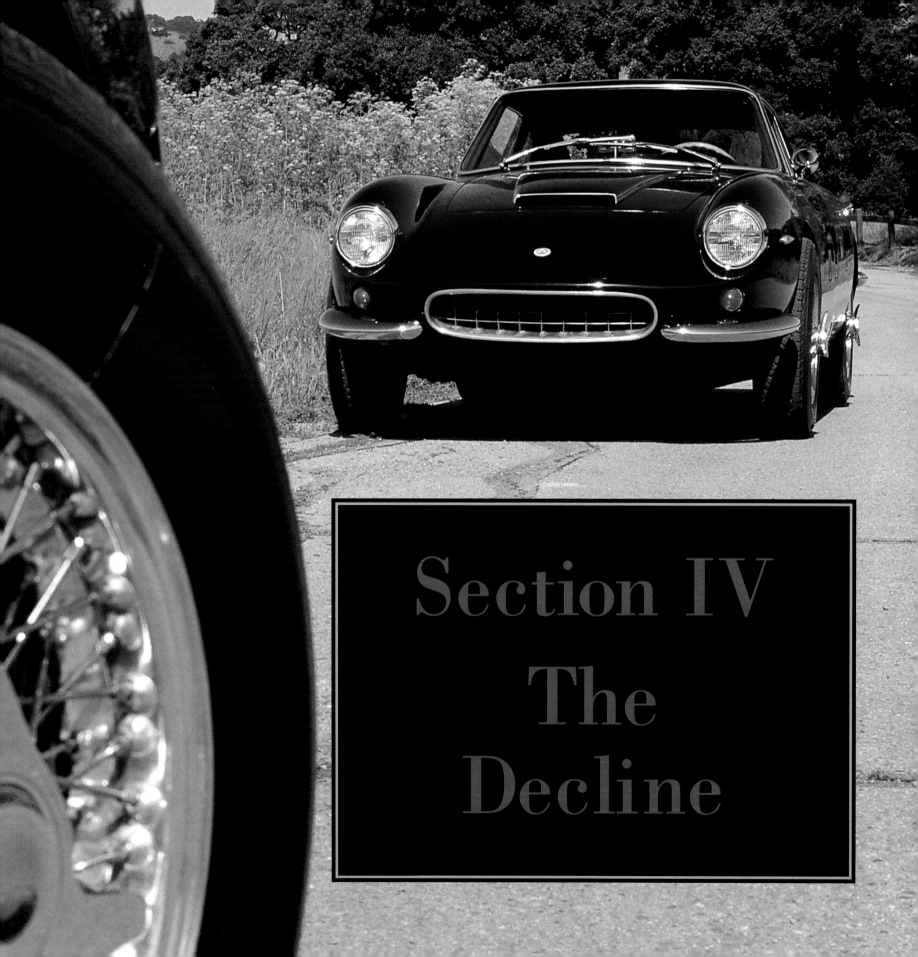

Section IV
The
Decline

Twilight
of the
Goddesses

1969-1973

Two disparate elements prompted Italy's decline in sports/GT production and styling: an American attorney named Ralph Nader and May 1968. Nader wasn't even a blip on the automotive world's radar screen when the 1960s began. Thanks to his controversial book *Unsafe at Any Speed* and General Motors ham-fisted response to his attack on its Corvair, the young attorney became a national figure in 1965. His subsequent testimony before Congress was instrumental in America enacting the National Safety and Motor Vehicle Act.

When the act went into effect on January 1, 1968, all of the world's manufacturers were completely unprepared. "The safety and pollution laws were a very big problem for us," said Maserati's Giulio Alfieri. "Being alone, like we were, it was very difficult."

Iso's Piero Rivolta agreed: "Everybody was intimidated. No one knew what to do. Even the big European manufacturers were unsure."

Most of Italy's design houses were sucker punched by the regulations. "Before," Bertone's Enzo Prearo said, "changes in styling were caused by trends. Now, [they] were dictated by law."

Marcello Gandini seconded Prearo's statement: "While the crash testing was influential, the bumper and light requirements caused most changes, [for] we were used to doing different types of bumpers on different designs. When I see designs from this period, it reminds me of how many uncertainties there really were."

As the world's top speed wars escalated in the late 1960s, Iso first showed the prototype Grifo 7-Liter at Geneva in 1968. Powered by a Corvette 427 engine, it had minor cosmetic differences from the standard Grifo. "I basically made the car as a joke," said former Iso president Piero Rivolta. The last laugh was on him, however, for customers immediately lined up to buy it. The 7-Liter would enter production later that year, then receive a facelift in late 1970 when the model's name was changed to Grifo Can Am (pictured).

The Maserati Ghibli Spider debuted in 1969 and saw 125 produced over a four-year period. "The story behind the car is quite simple," Giulio Alfieri said. "At that moment, it was necessary to have a spider version, and Giugiaro proposed a solution." Like the Ghibli coupe, it was first offered with a 4.7-liter V-8, then a 4.9 in the SS version. All Ghiblis were available with a five-speed manual or three-speed automatic transmission.

May 1968 was something else altogether and marked the end of the Era of Prosperity. The unions and students' rebellion had become a force, causing violence to erupt in major cities that fateful month. "Walking down the street suddenly became very dangerous," one participant recalled. "You would see numerous young people with broken heads."

A wave of chaos swept across Italy and the rest of Europe, propelled by improved media communication. Communism was now rampant in college, with many students firmly believing what the handful of leaders told them. With capitalism and private property a crime in their minds, their belief was so strong, it was if they were saying, "We are starting a war."

If this maelstrom wasn't enough, Italy saw a truly revolutionary faction emerge, the Red Brigades. This small group's goal was to eliminate capitalism and those who were its leaders. Believing change could only occur through revolution, rather than democratic processes, their propensity for "kneecappings" got them quickly noticed.

By the end of the year, and on into 1969, a display of wealth or opulence often attracted major attention, with negative consequences. At the 1968 opening night of Milan's famed La Scala opera house, the elegantly dressed patrons were pelted with eggs and tomatoes. "Rich people, enjoy yourselves. This will be your last time," one banner read.

Violence directed at the automotive manufacturers and suppliers intensified when negotiations over the industry's engineering workers' three-year contract appeared to flounder. Strikers would invade a sector of a factory, then attempt to take over the entire concern, wantonly destroying property in the process. Frequently, no one was sure where the strike began and what started the grievance. On-the-job habits became slack, undermining the morale of those who wanted to work.

For coachbuilders, the pleasure of making and producing designs disappeared, replaced by daily skirmishes with people who were against everything they did. Marcello Gandini remembers this "us versus them" mentality reaching its zenith just before the 1969 Turin Show when a group burst in to the Bertone design studios and damaged the two prototypes they were preparing.

The ensuing shouting match quickly turned into a scuffle, Gandini somehow managing to throw the disrupters out of the studio. The leaders then went to Bertone and issued an ultimatum: Either Gandini goes, or we don't sit down at the negotiating table. Bertone, not batting an eye, stood behind his styling chief.

Now fearing for the safety of their work, one night Gandini and crew removed the prototypes from the studios, taking one to a small building, the other to a cow farm! Such frequent disruptions caused Bertone and Pininfarina to establish design studios on the outskirts of Turin, away from their production facilities.

Modenese coachbuilder Sergio Scaglietti's life was also turned upside down. "The 10 years from 1957 to 1967 were wonderful," he said. "We often worked straight through the night, and I would pay the workers quite well, separate from the normal wages.

"Then, very quickly, everything went to hell. The unions spoiled it, deciding the workers shouldn't do the extra hours. People quickly became lazy."

The constructors were also hit. Piero Rivolta recalls a large group from nearby Pirelli travelling to Bresso to get his employees to join them in their walkout. "They broke some windows and such," Iso's chief remembered. "It was like dealing from inside a fort, and then figuring a way to leave the fort without anyone being killed."

The constant turmoil took its toll on Enzo Ferrari, causing Scaglietti's close friend to look for a way out. "The workers were giving him hassles and headaches," the humble coachbuilder remembered. "He was really fed up with the whole thing."

Ferrari found his answer by selling his company to Fiat in 1969. Keeping Sergio abreast of the situation, "One day he called me to Maranello and said, 'What do you think of doing something like I am doing?'"

Scaglietti didn't hesitate. "Give me the pen!" he replied. "I am ready to sign."

Surprisingly, Ferrari [and Scaglietti] were not the first to merge, for the Orsis sold Maserati to France's Citroen in 1968. "We really weren't surprised, for it was a long time coming," Giulio Aflieri reflected. "Frankly, Citroen's presence offered a sense of protection. Their immense size made us feel more prepared. Their assistance in rules and laws was something we never would have been able to do alone."

As the 1960s came to a close, the tide against gran turismos and sports cars had not turned completely. For a majority of the general public and industry alike, they still held great allure and fascination.

Although the Miura had opened the midengine floodgates, the front-engine berlinetta remained in the thick of the top speed wars. Alfieri and Maserati dipped into the American hot-rodder's trick of "there is no substitute for cubic inches" with their Ghibli SS.

Introduced in 1970, the year after the company launched the Ghibli Spyder, the SS's 4.9-liter V-8 had a slightly longer stroke, higher compression, and larger Weber carburetors. The new engine's output ranged from 335 to 355, depending on the source quoted.

Iso applied the same philosophy to its Grifo when it introduced the 7 Liter version at the 1968 Geneva Show. A Corvette 427 V-8 lurked under the Iso's raised bonnet, the model becoming a serious contender for the World's Fastest Car title when it received a five-speed transmission. "More than once," Iso engineer Guiseppe Caso recalled, "the car was still accelerating at 275 kilometers per hour [171 miles per hour] when I was testing it."

The berlinetta design was also used to great effect on four-seat GTs. Once again Lamborghini and Bertone led the way when they introduced the sensational Marzal show car in 1967. "Glamour on wheels has never been pursued more successfully," LJK Setright observed in *CAR*. "The Marzal is perhaps the most extravagant piece of virtuoso styling to have come out of Europe since the war."

"A lot of people wanted to buy it," Dallara remembered. As it was "simply a show car," the company's solution was the Espada. "Whenever there is a new Lamborghini," England's *Autocar* noted of the model's 1968 Geneva introduction, "it steals the show."

Like the Miura, the Espada was hustled into production. Overseeing its development was Paolo Stanzani, Lamborghini's technical office director who became its chief engineer when Dallara left in mid-1968 to go to De Tomaso.

With a rakish 46-inch-high body, a 350-horsepower V-12 and five-speed transmission, "Jaded though we are about exoticars, every Lamborghini we test turns out to be some kind of milestone for us," *Road & Track* said when it opened its July 1969 test. "The Espada, as it happens, is the most satisfactory combination of 4-passenger seating and practicality with thoroughbred GT performance and appearance we've yet encountered."

Bertone made a futuristic gullwing-doored one-off on a Lamborghini chassis in 1967. The Marzal was powered by a rear-mounted six-cylinder engine that was, in essence, half a Miura V-12. Just weeks after its Geneva Show debut in March, Prince Rainer piloted the car around the track at the Monaco Grand Prix. Although it went without a hitch, "I was extremely nervous," Gian Paolo Dallara smiled. "The Marzal had hardly done any testing, and my mind was filled with all the things that could go wrong."

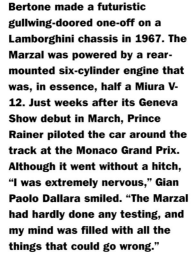

The Marzal was the inspiration for Lamborghini's Espada,(pictured). First seen in 1968, it featured a front-mounted V-12 and full seating for four in a package that was just 46.5 inches tall. Another example of the phenomenal creativity of Nuccio Bertone and Marcello Gandini, the Espada remained in production until 1978. More than 1,200 were built.

The Ferrari that first disappointed, then surprised everyone, was the 365 GTB/4. Commonly called the Daytona, its front-engine configuration was a letdown to those who thought Maranello would have a midengine reply to Lamborghini's Miura. Once tested by magazines, it was clear the Daytona was the Miura's superior in civility, acceleration, and top speed.

Although the 0–60 time of 6.5 seconds and estimated top speed at 158 miles per hour were impressive, the car had its faults. In addition to heavy steering and minor brake fade, its shoddy interior finish made R&T comment, "one would think a price of $21,000 allows sufficient time to do the job right."

Surprisingly, the Marzal/Espada saga had an adverse effect on Nuccio Bertone's relationship with Alfa Romeo. As he relates in *Bertone*, his 1967 Montreal show car for Canada's centenary exhibition was a very advanced sports coupe. Yet, before that Alfa was sent to the city after which it was named, the Marzal broke cover at Geneva. Bertone says Alfa chief Guiseppe Luraghi became furious, feeling the coachbuilder should have reserved his creativity and energy solely for their showcar.

Unfortunately, that anger negatively influenced the Montreal when it went into production three years later. Originally designed to use Alfa's four-cylinder engine, it ended up with a 2.5–liter V-8. Because Luraghi insisted the styling was to remain unchanged, the resulting series of compromises caused Bertone to regretfully observe "a rather ill-fated car came into being."

Just the opposite happened with the two-place Daytona, Ferrari's response to Lamborghini's Miura. Likely the era's greatest front-engine berlinetta, its roots can be traced back to late 1966 when Pininfarina's new chief stylist was inspecting a 330 GTC/GTS chassis.

Then 28, Leonardo Fioravanti had been with the coachbuilder barely three years. "That chassis really struck me as something unique," he said. "I wanted to follow its shape and dimensions, while paying close attention to aerodynamics."

He enthusiastically put the pen to the paper, then showed his renderings to Sergio Pininfarina. "He was so positive that he decided to present them to Ferrari, even though the 275 GTB/4's successor was not being discussed," the designer said.

"The fundamental objective we set for ourselves was to obtain a thin, svelte car like a midengine design," Pininfarina recalled. "The whole idea was really a search for this sense of lightness and rake, what could be referred to as a slender look."

Two prototypes were made before the definitive version broke cover at the 1968 Paris Auto Show. Called the 365 GTB/4, its "Daytona" moniker derived from Ferrari's 1-2-3 sweep in 1967 at the Florida race.

Its mighty V-12 engine displaced 4.4 liters and was crowned by an impressive stack of six double-barrel downdraft

Weber carburetors. Power output was a heady 352 horses at 7,500 rpm.

Called "the anti-Miura production car" by *Motor*, in one fell swoop Ferrari regained its lost laurels. "It might as well be said right now," *Road & Track*'s 1970 road test began. "The Ferrari 365 GTB/4 is the best sports car in the world. Or the best GT. Take your choice; it's both. And we really didn't expect it to be. After all, it is not the most exotic."

R&T's Daytona hit 60 in 5.9 seconds, touched 100 just 6.1 seconds later, and blasted through the quarter-mile in 13.8 seconds. Its 173-mile-per-hour top speed was the highest the magazine had recorded, besting the 168 miles per hour turned by a Miura S.

Other magazine results were much the same. The Miura S *Autocar* tested touched 172, while the Daytona did 174. Where the Lamborghini needed 14.5 and 26.1 seconds to cover the quarter-mile and standing kilometer, the Ferrari needed 13.7 and 24.3 seconds for the same distances.

"It is hard to capture in mere words all the excitement, sensation and sheer exhilaration of this all-time great among cars," *Autocar*'s test concluded. "This Ferrari did not disappoint us one iota, and the performance astounded us by surpassing our expectations by a substantial margin. For us it has become an important new yardstick, standing at the pinnacle of the fast car market."

Still, the midengine design was sweeping the world, and now everyone wanted in on the act.

Ferrari's first was Pininfarina's Dino. Named after Enzo Ferrari's beloved son who died from illness in 1956, "what you must realize is the Miura was a production car, while the Dino we showed at Paris in 1965 was a dream car," the coachbuilder reflected. "I was constantly telling Ferrari that we should also make a midengine car, and all the salesmen were with me. When Mr. Ferrari finally relented, he said, 'You make it not with a Ferrari name, but as a Dino.' Because it was a less powerful car, for him, this meant less danger."

Pininfarina quickly went to work. Four prototypes were constructed in 1966 to 1967, leading to the definitive car, the Dino 206 GT. Its shape was an all-time classic, a masterful blending of sensuous curves, outstanding surface development, and stunning proportions.

Under that memorable form, the Dino's transversely mounted 1,987-cc V-6 was housed in unit with the five-speed

"When I sketched a Daytona coupe, I did not plan to derive a spyder model," says former Pininfarina stylist Leonardo Fioravanti. "We did not foresee an open version because of stiffness and aerodynamics considerations." Yet, one year after the Daytona coupe's 1968 debut, the car was displayed at Frankfurt. The man behind the idea was Modenese coachbuilder Sergio Scaglietti, who found the coupe to convertible transformation "fairly easy to do."

The seed for Ferrari's midengine Dino was planted with this car, Pininfarina's Dino Berlinetta Speciale research prototype that debuted at the Paris Auto Show in October 1965; it used Ferrari's V-6 Dino racing car for the underpinnings. "This car was 100 percent a proposal by us," Sergio Pininfarina said. "I long wanted to do a midengine car for it has a lower center of gravity as there was no exhaust. It also allowed for very good visibility, for I would not have the problem of a big radiator."

With Ferrari giving the Dino the green light, this production prototype 206 Dino appeared in late 1967. Although its look drew heavily from Pininfarina's 1965 prototype, this is a much more refined car and has a transverse, rather than longitudinal, V-6 engine. "The Dino recalled the Cisitalia with fenders that were higher than the bonnet," Sergio Pininfarina noted. "The rear end's vertical rear window was done in such a way to make the front of the car man and bonnet, and the rear part of the car, the engine."

gearbox. The engine featured double overhead cams, three Weber carburetors, and produced 180 horsepower at 8,000 rpm.

When it made its debut at the 1967 Turin Show, the car had its own separate stand under the Dino name. Throughout its production over the next seven years, it would never be called a Ferrari.

Still, there was no hiding its origins. *Sports Car Graphic* dubbed it "an engineering masterpiece," had recorded it at 0–60 in 6.7 seconds and a top speed of 142 miles per hour in Enzo's personal car.

Where the Dino truly shined was on serpentine roads. Here, it "literally tripped from one curve to another with a light and fluid style which transforms driving into a sublime pleasure," the magazine said.

CAR agreed, its test concluding "the 206GT Dino . . . stands out as one of the most advanced grand touring cars of our time."

Reactions were much the same for the 2.4-liter 246 Dino that was introduced in 1969. "It is so right," Mel Nichols noted in his test. "In all of motoring's history there have been few vehicles so balanced, integrated and complete as this one."

Alfa Romeo's midengine marvel was the Tipo 33 Stradale. Introduced in 1967, its birth carried a simple edict: The street version had to offer performance no less than 95 percent of its competition counterpart.

The Stradale did just that, thanks to its 230-horsepower, 2-liter double-overhead-cam V-8, six-speed gearbox and ravishing lightweight Franco Scaglione–designed coachwork. Because Alfa never seriously promoted the Stradale, just 18 were built.

That didn't stop the chassis from becoming a coachbuilder favorite. Bertone's stunning Carabo of 1968 stole the Paris Show, its futuristic wedge shape becoming the starting point for many subsequent designs. Pininfarina's 33 Speciale was as beautiful as the Carabo was bold.

Also dramatic was Ital Design's Bizzarrini Manta. This midengine showcar debuted at Turin in 1968 and was Giorgetto Giugiaro's formal announcement that he had formed Ital Design with Aldo Montovani. An innovative one-box shape where the silhouette was one long continuous line, Giugiaro says the Manta was the starting point of all his future designs at Ital Design.

With the floodgates now open, Italy's first mid-engine production car to debut in the 1970s was Alessandro De Tomaso's Pantera. Now the owner of Carrozzeria Ghia (and one of the reasons Giugiaro left the concern), De Tomaso hired Tom Tjaarda as the company's chief stylist in early 1968.

A little more than a year later, De Tomaso traveled to America to meet with Ford president Lee Iacocca. "After his return, he

walked into the office and said, 'We are going to do a new car—a new Mangusta,'" Tjaarda remembers. "I was then given an assignment to produce a 1:5 scale model, but not much more information than this. I sensed something important was happening, and give De Tomaso credit for making me feel this without tipping his hand." The "extra effort" Tjaarda put into his work was reflected in the car's stunning, clean shape.

The chassis design fell on Gian Paolo Dallara, whom De Tomaso had lured away from Lamborghini in mid-1968 with his upcoming F1 effort. "De Tomaso wanted a derivative of the Mangusta," the engineer remembers, "the same kind of gearbox, engine, and basic dimensions." Dallara adds, "he also wanted easy production capabilities in reasonable quantities."

After several months of frenetic activity, Alessandro's new GT debuted to great fanfare in March 1970. Technician Venazio Di Biase then had the responsibility of taking the Pantera from concept to production in just eight months.

The man whom Tjaarda calls "the bull" relished the challenge and kept going seven days a week, organizing both technical staff and production processes. "I immediately hired 20 designers," said Di Biase, who was then only 28. "At night I hired another 50 designers who worked from 9 P.M. to midnight. I knew these moonlighters from my previous work at Bertone. They were kind of like engineering guns for hire."

The Pantera arrived at American dealerships in early 1971 with a price just under $10,000. As *Car and Driver* magazine was quick to note, "Even a thrifty bellhop can scrape up enough front money for a $10,000 car."

De Tomaso was once again haunted by refinement and quality-control gremlins. While *Car and Driver* recorded 0–60 in a sparkling 5.5 seconds, it found the Pantera had "a bad habit of oversteering abruptly when you lift off the throttle in a turn." Among other things, they also noted ventilation problems, excessive noise, and interior flaws. "You have to wonder if Ford Motor Company knows what it is getting into," was their conclusion.

De Tomaso, Iacocca, and Ford quickly set about making things right. Di Biase and one of his cohorts went to America to discuss quality control on both the Pantera and future De Tomaso products. "They were willing to instruct us," he says, and "to see if we were sensitive to their requests."

Those efforts did not go to waste. In 1973, *Road & Track* would conclude its test by noting, "As far as midship GTs go, the Pantera is a bargain." More impressive, America's *Road Test* magazine named the Pantera its Sports Car of the Year.

About the time the Pantera first went on sale, Maserati jumped into the thick of things with the Bora. "We recognized that times were changing," Giulio Alfieri said. "It was the moment of the mid-engine car, and if we didn't do one, it would demonstrate that we weren't in line with the times." His insight was impeccable, for when the Bora debuted, *Road & Track*'s test of a Ghibli concluded it was "a beautiful car that promises more excitement than it delivers."

The final Dino was the 246 GTS that broke cover in 1972. The main difference between it and its coupe stablemates was the removable targa top. Like all the 206/246 models, the 246 GTS was assembled at Ferrari, and never had any Ferrari badging.

Bertone's fantastic Carabo broke cover in 1968 and ushered in the "wedge" look. Built on an Alfa 33 chassis, this machine served as the starting point for a number of subsequent designs by Bertone and other coachbuilders.

Maserati's mid-engine masterwork was the firm's first street model with fully independent suspension and was markedly different from the competition. Not only would it make use of Citroen components (steering, brakes, hydraulic systems), it reflected Alfieri's preference for refinement above everything else. "When a man gets into a car," the engineer says with a twinkle in his eye, "he speaks to it, and the car responds. He is its guest, and I liked the car to be a good host."

The Bora's V-8 was rated at 310 horsepower at 6,000 rpm and placed longitudinally in the chassis. Later, it received the 4.9-liter, 330-horsepower engine.

The Pantera L

De Tomaso's Pantera was the result of the fiery ex-pat Argentinean's linking up with Ford in America; it would use a Ford 351 V-8 throughout its 20-year production run. "My goal was to create a design that was aggressive, almost beast-like in aspect, yet refined and delicate in proportion," designer Tom Tjaarda recalled about the car his name is most closely associated with. As this brochure of a 1973 Pantera L aptly illustrates, Tjaarda certainly fulfilled his desire.

Maserati's newest debuted at 1971's Geneva Show and went on sale the following year. "Human engineering is [much] better in the Bora than a lot of full sized Detroit cars," *Motor Trend* reported in 1973. "For example, although the car is many inches shorter than a Corvette, it has a larger interior, and luggage space as big . . . as a Mustang."

They also lauded its civilized nature, off-handedly complimenting Alfieri's philosophy in the process: "The Bora's derivability is superb throughout its speed range. On the road, the Maserati's demeanor sets the class standard."

Road & Track's assessment was much the same. "The Miura was great in its day," they concluded, "but the Bora far surpasses it in comfort and quietness while approaching its performance level. Everything considered, the Bora is the best mid-engine car we've tried to date."

Lancia's wild Stratos was a completely different animal. Originally a Bertone concept car that used a Fulvia 1.6-liter engine, the only Lancia person who expressed any interest at its 1970 Turin Show debut was the company's competition manager, Cesare Fiorio.

That spark would turn into a flame over the next 12 months. When Bertone drove the prototype to Lancia, it quickly became apparent the company was interested in small series production, using it as the basis for a rallye car.

The result was the Stratos HF that appeared at the 1971 Turin Show. Besides its all-new body, the other major difference over the prototype was its engine: It now had a 2.4-liter Ferrari Dino V-6.

This engine was the ideal solution: In stock form, it produced more power than any Lancia engine. It was also readily available since Lancia, like Ferrari, had recently become another part of the Fiat Empire.

A totally different midengine car stole the 1971 Turin Show where the production prototype Stratos appeared: Ferrari's Berlinetta Boxer. Also known as the "BB," it was powered by a flat-12 ("Boxer") engine that was loosely based on the company's

Formula 1 motor. "We were not going to be rushed into changing to the mid-engine format for our big GT car," Ferrari engineer Angelo Bellei told CAR journalist and author Mel Nichols. "But when we did make the decision to create the Boxer we had no qualms: our experience with the 246 GT and Formula One combined to give us the complete confidence in the path we wished to follow."

Pininfarina made a beautifully balanced shape for Ferrari's newest. "We had a running joke inside our company," Pininfarina laughed. "Because of the way it looked, when we called the car the BB, we were not only referencing its Berlinetta Boxer name, but Brigitte Bardot!"

The production Boxer debuted one year later at Turin, where it was officially dubbed the 365GT/4 BB. While the prototype's engine was quoted at 380 horsepower at 7,000 rpm, the production car's output was listed at 360. Still, it was enough for Ferrari to quote its top speed of 180-plus miles per hour.

As memorable as the Boxer, Pantera, et al. were, Lamborghini and Bertone would once again team up to produce the standard bearer, the midengine model that would come to define the word supercar. That immortal car was the Countach.

If Dallara was the father of the Miura, then this machine's padre was engineer Paolo Stanzani. Then in his early mid-30s, Stanzani was born in Bologna in 1936. Easy going, enthusiastic, and genial, he received a mechanical engineering degree from that city's university.

After working as an engineering assistant for one year, Lamborghini surprised him with an offer to join the firm in 1963. For his first five years, he assisted Dallara on the 350 and 400 GT, Miura, and Espada.

When Dallara left, Stanzani made the most of the opportunity. Although he would perfect the Miura with the SV, "I recognized

MASERATI BORA

in 1969 that we needed something all new, something that started from a clean sheet of paper," Stanzani said. "My basic concept was to make the McLaren F1 of its day," referencing the 1990s British supercar that totally rewrote the rulebook by offering an incredible jump in performance.

"The Countach was conceived and built for one singular purpose," test driver Bob Wallace concurred. "To go like hell."

Maserati's entry into the midengine sweepstakes was the Bora that debuted at the Geneva Motor Show in 1971. By design, it was the most refined and comfortable of the world's midengine GTs. "The interior noise was low, and there was no mechanical vibration at all," said Giulio Alfieri. "From a mechanical point of view, it demonstrated something different, if not new." The U.S. specification Bora (pictured) had much larger front and rear bumpers than its European counterparts.

Nuccio Bertone and chief stylist Marcello Gandini must have seen a number of War of the Worlds reruns when they came up with the 1970 Lancia Stratos prototype. Although the midengine machine used a Lancia Fulvia 1.6-liter engine, Bertone noted he made the car without Lancia's knowledge for fear they would negatively react to its audacious design.

When Nuccio Bertone drove his futuristic prototype Stratos to Lancia's headquarters in early 1971, he piqued their interest. The result was the Lancia Stratos HF that debuted at that year's Turin Auto Show. This car was powered by a 2.4-liter Ferrari V-6 engine and would go on to win three world rallying championships in the mid-1970s.

At the 1971 Geneva Show, Bertone and Lamborghini unveiled the Countach LP500. Its impressive mechanicals were the work of Lamborghini chief engineer Paolo Stanzani and included an all-new chassis and a 5-liter V-12 that was mounted longitudinally (hence, the LP500 name). While the press wrote that the Countach was just an "ideas car," "We always intended to put the car in production, right from the time it was first conceived," Stanzani said. This period photograph shows the beauty and absolute purity of Gandini's wedge-shaped design.

Contrary to what has frequently been written, this Lamborghini was no mere "ideas car." "From Day One," Stanzani notes, "the idea was to produce it."

Like Dallara with his Miura, Stanzani followed an original line of thinking. The V-12 would be mounted longitudinally, its bore and stroke enlarged so it displaced just under 5 liters. But unlike the Boxer and Pantera, Stanzani put the gearbox ahead of the engine, thanks to the driveshaft's sealed lubrication chamber that ran through the engine's sump. Not only did this offer better weight distribution, it made for cleaner shift action.

More important—and completely in line with McLaren's philosophy two decades later—Stanzani did everything possible to save weight. Thus, the Countach was originally envisaged without air conditioning, and magnesium was used in a number of components.

Bertone's shape beautifully reflected this "performance above everything else" edict. Using the Carabo as the starting

Once Enzo Ferrari endorsed the midengine concept with the 206/246 Dino, it was only a matter of time before the company would make a 12-cylinder model for the street. "He was fully behind the Berlinetta Boxer," Sergio Pininfarina noted of the car that broke cover in 1971. The basis for its look can be traced back to Pininfarina's 1968 styling exercise, the P6. The prototype Boxer first appeared at the 1971 Turin Auto Show and was the world's first production car to use a flat-12 cylinder powerplant. "I consider that type of engine one of my greatest achievements," said former Ferrari chief engineer Mauro Forghieri. The production Boxer went on sale in 1973 and was continually refined throughout its production life. The Boxer's beautiful shape remained largely unaltered.

point, Nuccio and Marcello Gandini created an even cleaner line, one that put the wedge at the forefront of performance car design.

The hastily finished prototype debuted at Geneva in March 1971; testing began soon after that spectacular debut. In short order, Wallace determined the Countach was superior to the Miura SV, with better handling and high-speed stability, more forgiving road manners, and quicker acceleration.

Mel Nichols found this out when he was given a ride from Monte Carlo to Sant' Agata. Unaware they had been travelling at 160-plus miles per hour, Nichols wrote that he could do nothing but stare at his typewriter when he was dropped off at the hotel. "After weighing it all up for a while," he reflected, "you find you're

asking yourself a question: Have I just ridden 250 miles in the ultimate road car?" His conclusion was yes.

Lamborghini took two years to develop the Countach. In addition to returning to a 3.9-liter V-12 for power ("the larger engine wasn't durable enough," Stanzani noted), the body and interior also underwent changes, as did the chassis.

The production Countach, now called the LP400, broke cover at 1973's Geneva Show. Yet it would still be some time before production truly ramped up.

This was undoubtedly due in part to Ferruccio Lamborghini losing his spark and passion for the company. Like Dusio and Cisitalia, Ambrosini and Siata, and Orsi and Maserati, Lamborghini's

After two years of testing, Lamborghini displayed the production Countach for the first time in 1973. Now dubbed the LP400, it was named after the car's longitudinally mounted 4-liter V-12 engine. The Countach LP400 is undoubtedly one of the finest postwar statements of pure automotive art, for it maintained the freshness and integrity of Gandini's original design. Because of the cutout in the roof that was originally done so the mirror could look down the channel, enthusiasts call these cars "periscope" Countaches.

profitable business dealings in South America would turn sour and greatly affect his personal and corporate fortunes.

In 1972 he built 5,000 tractors for the Bolivian government. Just before shipment, the government was overthrown, the resulting financial burden forcing the industrialist to sell 51 percent of Automobili Lamborghini to Swiss businessman Georges-Henri Rossetti.

In truth, this was likely just the straw that broke the camel's back. Like everyone else in the industry, Lamborghini was aware how radically public perception had turned against GTs since the start of 1970.

As the socialist mentality gained considerable strength in Italy and Europe, the American market always held hope. When small manufacturers were not able to meet smog and safety requirements in the early 1970s, that potential died. "When you lose some possibility," Iso's Piero Rivolta reflects, "you feel a little weaker. We always thought 'one year, there will be a market for us.' But when that hope was taken away, I began to sense the era of the GT was running toward its end."

Other factors would contribute to such a pessimistic outlook. In the fall of 1970, the industry experienced a period of high inflation. Partially due to a run up in petroleum costs, the specialist constructors' use of limited tooling caused the greatest increase. Because this manufacturing process gave crude results, the number of skilled craftsmen who corrected the flaws was decreasing at the very time their abilities were needed more than ever.

Moreover, the public no longer saw the GT as glamorous, but an evil that greatly contributed to civilization's problems. Stylist Gandini sensed this disdain, and remembers in 1972 the focus switched from berlinettas and midengine offerings to sedans that concentrated on packaging and use of space.

That year also saw a large increase in global conferences on safety and commuter congestion. Experimental Safety Vehicles took center stage, with Fiat, General Motors, Ford, Mercedes, Nissan, Toyota, and others displaying these ESVs.

Environmental concerns were also heightened. As fuel consumption became a major issue, Italy responded by instigating a string of new taxes aimed at larger autos and those with large displacement engines.

"Because the government stressed cars that used small amounts of gas . . . people who used GTs were considered someone damaging the community and spending money for nothing," recalls Iso's sales manager Piero Sala, who had the unenviable job of moving hardware in this hostile climate.

The instigation of speed limits by Germany and other countries put a further damper on the market. "Industrialists who drove expensive cars very often had their windows broken by the workers, or someone else," one engineer recalls.

Demand at home was also influenced by Italy's in-vogue "equality" ideology. As it received considerable press coverage, and thus much examination, equality started stripping away the incentive of rewarding oneself after successfully working hard.

Because everyone wanted to look like everyone else, mediocrity became the rule.

This stifled a company's ability to selectively reward key employees or those rank-and-file workers who performed exceptionally well. Everyone now received a pay raise in unison; those driven to excel were castigated by their fellow workers.

Pride in doing one's job vanished, for there was no longer any difference between the best and the worst. Not surprising, Fiat's absentee rate increased from 4 percent in 1960 to 8 percent in 1970, then to 15 percent in 1972. For comparison, Renault's was just more than 5 percent.

As the GT constructors' revenue dropped precipitously, they had nowhere to turn for financial assistance. "It was very difficult to find help in solving our problems," Sala summarized for many. "The banks, the government, everybody had the mindset 'You are not a useful industry, so you should change your product.' But even when we examined alternatives and talked to them about it, these people weren't interested in helping. Nobody was willing to give additional capital, nobody!"

All these factors brought the largest hit to the marketplace—the *complete* change in mentality to the vast majority of the car buying public. In previous bad times, there was almost always someone who was doing well and would purchase the object of their desire. But now, just five to six years after the GT's zenith, the decline was endless.

Jean-Francis Held aptly summed up this sudden and dramatic change in *Automobile Year*. In a piece entitled "Twilight of the Goddesses," "All of us who are in love with beautiful motor cars are conscious of living something of a paradox," he observed. "At a time when, on all sides, the automobile is being reviled and accused of killing, of polluting, and stultifying, those of us who carry on nurturing our passion are beginning to feel like criminals on the run.

"Have we arrived at the crossroads? Are we experiencing, in short, the twilight of those goddesses we persist in adoring, come hell or high water?

"Pride itself, the prestige one can derive from an image boost a dream car can give, has lost a lot of feathers in the winds of change. And that is the most serious factor of all, the one nobody can do anything about."

Held and the rest of the world would soon discover there was indeed another factor, one that would cause the situation to go from bad to worse.

Iso entered the mid-engine rush with its Varedo. Designed by former Zagato chief stylist Ercole Spada, the Varedo had a longitudinally mounted 325-horsepower Ford 351 V-8. "Our target customer was the type of person who was mostly interested in performance," Piero Rivolta said, explaining why the car diverged from the luxurious finish of Iso's other models. It remained a one-off, as Rivolta sold his ownership in Iso before production commenced.

Via Crucis

1974 - 1983

The oil crisis hit on October 21, 1973. America, the only market seemingly unaffected by Europe's Socialist movement, saw its GNP nosedive, and inflation and unemployment figures skyrocket. Gas lines quickly affected the country's psyche. "In this year of the fuel crisis," journalist Jan P. Norbye wrote, "pleasure driving is just a memory, the temptation of quick get-aways from a dead stop . . . and second cars have been put in mothballs."

Italy and other countries totally dependent on oil imports were hit much harder. Chaos raged throughout the southern European nation, the unions' now powerful enough to coerce Fiat into monthly wage increases and subsidies for transportation, meals, and schooling. The government banned all driving on Sunday.

Giorgetto Giugiaro knew he had to play hardball to survive. Informed that his workers were preparing to strike, he called a general assembly. "You can have the factory, for I am more than happy to go on a long vacation," he informed them. "But just remember, all our contracts were made by me. If I go, our clients will also go."

He then laid down the ultimatum: "You have two hours to inform me of your decision." Ital Design did not have any further problems with the unions.

Yet, the firm was more the exception than the rule. "I remember telling De Tomaso several months before the oil crisis that it seemed we were at via Crucis," Piero Rivolta reflected. "It was the crossroad, the street that brought Christ up to the cross. I was very concerned about the future."

Ferrari's first production car to use a V-8 engine was the Bertone-designed Dino 308 GT4. "I was certainly not pleased when Ferrari's management addressed Bertone for the design of the 308 GT/4," Sergio Pininfarina candidly noted, "for all Ferrari cars previously designed by us were accepted by the market with great success." Due to its "Dino" nameplate and wedge-shape design, the GT/4 initially stumbled in the market. By the end of its production run in 1980, however, it was (at the time) Ferrari's best-selling model ever.

Frank Reisner's Intermeccanica was a small constructor that flourished during the second half of the 1960s/early 1970s, then found itself floundering in 1973. Reisner's Italia also went under the names of Omega and Torino and was built from 1966 to 1971. These attractively styled coupes and spiders were powered by Ford V-8s and found an active market in America. Reisner said more than 500 were built.

He had every reason to be worried, for the manufacturers were hit the hardest. One that would disappear was Frank Reisner's Intermeccanica. Since splitting with Milt Brown and Apollo in the mid-1960s, Intermeccanica's fortunes blossomed. It first teamed with Jack Griffith, supplying the American with a striking Robert Cumberford–designed two-seat coupe body.

When Griffith ran out of money, "it became obvious the only way to build cars was if they left Italy fully assembled," Reisner commented. In 1966 he obtained a line of credit, found an American distributor, and started producing complete cars. Using Ford running gear, Intermeccanica's coupe and spiders carried several different names: first Omega, then Torino, finally, Italia.

Reisner had found his formula. For the balance of the 1960s, he consistently produced 100 to 200 cars a year.

The picture became rosier in 1970 when he formed an alliance with GM's German subsidiary, Opel. "I saw an Italia at an auto show

and was admiring it," said former Opel executive Bob Lutz, who later became president at Chrysler. "After speaking with Reisner, a light bulb went off, and I thought, 'He could do this for us.'"

And so was born the Indra. Debuting at the 1971 Geneva Show, the striking Franco Scalione–styled coupe and spyder used a GM 350 V-8 and was sold at Opel dealerships. After introducing an attractive 2+2 at the 1973 New York Auto Show, "GM changed its policy and stopped supplying us, and selling Indras," Reisner said.

As he weighed his options, the oil crisis hit. Reisner soon discovered a surprising potential savior in Rivolta's Iso. Yet, the man whose father founded the company was no longer there.

Like Intermeccanica, Iso experienced several twists of fate in the 1970s. When Piero Rivolta was unable to find additional capital in Italy, he turned to America. After teaming with refrigerator manufacturer Coolaire, the companies incorporated under the name "ISO Industries" and had a successful IPO.

While this gave Rivolta temporary breathing room, he felt he truly struck pay dirt when he was contacted by Ivo Pera, an extremely wealthy Italo-American financier. "The one thing I did not have was a stake in a publicly traded company," Pera said about why he was so drawn to Iso. Several months later, Rivolta was on the short end of the stick when Pera instigated a hostile takeover.

The financier became the center of Italy's struggling sports car universe when the oil crisis hit; contacting him first was Lamborghini majority shareholder Rosetti. "He was having problems with his banks, so we started talking," Pera recalls. "Lamborghini was very appealing to me, for it was much better known than Iso, and their cars were beautiful."

Then Reisner called, and Pera's mind went into overdrive. He felt he could emulate GM's successful business model on a much smaller scale. In addition to taking advantage of production and purchasing economies of scale, "we would have a car in several market segments," Pera noted. "Intermeccanica would supply the sporty convertible, Iso the luxury car, and Lamborghini the pure, high-performance sports car."

Pera says he then made a fatal mistake: "I underestimated the oil embargo's duration." When a refinery he purchased in early 1973 received no oil, he was left holding a costly empty bag. Like Billi and ATS years earlier, Pera was spread too thin. Reisner closed Intermeccanica in early 1974, and Iso declared bankruptcy several months later.

Lamborghini hung on by a thread, with Ferruccio selling his remaining stake to Rosetti's friend Rene Leimer. Both of the well-meaning Swiss businessmen were in over their heads, for neither had the leadership skills nor the deep pockets to weather such a storm.

Lamborghini started drifting, and key players such as Paolo Stanzani and Bob Wallace soon jumped ship. Suppliers began demanding cash up front, and production ground to a near halt. Only the juggling act of sales manager Ubaldo Scarzi kept any merchandise heading out the door.

Alessandro De Tomaso was well positioned to take advantage of the oil crisis, having completed his sale of Ghia and Carrozzeria

Vignale to Ford in January 1973. Now in Modena, he reached an agreement to continue Pantera production when the American company shut down Vignale, the car's manufacturing facility in Turin.

That was simply De Tomaso's warm-up act. "Through his contacts in Rome, he arranged to buy other automotive companies," Tjaarda says. Within months, the Argentinean owned Innocenti and motorcycle manufacturers Benelli and Moto Guzzi.

His biggest coup was Maserati. "GEPI, the government's financing company, told him he had to pay something," says Giordano Casarini, an ex-Ferrari man who would be instrumental in Maserati's future products. "So he offered 150,000 lire, or approximately $70.00."

De Tomaso ruthlessly gutted Maserati, one casualty being Giulio Alfieri. Suddenly, and without warning, this most gifted engineer was on the outside of the firm he helped make a household name. "I felt like a chicken in the center of the road, with cars zipping by in both directions," Alfieri reflects on being blindsided. "So what must the chicken do? Try to save himself." Within months, he was president of Honda's Italian factory.

Iso, Maserati, et al., were not alone in their plight. England's Aston Martin temporarily slipped into bankruptcy, and Jensen disappeared completely. Switzerland's Peter Monteverdi would eventually stop building GTs, producing off-road vehicles instead.

Only Ferrari survived relatively unscathed, its production dropping just 25 percent. Undoubtedly helping it was a tact all of Italy's GT constructors would follow—smaller displacement models.

Ferrari's first was its controversial 308 GT4. This midengine 2+2 used the firm's first street V-8 engine. In European trim, the transversely mounted 3-liter produced 255 horsepower at 7,700 rpm.

Most surprising was the model's wedge-shaped Bertone coachwork. The first non-Pininfarina production Ferrari since the mid-1950s, "It wasn't Ferrari asking us to manufacture the Dino

The car that knocked the GT4 from the Ferrari best-seller pedestal was the Pininfarina-designed 308 GTB. "Like the 206/246 Dino, the inspiration for this car's line comes from the Dino Berlinetta Speciale we exhibited at the Paris Show in 1965," Pininfarina stated. The traditionalists were most pleased with the return of rounded forms to Ferrari, and the 308 GTB remained in production for nine years.

Maserati's entry into the medium capacity displacement sweepstakes was the Merak. First shown in 1971 and powered by a V-6, Giugiaro drew heavily from the V-8 Bora for its style. "We wanted to utilize the engine we were building for Citroen's SM for a new model of our own," Giulio Alfieri noted. While earlier Meraks used a 190-horsepower 2.7-liter, the later cars, 3-liter V-6 was rated at 208 horsepower.

308," said Bertone's Enzo Prearo, "it was Fiat asking us to replace production of the Fiat Dino coupe with a new Dino. As Ferrari's coachbuilder had always been Pininfarina, we left Ferrari to them." While this clears up why the GT4 debuted under the Dino badge, Marcello Gandini says Enzo Ferrari was actively involved in the car's design.

The Dino 308 debuted at 1973's Paris Auto Show, with sales starting in 1974. "I can state that the new car is . . . better in every important aspect than the 246," *Autosport's* John Bolster declared. He recorded 0–60 in 6.7 seconds and saw a top speed of 160 miles per hour. "It is a delight to drive and worthy of bearing that famous name," he concluded.

Equally impressed was world champion Formula 1 driver Emerson Fittipaldi. Writing for Italy's *Quattroroute* magazine, he found it to be "one of the best GTs."

Still, the car languished on dealer lots. In America, its performance was lacking (*Road & Track* needed 8 seconds to hit

60), and the absence of Ferrari badges confused buyers. After the model received the coveted Ferrari name in 1976, it became Maranello's best-selling model that decade.

Those desiring a traditional Pininfarina-bodied Ferrari were satisfied by the 308 GTB. First presented at 1975's Paris Auto Show, the GTB's 92-inch wheelbase was 8 inches shorter than the GT4.

Autocar adored the new 308. "All round," the magazine said, "it is the best Ferrari we have yet driven."

Like the GT4, American GTBs' emissions equipment strangled performance: Where *Autocar* hit 60 in 6.5 seconds, *Motor Trend* needed 8.2. Still, "It has all of the good road manners, the fantastic roadholding and cornering, that make it feel as though it was an extension of the driver's body," *Motor Trend* concluded. "It is, in short, a true Ferrari."

Maserati's Merak came to market two years prior to the 308 GT4. With styling similar to the Bora, it had a V-6 engine and

meager back seats. "We wanted to utilize the engine we made for Citroen for another car, to increase our production," Alfieri reflected. "It was a small change for us to do."

Road & Track felt models like the Merak were the wave of the future. "Stressing total refinement instead of brute power, the Merak may be showing how the 'exoticar' is going to cope with the changing 1970s," it observed in its 1974 test. Despite needing 9.2 seconds to hit 60, the magazine felt the Merak was "an exciting and pleasing machine to look at and drive."

Lamborghini's Urraco was the first "small" car to come to market and was Ferruccio's ambitious attempt to dramatically increase Lamborghini's production by offering a more affordable model in Porsche 911 territory. Called "one of the most nimble cars we built," by test driver Bob Wallace, this extremely handsome Bertone design was powered by a 2.5-liter, 220-horsepower V-8.

The Urraco debuted to great fanfare at the 1970 Turin Show. "The P250 is an exciting, beautiful, fast and—hopefully—safe car,"

Road & Track summed up for many magazines. "Let's hope it will be available to us poor Americans, who would rather be happy in a fast and responsive car than ultra-safe in a padded crashmobile."

That reaction was exactly what Lamborghini hoped for. Commercial director Ubaldo Scarzi said he had several thousand orders from prospective customers and distributors within weeks of the launch.

Unfortunately, the Urraco debuted much too early. The car's heart—its V-8 engine—proved so unreliable that Bob Wallace says the first few test cars' engines wouldn't last 5,000 miles.

When production did start in late 1972, it was too little, too late. Ferrari's and Maserati's offerings were more refined and considerably faster. *Road & Track's* U.S. spec Urraco needed 10.1 seconds to reach 60 and came in last in the comparison test. "[It] remains an enigma," the magazine concluded. "By far the most sleek looking, it promises much but delivers little."

The financial drain on Lamborghini to tool up and expand the factory undoubtedly contributed greatly to the company's

The Silhouette was Lamborghini's attempt to boost sales by offering an open-air version of the Urraco. Unlike the variety of engines for its closed counterpart, the Silhouette was only offered with a potent 260-horsepower, 3.0-liter V-8 engine. Lack of operating capital caused only 54 to be built over a four-year period. Gandini and Bertone were responsible for the car's effective angular styling.

While a later brochure would say Fiat's mid-engine X1/9 had "the energy and excitement of a small Ferrari," it would have been more appropriate to call the car a "miniature Miura." Prior to its introduction in 1972, coachbuilder Nuccio Bertone says he was frequently chided by Fiat's management as wanting to build a down-market Miura. The nimble X1/9 was the perfect sports car for the oil crisis, for it returned more than 35 miles per gallon on the freeway.

Fiat X1/9

FIAT

subsequent misery. Not even the best of the Urracos—the magnificent 157-mile-per-hour P300 and open air derivative Silhouette, and their properly developed 260 horsepower V-8s—could save the day.

For enthusiasts on a budget, Fiat's X1/9 and Lancia's Beta Montecarlo were mass-produced alternatives.

The former was the replacement for the successful 850 Spyder. Nuccio Bertone told author Luciano Greggio that when he presented a midengine proposal to Fiat director Oscar

Montabone, the Fiat man replied, "All you want to do is build a poor man's version of the Miura."

Thanks to the coachbuilder's persistence, the car was given the green light in October 1969. With Montabone and Gianni Agnelli now two of the car's biggest supporters, Fiat's "baby Miura" was powered by a 1,290-cc inline four-cylinder engine developed from the company's popular 128 Sport Coupe. The X1/9's suspension was independent, and disc brakes were used on all four wheels.

One year prior to the car's launch, Bertone and Fiat got quite a start at the 1971 Turin show when De Tomaso exhibited a small, midengine prototype that was a dead ringer for the upcoming model. Causing tremendous controversy at the time, "that was typical of the man," Tom Tjaarda laughed. "De Tomaso would often do something to see how people would react. One day he instructed me to visit him in a carrozzeria where a prototype X1/9 was standing, and copy it. So I did."

The Real McCoy's unveiling was cause to rejoice, the enthusiasm becoming even greater in actual road tests. "With the X1/9," *Car and Driver* wrote, "Fiat has produced an object of high fashion, and reduced its competition to the status of period pieces." Lauding the car's balance, suspension, gearbox, and brakes, the writers felt it was "kind of like a motorcycle, only with twice as many wheels."

Road & Track reached the same conclusion, twice. "Even with our high expectations," they noted in their first road test, "the mid-engine roadster was a pleasant surprise." Their later comparison against a 124 Spider, MGB, MG Midget, Triumph Spitfire, and TR7 saw the X1/9 the runaway winner.

Pininfarina's attractive upmarket Fiat X1/20 ended up becoming the Lancia Beta Montecarlo when it was introduced in 1975. Sold in America as the Lancia Scorpion, any chances of its success were ruined by its emissions-strangled four-cylinder engine. A number of economy cars offered equal or superior acceleration, and the Scorpion couldn't hold a candle to the 120-mile-per-hour performance offered by its European counterpart.

Not as successful was Lancia's Beta Montecarlo. Originally dubbed the X1/20, it was to use a V-6 from Fiat's 130 series and be positioned above the X1/9. When Italy's economic and political turmoil affected Fiat's bottom line, Umberto Agnelli assigned the X1/20 to Lancia.

The model debuted in Europe in 1975, powered by a 2-liter inline four. It went on sale in America the following year as the Scorpion.

Because Lancia was absent from America for several years, the lack of name recognition hurt demand. Even more damning, the U.S.-spec engine was out of character with Pininfarina's racy coachwork. Where the Beta Montecarlo produced 120 horsepower (delivering 0–60 in 9-plus seconds and a 120-mile-per-hour top speed), the Scorpion's emissions-emasculated 1,756-cc engine made just over 80. The resulting acceleration was so leisurely that *Road & Track's* succinct summary was, "so lovely, so agile, so ingenious, so slow." Just 7,500 were made over the next several years.

Ferrari's 365 Boxer and Lamborghini's Countach LP400 had just gone on sale when the oil crisis hit. Despite the general backlash against such models, the fascination with such "ultimates" never left the world's automotive journals.

Australia's Peter Robinson was one of the first to try Ferrari's newest and was enraptured by its stunning looks, silky smooth engine, and relaxed road manners. After noting its phenomenal acceleration, cornering, and high-speed capabilities, "It has enough of everything to make a nonsense of other cars," he reflected. "You could drive a Boxer at five-tenths and still be king of the road, but run it out and you know that you are experiencing something whose dynamics are unbeatable, and simply beyond the reach of other cars."

Road & Track's 1975 test came to the same conclusion, though low-rpm carburetion flooding and a slipping clutch hampered its car's acceleration times. After recording 0–100 in 14.8 seconds and a top speed of 175 miles per hour, it was the fastest car they had tested. "As an ultimate road-going performance machine," the magazine concluded, "the Boxer has few equals."

The "fastest/ultimate" title fell to Lamborghini's Countach just months later. Using a cautious starting technique, *Road & Track* recorded 0–100 in 13.4 seconds. As the LP400's V-12 was pulling so strongly at 7,000 rpm in fifth (170 miles per hour), its estimated top speed was 192 miles per hour. *Road & Track* "couldn't remember testing another car that felt more stable above 130 mph," and lauded its "exemplary road manners," cornering, and "comfortable" ride.

Car and Driver was not as enamoured as *Road & Track*, but still couldn't deny that Lamborghini's newest was the pinnacle in performance. Testing a factory hot rod LP400 in which a test driver reportedly cracked the 200-mile-per-hour barrier, "Take a run through the gears in a Lamborghini Countach and you eclipse every speed reference on the books," they noted.

Likely the only journalist to have the 365 Boxer and Countach LP400 meet face to face was Australia's Mel Nichols. In

Sports Car World's "Ultimate Comparison," he also included Porsche's Turbo Carrera.

Nichols needed almost a year to get the three cars together and would spend more than a week with them to render his decision. For long trips and tackling sinuous roads, "It is here—in the domain of the supercar—that the [Lamborghini] is superior," he wrote. "It corners faster and more easily, and gives the driver more pleasure," leading him to conclude, "The Countach is the ultimate supercar."

As the market rebounded from the first oil shock, things got worse in Italy. America's *Forbes* magazine noted this in the mid-1970s, observing that "Italy, once again, is the sick man of Europe. There are bombings and strikes and a breakdown of public services. . . . [The country] faces an oil import bill as big as Japan's but without Japan's still formidable economic strength.

"For Italy," the magazine summarized, "the oil crisis is not over. It is just beginning."

Forbes was right. When the world's second shortage hit in 1979, every business became targets of the unions' wrath. Lamborghini's production was just 55 cars that year, and the company declared bankruptcy. Maserati survived only by completely abandoning its roots as a sports/GT car constructor.

Turin was a city under siege, the turmoil in Fiat, endless. Tom Tjaarda was now its director of advanced design and recalls "the place was total chaos, for nobody had a clear idea as to what direction the styling profession would take. The violence forced Agnelli to hire a new kind of manager and executive, tough-guy types with no background in the automotive field. Their principal role was to fire people, and try and control the outbreaks. No one concentrated on production, only on trying to survive."

That last word was particularly prevalent to Sergio Pininfarina, who endured one episode that perfectly illustrated Italy's radical transformation in little more than a decade. Since Pinin passed away in 1966, Sergio's integrity, business acumen, and

A good indication of how hard the labor and political unrest hit Italy during the 1970s was the country's lack of all-new sports cars. "The fact that our Alfa Romeo Spider was first introduced in 1966 and was still on sale into the 1990s, largely unchanged, reminds me of this," said Sergio Pininfarina. Shown here is a version from the late 1970s.

A timeless Pininfarina design that also lived a long life was Fiat's 124 Spider. To help offset the power loss and additional weight of the large bumpers, starting in 1981 U.S. buyers could order the Fiat Spider Turbo. The installation was done by Legend Industries of New York and greatly increased the car's midrange performance. Unreliability saw the option pulled at the end of 1982.

After Alessandro De Tomaso purchased Maserati in 1975 with governmental financial assistance, Rome's bureaucrats wanted to make sure its employees stayed employed. "They put pressure on him to offer a car that had a wider audience appeal," says Giordano Casarini. The resulting Maserati Biturbo was unveiled in 1982 and broke from company tradition by having a (relatively) more affordable price and conservative, boxy styling.

hard-charging character made him a nationally prominent figure and an elected member of European Parliament.

He recalls the love and affection the country gave him after his father's passing, for the average Italian understood the Pininfarina name promoted Italy globally. He relished the role of ambassador and never lost the importance of remaining in touch with the people.

His humanity was completely lost to Italy's agitative element in the late 1970s. As the president of Turins' Industrialist Union, Pininfarina became a target.

This fact was made all too clear following an overnight flight from America. After working for several hours, he went home. His chauffeur smoothly navigated through the city's traffic, his bodyguards trailing in a separate car immediately behind them.

As they pulled up to a red light, Pininfarina slumped his tired body deeper into the back seat. Now completely surrounded by traffic, he heard an unfamiliar sound on the window beside him. Immediately glancing to that side, a bullethole's web accented the glass. His heart pounding, another suddenly appeared. He dove to the floor, the several seconds of waiting for the car to move, an eternity.

He escaped unscathed, and to this day does not know if it was a warning, or an attempted assassination. The assailants were never apprehended.

Pininfarina and all of Italy's industrialists got their reprieve on October 14, 1980. Tjaarda recalls the day when Fiat was so paralyzed by a particularly brutal strike that everyone was sent home. But rather than heading straight back, he decided to head to the center of town.

Within minutes, he learned everyone else was doing the same. Workers and executives had reached their limits and wanted to send a strong message to the unions. As if by osmosis, a groundswell movement ran rampant through Turin, and others soon joined them.

Lamborghini introduced the Countach LP 500 S in 1982. Also called the 5000S, it featured a larger and heavier body, flared fenders, larger wheels with sticky Pirelli P7 tires, and a 5-liter engine that had a longer stroke than the earlier 4 liter. This model clearly marked the turn away from Stanzani's "performance above all else" vision for the Countach.

At the time, Pininfarina was chairing a stressful meeting with the city's business leaders. As he fought to rally the troops, an underling interrupted him. "Five thousand workers are marching through downtown," he informed the group. Within minutes, Pininfarina had an update: The number was 10,000. Several minutes later, the figure had doubled again. Then it doubled again.

Known as The March of 40,000, news of the spontaneous populist uprising swept across the country: The unions' stranglehold had been broken. For the first time in years, the average working Italian was smiling.

Emergence

The March of 40,000 was the turning point. The unions struggled fiercely to maintain their turf, causing strikes to remain an integral part of Italian life for several more years.

It only delayed the inevitable. By the mid-1980s, the unions no longer held sway over the public and industry.

Still, the Decline's scars remained long after the battles had ended. "When the first real wave of student protests hit, they intimidated what was an already shaky society, subduing enthusiasm for GTs," Tom Tjaarda reflected. "The first oil crisis was the final nail in the coffin and put a halt to the exotic sports and GT-type car market."

Now that exotics were taboo in Italy, "it really marked the beginning of the decline of Italian styling," Tjaarda continued. "In the mid-1970s, stylists became 'designers,' where you had to adapt a new approach. Italy found itself replaced by the 'Californian art school' type of design, with rounded shapes and low Cd numbers."

Indicative of this trend was the Turin Show. Long the Mecca of design and styling trends, it became a biannual affair starting in 1972. By the mid-1980s, it had disappeared altogether.

The damage inflicted during the Decline extended far beyond styling and coachbuilding, for the battle to survive had literally sapped the vitality out of Italy's auto industry. For a number of years, no one conceived and created truly new products, especially sports and GT cars.

"When I see our Alfa Romeo spider, it reminds me of how little was done during that period," Sergio Pininfarina noted. "The car was introduced the mid-1960s, yet here it was, the same model, a decade-and-a-half later."

Alfa was not alone. Fiat's 124 Spider and X1/9 only received minor mechanical updates and would remain in production into the mid-1980s.

Most damning was quality control. Where magazine articles from the 1960s often referenced an Italian car's outstanding durability, rust and fragility became an owner's operative words.

Surprisingly, Alfa and Fiat fared better than most. Because sports, GT, and performance cars remained the scourge of society for the better part of a decade, MG and Triumph fell by the wayside. Lancia would soon leave the sports car segment altogether.

Maserati also exited the market in 1982 when it introduced the Biturbo. According to Giordano Casarini, the 2+2 was born in the late 1970s. "When I arrived at Maserati in 1976, the French had completely robbed the technical department of all drawings and information about certification," he said. "So here we were,

Lamborghini resurrected the highly regarded Silhouette in 1981 with the Jalpa. Bertone massaged the design and revised the interior. Lamborghini enlarged the V-8 engine from 3.0-liters to 3.5. The Jalpa remained in production through 1988 with 410 made.

The result was the Biturbo. Assembled at Innocenti in Milan, the compact angular coupe had a 2.0- or 2.5-liter twin-turbo V-6. BMW's 3-series was now the chief competition, not a product from fellow Modenese constructors Ferrari and Lamborghini.

When *Road & Track* compared the Biturbo to a 325e in 1983, "If you are a driving enthusiast who loves cars, hungers for something exotic in the mid-$20,000 price range, and have a strong streak of automotive romance in your makeup, the Maserati is for you," the magazine concluded. "In short, it makes you glad your hobby is cars rather than bowling."

Unfortunately, durability and mechanical reliability issues would haunt the Biturbo for several years. Coupled with the model's vast departure from its predecessors sporting and GT roots, by the late 1980s, the Maserati name had lost the luster that surrounded it during the Era of Prosperity.

Lamborghini was fortunate to even survive the 1970s. Crippled by the oil crisis of 1973 and 1974, a lack of operating capital, a revolving door of personnel, and some less-than-honorable buy-out attempts, the company struggled to produce the much-in-demand Countach. With just a handful of LP400s and Urraco P300s being made every month, in August 1978 it went into receivership, in accordance with Italian law.

Local authorities started running the firm, one of their first moves being the hiring of Giulio Alfieri as technical director. Not surprisingly, it took the engineer time to adjust to his new home. "Lamborghini's philosophy was completely different from Maserati's understated, comfort-first approach," the engineer said. "At first, it was difficult for me, but I eventually interpreted my line of thinking with that at Lamborghini."

In mid-1980, France's Patrick Mimran purchased the firm. Then in his mid-20s, the Mimrans were one of the country's wealthiest families, owning a large commercial and industrial group. "Patrick and his brother Jean-Claude were very clever," Alfieri recalled of the men who brought financial and management stability to Lamborghini. "They had confidence in me, and we worked very well together."

starting from scratch in modifying cars for the American market's safety and emission standards."

To enhance horsepower, Casarini relied on experience he gained while spending a year in the world's hot rod Mecca, southern California. "Unbeknownst to anybody, we made a turbocharged Merak," he said. "There were two versions—one with a single turbo placed on top of the engine and another with twin turbos. The second was so powerful, it would make the car's front end lift when you stood on the gas!"

Casarini then presented the bi-turbo Merak to De Tomaso, and Maserati's future was born. "But the government was pressuring the company to make a less luxurious, more affordable car, something with large production numbers," Casarini pointed out. "De Tomaso had purchased both Innocenti and Maserati with government funds, so they wanted all those workers to remain employed."

Thanks to the hit television series *Magnum PI*, the 308 GTS was the model that brought Ferrari into living rooms around the world. Its looks were nearly identical to the 308 GTB, save the removable roof panel. Both models received fuel injection in 1981 and four valves per cylinder in 1983.

Over the ensuing years, the Countach would stray away from Stanzani's and Bertone/Gandini's original vision of being the ultimate performance car with purity of line for the serious driver. Now it would metamorphose into the "bad boy" machine of choice and go on to become the company's best-selling model ever.

Typifying this new image was the Countach LP 500 S. Introduced in 1982, it was taller, wider, and heavier than the LP400. Its interior was more luxurious and fitted with an updated air conditioning system.

To offset the additional weight, the V-12's displacement increased to 4.7 liters. Fender flares that were first seen on 1978's 400 S remained and were usually augmented by a rear wing that typified the car's new persona.

With Lamborghini's future secure, magazines couldn't get enough of the world's wildest supercar, even if its performance was below that of the LP400. Throughout the 1980s, the Countach would grace more magazine covers and posters than any other car.

Lamborghini also introduced the Jalpa. Breaking cover at 1981's Geneva Show, the Silhouette's targa-topped successor had a 3.5-liter V-8 and was, in essence, a more refined version of that much appreciated, but rare, Lamborghini.

The Jalpa's main competitor was Ferrari's 308 GTS. This open-air version of the 308 GTB also had a targa top and was introduced at 1977's Frankfurt Auto Show. It shared its enclosed counterpart's transverse 3-liter V-8, tubular steel chassis, and independent suspension.

Like Lamborghini, Ferrari's cars had lost their performance edge in the late 1970s. With the constant battle against strikers and public opinion only exacerbating the already difficult task of trying to meet ever more stringent emissions requirements, in 1978 the 308's engine produced just 205 horsepower.

Things became worse when Ferrari introduced fuel injection in late 1980. Although quoted power remained 205, *Road & Track's* 308 GTBi was slower to 60 and 100 miles per hour than a carbureted 308 GTB.

The Berlinetta Boxer also underwent changes. At the 1976 Paris Auto Show, Ferrari introduced the 512 BB. The flat-12 engine was now enlarged to 5 liters and was modified to deliver smoother, midrange acceleration.

When *Road & Track* tested one in 1978, it recorded 0–60 in 5.5 seconds and 0–100 in 13.2 and estimated its top speed at 180-plus miles per hour. Although the Countach LP400

In 1982, Lancia introduced the Rally 037. This midengine machine had a Pininfarina body and was constructed to compete in Group B rallying. Its 2-liter, inline four-cylinder engine was designed and developed by Abarth, which was now a part of Fiat. The street cars' engines produced just over 200 horsepower, while competition versions fitted with direct fuel injection and an Abarth supercharger churned out 280 to 310 horses. In 1983 the 037 won the World Rally Championship.

Ferrari's first full convertible since it discontinued the Daytona Spider in the early 1970s was 1984's Mondial Cabriolet. The Mondial model line was introduced three years earlier at the Geneva Auto Show and was a Pininfarina midengine 2+2 coupe that succeeded the Bertone-designed 308 GT/4. The version seen is a 1989 Mondial T Cabriolet.

remained the magazine's fastest car, "the Ferrari 512 Boxer wins a more important award, as the best all-around sports and GT," the magazine noted.

The Boxer would also gain fuel injection in late 1980. The engine's even greater tractability helped make the 512 BBi the most refined of the series.

As impressive as the Boxer and Countach were in the early 1980s, Italy now faced its greatest attack in two decades and Jaguar's E-type as the undisputed king of speed. Compared to Ferrari's 308 and recently released Mondial, and Lamborghini's Jalpa, Porsche's 911 and Chevrolet's Corvette offered superior acceleration, had similar cornering power, and nearly identical top speeds. While they couldn't match the Italians' panache, they cost thousands less.

More damning was Porsche's muscular Turbo, the car Nichols included in his Ultimate Comparison. Not only did it undercut the 308's and Jalpa's price tags, its formidable performance had been boosted to even greater heights so it could easily see off Italy's V-8s without even breathing hard. Although the Boxer and Countach were ultimately faster, the Turbo's acceleration was their equal to 100 to 120 miles per hour.

For ultimate top speed, a new challenge came from England's rejuvenated Aston Martin. Given enough room, the front-engine V-8 Vantage would see 170 miles per hour.

Fortunately for automobile enthusiasts everywhere, by the early 1980s Italy's veil of scorn had lifted, and Ferrari and Lamborghini were shaking off the cobwebs. By successfully teaming up with Turin, they would soon attack the ultimate speed and glamour titles with renewed vigor.

Section V
Revolt
& Rebirth

Backlash, Boom, and Bust

1984 - 1996

Ferrari's first shot against the German and English encroachment was the 308 Quattrovalvole. The model debuted at the 1982 Paris Auto Show and looked nearly identical to its predecessor GTB and GTS. The biggest change was found under the rear bonnet. The 3-liter engine now had four valves per cylinder and bumped horsepower for the critical U.S. market from 205 to 230. This was the shot in the arm Ferrari's V-8 models needed. When *Road & Track* tested a four-valve in 1983, it was more than a second quicker to 60 and through the standing quarter-mile than the two-valve 308. It also had superior performance to the Corvette, Porsche 911, and 928.

When the magazine compared the Ferrari to a 911 and Corvette, the editors chose the 308: "It's fast, fine handling, beautiful, [and] handbuilt in the best sense of the word. [A]fter eight years of exposure to the public the Pininfarina body still provokes more praise, excitement and public admiration than any of the others."

England's *Motor* came to the same conclusion when it pitted a GTB against a 911. After trying the cars on public roads and the track, "Our enthusiasm for the Porsche remains undiminished. Yet [t]he feeling sneaks up on us at first, then takes hold with growing conviction. We like the Ferrari better. [W]hen we parted that evening after 12 long hours of driving and testing, the car in which we both wanted to drive home was the [308]."

Ferrari upped the ante in September 1985 when it introduced the 328 range at the Frankfurt Auto Show. The Pininfarina body was an effective update of the 308's lovely form and was available as a coupe (GTB) and spider([GTS).

The model's name reflected its new V-8: the engine's capacity was now 3.2 liters and was also used in the updated version of the mid-engine Mondial 2+2 coupe. Power output for European cars was 270 at 7,000 rpm and just 10 less for the American market.

Any performance advantage Ferrari lost during the first half of the 1980s was regained in the 328. First seen in 1985, the car's Pininfarina-designed body was an effective evolution of the earlier 308. It offered considerably more performance than its predecessor, thanks to its larger, more muscular 3.2-liter V-8.

De Tomaso's Pantera GT5 illustrates a trend that took hold as the 1980s progressed: the more flamboyant the look, the better. Several people interviewed attribute this "backlash" to the oppression Italy's manufacturers and coachbuilders felt during the 1970s. Like earlier Panteras, the GT5 continued to use Ford's venerable 351 V-8 engine. This particular Pantera is one of just a handful that had the Carrozzeria Pavesi–manufactured, factory-commissioned targa top.

By spring 1986, the 328 was gracing magazine covers around the world. "By far the most significant improvement is the horsepower increase," *Car and Driver* noted in its road test. The GTS proved to be considerably quicker than a four-valve 308, arriving at 60 1.8 seconds sooner (5.6 vs. 7.4). Its top speed of 153 was 9 miles per hour greater.

Autocar's figures were much the same, with 60 needing 5.5 seconds, 14.2 for 100 miles per hour, and the top speed being 154. "On performance, handling and build quality [the 328 GTB] is more than a match for its [German] competitors," the magazine concluded.

Matching the Ferrari's speed was a well-aging cross-town warrior, De Tomaso's Pantera. In late 1984, the company introduced the GT5. Available as a coupe or targa, the GT5's Ford V-8 now packed 350 horsepower. Its appearance followed Lamborghini

Countach's lead, being bigger and more hairy looking than the original, thanks to flared fenders, bulging tires, air intakes, and a rear wing. The interior was also more luxurious.

The GT5 tested by *Fast Lane* clocked almost identical times to *Autocar*'s 328. *Fast Lane* quoted 0–60 in 5.5 seconds, 0–100 in 13.5, and saw a top speed of 156 miles per hour. Although the right-hand-drive car had poor rear vision, a low rpm resonance, and an awkward driving position, the testers were surprised by its composed ride over broken surfaces, triple-digit speed stability, and "flat as a skateboard" cornering ability.

"For all its deficiencies and impracticalities, the faster and further we drove this car the more we grew to respect and like it," the testers wrote. "It is a machine of towering capability and stature, a car for the disciplined, discerning enthusiast skilled enough to exploit its colossal, dynamic abilities."

The real jump in performance was seen in the market's upper echelons. Now that manufacturers such as Ferrari had finally mastered the elusive art of the world's emissions standards, Maranello took a new course when it introduced the 288 GTO.

The first of the company's limited production cars, this memorable model marked Ferrari's return to its competition roots. In the early 1980s, rallying came to the fore of street performance when FISA instigated a series of new rules. Attracting considerable manufacturer interest was "Group B," international competition's top level. The boom to enthusiasts was the key regulation: Two hundred examples of any car competing had to be produced within 12 consecutive months.

Ferrari's entry into the Group B ring debuted at the 1984 Geneva Show. A leap forward for the company, the 288 GTO's body was a combination of fiberglass, Kevlar composites, and aluminum. The resulting Pininfarina shape looked like a 308

Ferrari's second new model introduction in 1984 was the Testarossa. It had a flat-12 engine that produced 390 horsepower and pushed the car to 180 miles per hour. Like the 308, the Testarossa gained mass exposure, thanks to television. In this case, it was chariot of choice for *Miami Vice*'s Sonny Crockett.

GTB on steroids, yet was even more beautiful, thanks to its longer wheelbase.

Its 2.9-liter V-8 was mounted longitudinally and featured four valves per cylinder and two turbos. "We tried many turbochargers to find the best full range of characteristics we wanted, [which was] refined power production, available progressively through the whole rev range," Ferrari's managing director Giovanni Squazzini noted at the car's introduction. Final power output was 400 horsepower at 7,000 rpm.

When word got out that Maranello was making an upcoming limited production model, the allotted run was sold out without one client knowing what it would look like. That pandemonium continued at the 288's Geneva introduction, for there were "a struggling mass of media men and hangers on," journalist Doug Nye observed. "Within 20 minutes, every scrap of GTO information had been removed from the Ferrari stand."

Checkbooks were being waved, as well. Nye reported that Aston Martin company owner Peter Livanos paid 20,000 Swiss Francs "for a piece of paper saying if a car becomes available, or if they build 201, his will be the 201st." He was in luck, for Ferrari produced 272 from 1984 to 1986.

Although FISA would kill Group B before the competition-minded 288 GTO Evoluzione hit the circuit, the standard GTO set impressive performance benchmarks. In *Road & Track*'s test, former Formula 1 champion Phil Hill found its roadholding "phenomenal, noticeably increasing with speed."

He recorded 0–60 in 5 seconds and 0–100 in 11. These times paled in comparison to *Automobile Revue*'s figures, which were 4.8 seconds to hit 62 miles per hour (100 kilometers per hour) and just 9.7 to reach 100 miles per hour. They saw a top speed of 180 miles per hour.

"In total," Hill concluded, referencing Ferrari's immortal 250 GTO that won three endurance-racing championships from 1962 to 1964, "the new GTO is miles ahead of its 22-year-old predecessor in performance, yet offers the option of air conditioning and Leoncavallo's Pagliacci in full stereo."

Several months after the GTO's launch, Ferrari unveiled the Testarossa at the Paris Auto Show. Like its mass-produced 512 Boxer predecessor, the TR used a 5-liter flat-12 engine. Yet, the new motor featured four-valve heads and numerous other updates. It was also the first 12-cylinder Ferrari homologated for the U.S. market since the Daytona, for all Boxers entering that country were gray market imports.

Although the Testarossa would become a styling trendsetter, its coachwork was quite controversial when it debuted. Because the engine's radiators were on the sides, rather than up front, "the model was quite a novelty with its [aggressive] side air intakes, and a rear track that was wider than the front track," Sergio Pininfarina notes.

In retrospect, he feels the car's flamboyant design was reflective of the era. "It was probably a backlash to the environment felt in the 1970s," the coachbuilder reflects. Observing that an almost blatant "over the top" type of consumerism and style had taken hold, "our Testarossa did not have the purity of line that the Boxer had."

Tom Tjaarda also felt a rebellion took place against the 1970s stifling atmosphere, and pointed to the Countach and his Pantera design as additional evidence. "People had been

Ferrari introduced a new line of ultra-high-performance, limited-production models with the 1984 288 GTO. Originally conceived to participate in Group B rallying, the GTO had a 400-horsepower twin turbo V-8 and 180-mile-per-hour top speed. The 288 marked the beginning of the "instant collectible"—those cars that instantly appreciated in price once they left the factory.

Lamborghini's "Quattrovalvole" Countach was the fastest of all the production Countaches. Its four-valve, 5.1-liter V-12 produced 455 horsepower and saw the car clear 180 miles per hour. America's popular *60 Minutes* news program brought the company's mystique to the forefront of John Q. Public's consciousness when it aired a most memorable segment on the model in 1987.

Ferrari's second limited-production car was the F40. Made to commemorate Ferrari's 40th anniversary, it was the fastest street Ferrari ever made. Made primarily from carbon composite materials and having a 478-horsepower twin-turbo V-8, production ballooned from an original 400 to more than 1,300.

repressed for so long, they wanted to show they were now free," he observed. "Everything became excessive and overly embellished, for the sense of proportion and refined surface treatment you saw before the 1980s was lost."

The Testarossa was larger, heavier, and more luxurious than any other two-seat Ferrari, but its performance again demonstrated Maranello had recovered from its late 1970s/early 1980s slumber. *Motor Trend* bettered the factory's performance figures, hitting 60 miles per hour in 5.29 seconds, seeing 100 in 11.3, and ripping through the quarter-mile in 13.4 at 110 miles per hour.

"Once you get beyond the way you expect its size and weight to feel," the magazine observed, "the Testarossa is surprisingly cooperative to drive, particularly in comparison with its Boxer forerunner, and even, we think, its smaller 308 GTBi/GTSi siblings. It is an all-around delight to drive, fast or slow, and is a hospitable grand tourer."

No sooner had Ferrari dropped its 12-cylinder production gauntlet, than Lamborghini fired back with the Countach Quattrovalvole. Introduced at the 1985 Geneva Show, Giulio Alfieri used the same principles that made the 328 and Testarossa sterling performers: four valves per cylinder.

Lamborghini's newest V-12 now measured 5.1 liters. Those four valves, coupled with six larger Weber carburetors for European versions, fuel injection for the American market, a longer stroke, and a host of other advances, produced 455 horsepower at 7,000 rpm.

When *Car and Driver* tested a fuel-injected Quattrovalvole, it recorded 0–60 in 5.1 seconds, 0–100 in 11, and believed the factory's claim of a 173-miles per hour top speed.

England's *Fast Lane* magazine was unequivocal in its position on who was indeed the king of speed. "Ignore those who claim the Testarossa's 181 mph top speed makes it the world's quickest production car," the road test started.

While the Quattrovalvole Countach's two-way average speed of 190.1 miles per hour was by far the highest any magazine recorded, even more startling were the acceleration times: 0–60 in 4.2 seconds, 0–100 in 10, 0–140 in 20.5, and the standing quarter-mile in 12.5. "The Countach is the king of supercars," the magazine concluded, "and nothing else even comes close."

Porsche would soon prove them wrong when it debuted the high-tech 959 in 1986. Like Ferrari's 288 GTO, this limited production model (283 made) was born to satisfy Group B homologation requirements. Featuring four-wheel drive, a sleek aerodynamic body, computer-controlled suspension, 450 horsepower twin-turbo engine, and six-speed transmission, Porsche listed its top speed at 195 mph.

In 1987 it became very clear that Modena's speed merchants had no intention of relinquishing their claim to the crown to the proud German firm. "A little more than a year ago, I expressed a wish to my engineers," 89-year-old Enzo Ferrari said to the assembled throng of media in Maranello that summer. "Build a car to be the best in the world. And now that car is here."

With that, a red cover was swept aside, revealing the F40. The journalists broke into spontaneous applause, everyone taken

by the Ferrari's serious but sensuous Pininfarina shape. "To put [it] in perspective," *Road & Track*'s Dennis Simanaitis noted at the time, "recall how jarring the Testarossa first looked. By contrast, the F40 looks immediately right."

This astounding model's origins can be traced back to the 288 GTO Evoluzione. While that competition Ferrari never raced, it proved to be the perfect starting point for the F40 and helps explain why such a potent machine could come to market in a little over a year.

Like the 288, the F40 had a tubular steel chassis, but differed in its extensive use of composites in the floorpan, dashboard, front bulkhead, and other areas. The body was also made of composites, in this case a Nomex, Kevlar, and carbon-fiber weave.

The engine was as potent as the body was light. The twin-turbo, double overhead cam V-8 produced 478 horsepower at 7,000 rpm. The transmission was a five speed, and the car's final weight was listed at 2,425 pounds.

It was the perfect response to the 959. When *Road & Track* tested the Porsche in its World's Fastest Cars shootout, the 959

Deluxe turned 0–100 in 9.4 seconds, the quarter-mile in 12.4, and saw a top speed of 197 miles per hour. The F40 the magazine later tried hit 100 in 8 seconds flat, and the standing quarter-mile 11.8; these latter times were even quicker than the lightweight 959 Sport. The F40's top speed was nearly identical at 196 miles per hour.

Ferrari wasn't the only Modenese constructor playing with carbon-fiber. In the mid-1980s, Lamborghini proved it was also adept at the "De Tomaso game" when it approached the Italian government for assistance in subsidizing research and development of the space age material for road cars.

Test driver Valentino Balboni, the man who was taught by Lamborghini's original maestro Bob Wallace, recalls that "we knew the big advantage would be lightness and rigidity. We wanted to see if composites could be effectively used in our future production."

The resulting Countach Evoluzione was constructed in the hastily formed Composites Department, run by a young, enthusiastic ex-pat Argentinean named Horacio Pagani. The Evoluzione's shape aped the Quattrovalvole, save some minor differences. The wheels

Although it could touch 170 miles per hour, Ferrari's 348 did not meet the universal praise its predecessor 328 received. Launched in 1989, not everyone warmed to its Testarossa-inspired styling, while others found its handling to be a handful. The last of the series was the 348 Spider, which was first seen in 1993. The model was the first of Ferrari's mid-engine, two-seat roadsters.

Ferrari gave the Testarossa a cosmetic and mechanical once over to come up with the 512 TR that debuted in 1992. The front-end treatment was revised, and the wheel size increased from 16 to 18 inches. More important, the engine now produced 428 horsepower, and the car's structural rigidity was vastly improved while it shed approximately 50 pounds of weight. Listed top speed was 192 miles per hour.

were pancake-type discs, the air intakes were subtly revised, and it had a cleaner front end, thanks to its sloping, integrated spoiler.

The final stripped-down car weighed some 800 pounds less than the production Countach. "It was an animal," Balboni smiles, recalling the countless hours of driving it.

Paul Frère certainly agreed. When he tried it for *Motor*, "Acceleration was so quick that even on secondary roads, we touched speeds of around 170 mph," he observed. "After an incredibly short time, we were back at the factory, having covered 55–60 miles in what must have been the quickest car I have ever driven on the road."

There were other reasons Frère would call this one-off special "a handful." "We didn't anticipate how its lightness would alter the Countach's balance," Balboni reflected. "Now, there was a lot more weight over the rear wheels."

Still, through trial and error, the legendary test driver says the team "developed special suspension settings to get it as good as possible. It was a really fast car, capable of hitting 100 kilometers per hour (62 miles per hour) in 3.2 seconds. I also saw a top speed of 330 kilometers (205 miles per hour)."

That experience would prove most valuable. In a little more than two years, Balboni and company would make the world's first production car to break the 200-mile-per-hour barrier in independent testing.

Boom and Bust

As the 1990s dawned, Italy and the world's automotive industry was in the midst of a performance boom not seen since the glory days of the 1960s. Manufacturers had a firm grasp on emissions and safety regulations and introduced a dizzying array of new, ever faster, and flamboyant machines.

Ferrari's successor to the 328 typified the explosion. The 348 that debuted at the 1989 Frankfurt Auto Show looked much like a miniature Testarossa, thanks to its side-mounted radiators

and dramatic side air intakes. On why Ferrari would replace its most popular car, the company's head of technical development Fabio Giunchi's answer was two simple words: *more performance*.

Thanks to the 348's new, longitudinally mounted 300-horsepower V-8, that was a given. *Road & Track*'s 348 GTS hit 100 miles per hour 1.5 seconds more quickly (14.5 vs. 15.9) than the outgoing 328 and estimated the new car's top speed was 20-plus miles per hour greater than the earlier model's 149 maximum. The magazine would subsequently name the 348 one of its Ten Best Cars in the World in December 1990.

Yet such praise was not universal. Several magazines found the 348's handling tricky at the limit, causing *Car & Driver* to observe "the car is a challenge to keep under control."

Two years later, the Testarossa received a boost in performance when Ferrari debuted the 512 TR at the Los Angeles Motor Show. The model's engine now produced 422 horsepower and made a good thing even more desirable. "[It] looks and handles better than its replacement," *CAR* noted in its January 1992 test, "but its greatness lies in that glorious flat-12 [engine]."

Road & Track's 512 blistered the drag strip, hitting 60 in 4.7 seconds, the standing quarter-mile in 12.9, and having an estimated top speed of 192 miles per hour. "What impressed me most is the Ferrari's impeccable manners," Phil Hill noted in the June 1992 issue. "It's a smooth relaxed highway machine, with none of the nervous or high strung feedback one gets in some exotic cars."

As impressive as the 512 TR and 348 were, the machine that captured the world's headlines at the decade's turn was Lamborghini's striking Diablo. This landmark model's roots can be traced back to June 1985 when company president Emile Novaro issued a short engineering brief to his men: Make a Countach successor.

Engineer Luigi Marmiroli went to work on an all-new car, using the just released Countach Quattrovalvole as his reference point. Working closely with IFOA, a Modena-based firm specializing in structural research, Marmiroli's goals were simple: higher performance, better visibility, more room, and emissions compliance.

Lamborghini boosted its V-12 output by increasing displacement to 5.7 liters, thanks to a larger bore and longer stroke. Coupled with a new fuel-injection system and higher compression ratio, the new engine produced 492 horsepower at 6,800 rpm.

As the experimental department completed the first Diablo prototype in April 1987, Marmiroli and all in the company were stunned to learn that the Mimrams had sold the firm to Chrysler Corporation, which was in a bidding contest with wealthy American enthusiast Ron Miller. This change of ownership radically altered the Diablo's planned May 1988 launch date, for Chrysler wanted to address quality control and manufacturing techniques, and refine the car's Marcello Gandini-designed shape and interior.

Lamborghini's maestro tester Valentino Balboni recalled numerous forays in the prototype Diablo. "We would go out late at night, where my job was to see how the car and its components would react under certain conditions," he smiles. "I often had an engineer with me, who would monitor the engine's functions on his computer. One night we got quite a start when, doing around 120 miles per hour, the headlights suddenly went out!"

Shortly after the Diablo's rousing 1990 introduction, it was immediately clear that Lamborghini had produced the world's first production 200-mile-per-hour car—every magazine that tested it cleared that magical barrier. Italian journalist Giancarlo Perini tried a privately owned Diablo and stormed to 60 in 4.2 seconds, hit 100 in 8.5, the quarter-mile in 12.3, and saw 150 miles per hour in 18.5.

Regarding its top speed, "the average [we saw] worked out to 205.22 mph," he noted in *CAR*'s September 1991 issue, bettering the factory's claimed 202-mile-per-hour maximum. "The Diablo just proved itself the fastest production car in the world."

Other magazines quickly followed suit. *Autocar* tested another Diablo on Germany's autobahn and saw more than 200 miles per hour. *Road & Track* found much the same, recording a top speed of 202 miles per hour in a third car. "It's not so much a car as a phenomenon, not so much a Countach successor as it is heir to the Lamborghini throne," the *American* magazine summed up in its August 1991 issue.

A number of companies were determined to wrest that coveted "fastest in the world" title from Lamborghini, both in Italy and abroad. Jaguar was working feverishly on its 211-mile-per-hour XK220, the principality of Monaco's Centenaire introduced its lightweight, twin-turbo, V-12-powered Monte Carlo GTB, and McLaren was hard at work on its $1 million-a-copy, 230-mile-per-hour F1.

Numerous other manufacturers teased they were going to enter the double century sweepstakes. As the 1990s began, auto shows were inundated with midengine prototypes that boasted the latest in steering, drivetrain, suspension, and construction technologies.

One of the most interesting dream cars from this pervasive period was Cizeta's Moroder V16T. Built in Modena by former southern California exotic car fixture and ex-Lamborghini man Claudio Zampolli, the Cizeta was powered by a spectacular 6-liter V-16 engine. Mounted transversally in the frame, it featured four valves per cylinder, an electronic ignition, and mechanical fuel injection. Quoted horsepower was 560 at 8,000 rpm.

When Italian journalist Luca Ciferri asked why he resorted to such a radical powerplant when Ferrari and Lamborghini were satisfied with 12 cylinders, Zampolli replied, "When you don't have an established name you should build something special."

And special it was. "A V-16 is smooth by definition," *Autocar* noted in its May 1989 comparison with Lamborghini's 25th Anniversary Countach, "but this 6-liter monster defies belief. It's just perfectly balanced, completely vibration free. The throttle response is so immediate and consistently smooth that you wonder if you are driving an electric-powered car."

CAR was given an even greater opportunity with the V16T when they compared Cizeta's prototype to a Ferrari F40, Anniversary Countach, and Porsche 959. "The V-16 easily has the biggest rev band, [and] is capable of pulling cleanly from as little as 1,000 rpm," Giancarlo Perini and Jose Rosinski marveled in the magazine's November 1989 issue.

Because the Cizeta's suspension wasn't fully sorted, they limited its speed to "just" 140 miles per hour. Although the two journalists preferred the F40 above the others, they were impressed by the V16T's comfort, ease of driving, and felt its projected performance (0–60 in the four-second range and a top speed of 204 miles per hour) seemed within reason. They concluded the Cizeta was "*potentially* the winner of this contest," noting it needed "more development before we can award it victory in such esteemed company."

An even more ambitious effort was the rebirth of Bugatti. Prior to World War II, this famed company was revered as the pinnacle of styling, performance, and engineering excellence.

The man behind the renaissance's goal was to once again capture that mystique. Born on December 5, 1932, Romano Artioli began his automotive career humbly at age 17 when he opened a small workshop in Bolzano, near the Italian/Swiss border. After he completed his studies at a local industrial school, he started a new business with his brother, the "Garage Mille Miglia."

Warm, likable, and cultured, Artioli harbored great ambition, and represented Ferrari, Renault, and Opel by age 30. Later, he expanded into Chevrolet, became the Suzuki distributor for all of Italy, and imported two lines of motor homes.

A true automotive enthusiast, Artioli says he fell in love with the Bugatti marque as a teenager. "In 1953," he recalled in

Lamborghini's Diablo was the first production car to repeatedly break the 200-mile-per-hour barrier in independent testing. So confident was the company of its new model that one of the first brochures compared the Diablo to Ferrari's F40 and 512 TR, using performance figures taken from America's *Car and Driver* magazine.

Bugatti's magnificent publication, *EB*, "I was shocked by the news that [the company] had retired from the automobile industry. . . . I decided that if nobody did anything about 'reviving' it, I would."

By the mid-1980s, this true gentleman had the financial means to pursue his lifelong dream. Yet there was much more to his effort than making the most prestigious car on the market—everything had to represent the ultimate. "Bugatti cannot be revived inside a commonplace factory, [with cars] coming out of an ugly box," he noted in 1991. "[I]t must have sunlight around it, in a spotlessly clean atmosphere, just like Ettore would have liked."

Bugatti's factory was erected outside Modena in Campogalliano and was an architectural marvel. Unparalleled in beauty, detail, and atmosphere, Artioli filled it with outstanding engineering talent. He first used ex-Lamborghini man Paolo Stanzani, then turned to Nicola Materazzi, an ex-Ferrari engineer responsible for the 288 GTO, Testarossa, and F40, to head the effort.

The ever-prolific Marcello Gandini originally penned the Bugattis in vogue wedge-shape. Because his prototype lacked styling cues to tie it in with the marque's tradition, Artioli had Bugatti's architect Giampaolo Benedetti modify the design.

The production Bugatti EB110 was unveiled in September 1991 in a ceremony that rivaled any royal wedding; it would be the first in a long line of lavish affairs to promote the marque. Underneath the EB110's racy but traditional skin was an engineering masterpiece. The engine was a 3.5-liter V-12 that featured four turbochargers, five valves per cylinder, and Bugatti's own fuel-injection system. Its output of 550 horsepower at 8,500 rpm was driven to all four wheels via a six-speed transmission.

Stopping power came from 13-inch ventilated disc brakes that featured ABS. The suspension was independent front and rear.

Leading Bugatti historian and author Griff Borgeson toured the factory and was given a ride in a prototype EB110 in late 1991. "After years of reserved judgment," he noted in *Road & Track*'s January 1992 issue, "I now cannot conceive that Ettore Bugatti and his heirs are not gratified by the new legend that is being created in the great man's name."

The EB110 delivered blistering performance. Despite severe turbo lag under 4,000 rpm, Germany's *Auto Motor und Sport* recorded 0–62 in 3.6 seconds, 0–124 in 14 seconds, and a top speed of 209 miles per hour. *Road & Track*'s USA-spec Bugatti needed 4.4 seconds for 60, 9.1 for 100, and 12.5 to cover the quarter-mile.

They would later record a top speed of 212 miles per hour in one of the magazine's famed top-speed "shoot-outs." "It drives like the most beautifully developed car you could imagine," Phil Hill and Paul Frère enthused in the January 1995 issue. "You can cruise at over 200 mph like you're on an ordinary road. The steering is lovely, and the gearbox delightful. It's just an outstanding car."

But much like ATS 30 years earlier, such publicity was too little, too late. Artioli followed in Giorgio Billi's footsteps by erecting an unforgettable monument of a factory, sapping up valuable cash in the process. That the car was indeed the most advanced machine on the market didn't matter, for any type of financial staying power was now gone.

Worse, the late 1980s/early 1990s demand for faster and more flamboyant supercars was artificial. As the world's economy went from bust in the early 1980s to boom several years later, the need to display one's wealth became a global obsession. Rapidly increasing real estate values, particularly in Japan and California, fed into the movement, as did a new mentality sweeping through America's stock market. Leveraged buyouts and merger mania created a new breed of wealth, one that rewarded key players with "telephone book number" paychecks.

The effect on the automotive market's upper echelons was enormous. As bankers eagerly lent against constantly increasing paper net worths, the era of instant collectibles was born.

Ferrari's 288 GTO initiated the craze. "The first 288 we received had a price of approximately $80,000, and we sold it for $115,000," says Brandon Lawrence, who then worked for a large California Ferrari dealership. "We bought our next one from another Ferrari dealer, priced it at $125,000, and sold it immediately."

Values quickly skyrocketed as too much money chased too few goods. "Three years later," Lawrence chuckles, recalling the lunacy, "we bought that first 288 back from the original owner for $950,000. We immediately flipped it for $1,050,000."

Ferrari responded with a much higher sticker price on the F40, then tripled its original production of 400 to meet demand. The price on the secondary market did the same, jumping from a sticker of approximately $400,000 to well over $1 million. Other cars, such as the Testarossa, Lamborghini's Countach, and Alfa's radical, limited-production SZ coupe by Zagato, also saw large price increases in the secondary market.

In the early 1990s, Italy's most sophisticated and highest performing road car was Bugatti's spectacular EB110. Its wedge-shape profile covered a V-12 that featured four turbochargers, four-wheel drive, and a six-speed transmission. The model pictured here was the ultra-high-performance EB110 SS, which produced 610 horsepower. The factory interior was always kept immaculate, all the better to dazzle prospective purchasers. Unfortunately, the car was let down by its conventional styling and controversial front end. It was launched just as the early 1990s worldwide recession hit. The company lasted until 1995, then declared bankruptcy.

True collector cars were also in the midst of an unprecedented boom and were swapped around like baseball cards. In the late 1980s, numerous historic Ferraris traded hands in the millions, with everything coming to a head when a Japanese collector paid $14-plus million for a 250 GTO in October 1989.

It is thus no wonder that companies such as Bugatti, Jaguar, and McLaren thought there was an insatiable demand for cars costing in excess of $300,000. There was just one problem: The instant collectible fad was sending a false signal, for many buyers had no intention of using, or keeping, their cars. "Groups of doctors and lawyers would come together to buy things," Lawrence noted. "These guys couldn't tell the good from the bad. Worse, they just viewed cars as investments."

Like tulip bulbs in the 17th century, the instant a greater fool no longer existed, the market would crash. And so it happened with the early 1990s bubble economy. When the wicked worldwide recession hit in 1991–1992, property values plummeted, and paper net worth suddenly evaporated under a barrage of debt.

Demand for the new breed of 200-mile-per-hour ego machines and instant classics completely dried up, ringing the death knell for a number of models and constructors. Claudio Zampolli's Cizeta produced just seven cars, while other names such as Piero Rivolta's new Iso Grifo and Giotto Bizzarrini's midengine Picchio, remained stillborn. Jaguar was left with a number of unsold XK220s, and McLaren had to reduce its F1 production run from 300 to just 100.

Hardest hit was undoubtedly Bugatti. Romano Artioli was a throwback to Italy's classic *capitano d'industria* days: He was *sure* he would succeed. Thus, in place of a business plan with hard numbers, several employees recall there was only a nebulous concept that one day the company would go public after the car had come to epitomize a luxurious lifestyle. Just as Bugatti luxury goods went on sale and a handful of Bugatti hotels were being drawn up, the funds ran out.

Several suitors, including Mercedes-Benz, expressed a serious interest in buying the firm. Unfortunately, Artioli remained as truculent as ever, wanting the deal to be done his way. In the mid-1990s, Bugatti was forced to declare bankruptcy.

Although it was a painful period for Italy and many of the world's manufacturers, it provided a valuable lesson. "Statement" cars were not necessarily better cars.

De Tomaso completely updated the Pantera in the early 1990s. De Tomaso often modified its Ford V-8, and later cars had a six-speed gearbox. Marcello Gandini designed the car's new look. Very few were made with a targa top.

Return to Roots

12

1996-TODAY

Three letters summed up the shortcomings of the so-called statement cars: *NSX*. This brilliant mid-engine 160-mile-per-hour Honda was introduced in 1990 and totally rewrote the supercar rulebook. Sold under the Acura name in America, it proved that an involving high-performance sports car could be as easy to live with as a typical family sedan. Ferrari would take the lesson to heart with the 355 that debuted in the spring of 1994. The 348 successor's 3.5-liter V-8 was a true marvel. With five valves per cylinder, titanium connecting rods, and sophisticated electronics, it produced 380 horsepower at 8,250 rpm.

The 355's coachwork was a Pininfarina masterpiece and featured perfect balance and proportioning, outstanding surface treatment, and air intakes that integrated nicely into the design.

From the first road test, it was clear Ferrari was on top of its game. "Anyone who ever attempted to drive a 348 hard over a good road or around a circuit and scared themselves will revel in what Ferrari has achieved with the 355," *Autocar*'s October 19, 1994, issue noted. "At a stroke it has created a new supercar class of its own, leaving the 911s and NSXs for dead. More than that, the 355 is the first car that brings into question the logic of spending seven times more on a McLaren F1 when in useable terms [the Ferrari] achieves at least 95 percent as much."

The magazine's acceleration figures only underlined the observation. Their test car hit 60 in 4.6 seconds, 100 in 10.6, and the quarter-mile in 13.0. Its top speed was 173 miles per hour.

More proof that Ferrari had blown off its late 1980s/early 1990s malaise was the 456 GT. Called by Sergio Pininfarina "probably the best Ferrari," this 185-mile-per-hour 2+2 broke cover at the 1992 Paris Auto Show and marked the return of the front-engine berlinetta.

Ferrari's 355 was one of the 1990s most beautiful road cars and is a perfect example of how far the performance envelope moved in two decades. This V-8 model was faster and quicker than a number of Ferrari's previous mass-produced 12-cylinder benchmarks: the 275 GTB/4, the Daytona, the Boxer, and Testarossa.

The 456 GT proved to be a turning point for Maranello: Blatant flamboyancy was out and understatement was in. "My father saw the original version of this car before he died," Piero Ferrari observed at the model's introduction. "It is his last car, and I think he would have liked (it)." Autocar's summary of the model was this: "Elegant, awesomely fast, breathtakingly beautiful—the crushing cool of Ferrari is back."

Its deliciously elegant understated coachwork and all-new V-12 captured everyone's attention. The engine measured 5.5 liters and featured four valves per cylinder, aluminum construction, and Bosch Motronic fuel injection. Its 442 horsepower were driven to the rear wheels via a six-speed transmission.

"It has been 20 years since we had a car like this at Ferrari, a car with so strong a personal touch," company president Luca Cordero di Montezemolo noted at its introduction. "It will only be built in very small numbers and will have a unique appeal to our most special customers. I don't think it will bring the speculators back on to our order books—this is not a car for them."

Road tests were ecstatic about Ferrari's return to the "classic" GT formula. "It is more refined, more comfortable and a sight more sophisticated than any car ever to be built at Maranello," Autocar's 1993 road test concluded. "Whether you look at it, sit in it or drive it, it all adds up to one simple fact: the 456 is the greatest Grand Tourer the world has seen."

Yet Ferrari was not done. For those who desired a pure two-seater, the company introduced the 550 Maranello in July 1996. On why Ferrari's production flagship didn't follow in the midengine footsteps of the Testarossa/512TR, "I was a little disturbed by a car that was too much of a show-off, too difficult to use," Montezemolo noted.

Sergio Pininfarina loved the challenge of creating 550. "It reminds me of how I felt in the 1950s, when I was first working with Ferrari," he said. "Ferrari returned to the front-engine configuration with this car because the progress of technology allowed us to reach the same performance of a midengine design with better comfort and luggage room."

Ferrari's test drivers put an exclamation point on this last observation. They could lap the company's demanding Fiorano test track 3.2 seconds quicker than the 512 TR.

One year before the 550 Maranello's launch, Ferrari debuted a limited production successor to the commercially successful 288 GTO and F40. That car was the F50.

Luca Montezemolo noted the model was "born at the onset of the 50th anniversary of Ferrari, [and] is the first and last street legal Formula 1 car." This last criterion separates it from McLaren's $1 million F1, for Ferrari wanted the ultimate in driver involvement, rather than out-and-out top speed and maximum performance.

Lamborghini's third Diablo model was the Diablo SE. Made to commemorate Lamborghini's 30th anniversary, just 150 were made. It boasted special bodywork, a 525-horsepower V-12, and a quoted top speed of 206 miles per hour.

Its voluptuous Pininfarina coachwork ensured this would happen. Unlike the British supercar, the F50's top was removable, making it a full roadster.

Its chassis was a tub made entirely of carbon composites and adhesive materials and followed Formula 1 principles in being the central part of the car's structure. The centrally mounted engine acted as a support for the rear suspension and bodywork.

The F50's 4.7-liter V-12 derived directly from Ferrari's 1990 multiple race-winning F1 engine. It had five valves per cylinder, double overhead cams, an 11.3:1 compression ratio, and produced 513 horsepower at 8,500 rpm.

This Ferrari proved quicker than an F40 when tested by *Road & Track*. Their F50 needed just eight seconds to hit 100 and 12.1

Marcello Gandini designed Lamborghini's Diablo Roadster. It offered a most interesting solution on where to store its one-piece top: It was secured on top of the rear decklid.

The Diablo SV was Lamborghini's successful attempt to enter a different marketplace. "The model was about pure performance," said company test driver Valentino Balboni. "That is why it had a more sporty interior, lower gears, and less weight."

for the quarter-mile. "More than anything," the magazine summed up in January 1997, "the F50 feels like a racing car."

Lamborghini also upped its performance benchmark with the Diablo SE. This special limited production model was made to celebrate the company's 30th anniversary and had a more powerful engine (now at 525 horsepower) and less weight. Styling cues included special badges and slats behind the driver's compartment that paid homage to the Miura. Quoted top speed was 210 miles per hour.

It was clearly the best of the Diablo range. "As a road car," CAR's September 1994 test concluded, "the SE is fast enough and good enough to put Lamborghini back in the top rank of supercar makers. Its looks are strikingly dramatic—a good enough reason alone for having one in the garage. It brakes and steers more engagingly than does McLaren's F1, and shades the Jaguar XJ220 in every respect except outright performance."

Lamborghini would introduce another engaging Diablo in 1995. What gave the Diablo Roadster a totally different flavor was its removable top. Available in both two-wheel and four-wheel drive, the model was powered by the standard 492-horsepower V-12, and quickly became Lamborghini's bestseller.

"The Diablo Roadster is the sort of car you would take out simply for the joy of driving it, but would it be the supercar of my choice?" racing driver and journalist Tiff Needell pondered in England's *Top Gear* magazine. After comparing it to Jaguar's XK220, McLaren's F1 and Ferrari's F50—all of which he had driven—"I'd go straight for the Roadster," he concluded, "with a special request for rear wheel drive only."

Lamborghini broadened the model range further by introducing the SV in 1996. Costing more than $50,000 less than the Roadster and four-wheel-drive VT, the SV was available only in rear-wheel drive and featured a 500-horsepower V-12 and stripped-down interior. Thanks to its lower final drive ratio, Lamborghini listed its top speed at "just" 185 miles per hour.

In 1993, Fiat and Alfa Romeo signaled they were returning to their roots by once again manufacturing the cars that brought them worldwide acclaim: outstanding sporting coupes and spiders.

Alfa's GTV was first shown late that year and resurrected the initials that were made famous by later versions of the Giulia GT. Like that earlier car, the GTV's underpinnings derived from a mass production model, in this case the sporty 155 sedan.

The GTV's highly individualistic form derived from the attractive Proteo concept car that was shown at Geneva in 1991. The GTV Spider's look had even more personality than the coupe, thanks in great part to the top being concealed beneath a hard cover that accentuated the cut line along the side of the body.

The GTVs were initially powered by several engines: a 150-horsepower 2-liter inline four; a 200-horsepower tuborcharged, 2-liter V-6; a 192-horsepower 3-liter V-6. In 2000, Alfa introduced a 155-horsepower inline four and a 220-horsepower V-6. All use five-speed transmissions, and a six-speed is optional today.

Although the GTVs broke with Alfa's sports car tradition by using front-wheel drive, road testers found this had little effect on the model's character. "We won't tantalize you," CAR's May 1995 road test of a normally aspirated 2-liter spider began. "[T]he new Alfa is fantastic. It looks wonderful, has terrific engines, and handles superbly. It marks a return to form for one of Italy's most famous makers."

The same could be said about Fiat's startling Coupe. Also introduced in 1993, the Coupe featured flavorful styling that did a masterful job of covering its mass-production—based platform.

The powerplant that truly fits the Coupe's sporting character was a turbocharged, 2-liter inline five cylinder. Introduced in 1995, it had a four-valve head and the requisite balance shaft for smoothness. Quoted power output was 220 at 5,750 rpm.

This Coupe was a stormer, hitting 60 in 6.6 seconds, 100 in just over 16, and returning 35-plus miles per gallon on the freeway. Top speed was 150 miles per hour. *CAR*'s February 1997 comparison named it the class leader, as their testers easily chose it over a Honda and Nissan.

Fiat's "barchetta" also received an enthusiastic reaction when it was introduced in 1995. Its chassis derived from the Punto coupe and sedan, the suspension was independent front and rear, and the disc brakes had ABS as an option.

One of Italy's and Modena's newest constructors is Pagani. Horacio Pagani says the inspiration for the Zonda C12's voluptuous shape was early 1990s Group C race cars, and the hourglass figure of his wife, Cristina. The result is likely the world's wildest looking street machine.

Like the Coupe and Alfa's GTVs, the barchetta has front-wheel drive. In this case, the engine was a free-revving, 1.7-liter inline four that produced 133 horsepower at 6,300 rpm.

It was clear Fiat hadn't missed a beat in the 10-plus years since it last built a roadster. "Its lovable for its looks, admirable for originality, delightful for its detailing," *CAR* enthused. "It's also fun to drive, and it scores a direct hit as a fashion accessory."

Performance Car agreed, the British publication's test car hitting 60 in 7.9 seconds and topping out at 120 miles per hour. "Fun, fruity and a few more words beginning with 'F,'" it summed up in the April 1995 issue, "the fabulous new Fiat is

a fine alternative to the (Mazda Miata), and a worthy alternative to a hot hatch."

As the new millennium unfolds, Modena is once again reasserting its position as the world's sports car capital. The city and its exotic car industry are in the midst of the greatest boom since the glory days of the early 1960s.

Ferrari is leading the way with its 360 Modena. This 355 successor was introduced at Geneva in 1999 and "represents the new reality of today's world," Sergio Pininfarina said. "It is a good expression of innovation, for it combines new technology, better performance, and a lot of creativity."

Its voluptuous (and somewhat controversial) shape demonstrates all these points, taking aerodynamics to new heights on road cars. The result of extensive wind tunnel testing, it emphasizes airflow above and underneath the car, and delivers more downforce than any previous road Ferrari.

Its new aluminum monocoque/spaceframe construction is revolutionary. It replaces the 355's traditional steel frame and tubular steel subframes, and it is lighter and considerably more rigid.

Why is the Modena larger than its predecessor? "Ferraris shouldn't be gadgets for rich people," Montezemolo told *Autocar*. "I want a Ferrari to be a car you can use, that has enough room so you can take your wife driving, a car with easy access, even a car that allows you to play golf and take the Ferrari."

The engine and transmission reflect this user-friendly edict. The Modena's 3.6-liter V-8 produces 400 horsepower at 8,500 rpm, yet its wide torque curve makes it as easy and tractable to use as an American V-8.

In July 1999 the factory that produces the Qvale Mangusta didn't even exist; what makes the car even more remarkable is the rigidity of its chassis. "It doesn't need any type of body to be able to survive a crash test," says Qvale engineer Giordano Casarini. This makes it no surprise the company is examining a number of alternative models for its Ford-powered platform.

But even with its civility and usability, the Modena is likely the greatest sports car Maranello has produced. *Autocar*'s 360 screamed to 60 in 4.2 seconds, touched 100 in 8.8, and saw a top speed of 184 miles per hour.

Lamborghini is also in the midst of a boom. After being sold twice in the 1990s, its current parent, Audi, plans to rekindle the type of rivalry Lamborghini had with Ferrari back in the 1960s and early 1970s. The current Diablo is now more refined than ever and remains a fearsome performer.

At the top of the pecking order is the Diablo GT, the fastest car Lamborghini has ever produced. It follows in the Diablo SE's footsteps by offering more power (in this case 570) in a lighter, limited-production package.

Several miles to the north of Lamborghini is Pagani, the brainchild of ex-Lamborghini man Horacio Pagani. As he worked on the lightweight Countach Evoluzione, "I saw the increasing importance of carbon-fiber in our industry," he said.

In the late 1980s, Pagani left Lamborghini to start his own firm, Modena Design. Within a decade, the composite manufacturer's clients included former employer Lamborghini, Ferrari, multiple Indy 500–winning chassis supplier and former Lamborghini chief engineer Gian Paolo Dallara, and several other automotive and nonautomotive concerns.

As business boomed, Pagani pursued his dream to design and construct his own car and began creating it in the early 1990s. The result was the Zonda C12, named after a wind in the Andes.

Made out of carbon-fiber, the Zonda is likely the world's finest machine in terms of craftsmanship, exceeding even the standards found at the renown Pebble Beach Concours d'Elegance. It weighs just 2,700 pounds and is powered by a 400- or 500-horsepower Mercedes-Benz V-12 that comes directly from Germany.

The Zonda is a throwback to Modena's golden years, being one man's vision of what a car should be. Its shape looks like nothing else, and the interior and dash are highly original. Maximum annual production of this $300,000, 200-mile-per-hour machine is just 30 a year.

Surprisingly, Pagani is not the region's newest constructor, for that distinction belongs to Qvale Modena. Behind this effort is California's wealthy Qvale family that has six decades of experience in the automotive industry.

Qvale patriarch Kjell Qvale was one of the founders of America's sports car movement in the late 1940s and introduced a number of European marques to the United States. He also owned England's Jensen in the 1970s and was instrumental in the success of De Tomaso's midengine Mangusta.

Spearheading Qvale Modena is his oldest son, Bruce. "This is the only area in the world where you have everything in such close proximity," Bruce said about why his family went to Modena to produce cars. "Within minutes of each other, there are engineers, designers, subcontractors, test drivers, and skilled labor who excel in manufacturing by hand."

Another reason why he uprooted his family from northern California is much more personal. "I remember being here as a 10-year-old kid," Qvale beamed, "sitting in the prototype De Tomaso Mangusta back in the 1960s."

Before the Qvales erected their own production facility, they secured the rights to manufacture De Tomaso's newest car, also named the Mangusta. Originally called the Bigua, this $80,000 front-engined machine is powered by a 320-horsepower Ford V-8 and uses one of the world's most advanced chassis. Marcello Gandini designed its innovative coupe-targa-roadster body.

The Guara marks the first De Tomaso car to be powered by BMW engines. "When we were designing it," Santiago De Tomaso reflected, "we felt the BMW V-8 was the world's best engine. That is why we decided to use it."

While Maserati's offerings of the 1980s and first half of the 1990s all delivered sparkling performance, the element of style was missing from the product mix. The 170-mile-per-hour 3200 GT 2+2 designed by Giugiaro attempts to remedy that. First seen in 1998, it is powered by a twin-turbo V-8 that produces 370 horsepower.

Early in 2000, Qvale determined it was best to be master of his own destiny, and broke away from De Tomaso. With engineer Giordano Casarini, one of the sports car industry's best kept management secrets, overseeing the production and development of the company's products, Qvale Modena is busy constructing Mangustas and selling them through their own dealer network in the United States and around the world.

De Tomaso continues to soldier on, with Alessandro's son Santiago firmly entrenched in the company. His first order of business was making a new Pantera in the early 1990s that featured an all-new body designed by Marcello Gandini. "The only thing that was the same between the new version and the old was the windshield," Santiago said. "The chassis, suspension, everything was new."

He followed this up with the company's current production car, the mid-engine Guara. This lightweight, compact machine features a racing-derived pushrod suspension and is powered by a BMW V-8. Available as a coupe or low windshield barchetta, in many ways it marked a return to the company's roots. Made in small numbers, outright performance and individuality, rather than comfort and refinement, are its strong points.

In a further demonstration of how times have changed, today former antagonist Ferrari owns Maserati. After Maranello bought the company from De Tomaso in the late 1990s, Maserati launched the 3200 GT in 1998.

This model marks the firm's return to its gran turismo heritage. Originally under development prior to Ferrari's purchase, the 3200 was designed by the man responsible for a number of Maserati's most famous GTs, Giorgetto Giugiaro.

The 2+2 coupe is powered by an exhilarating 370-horsepower twin turbo V-8 that is mated to a six-speed manual or four-speed automatic. The 3200 sprints to 60 in approximately five seconds and has a top speed in the region of 170 miles per hour.

So what does the future have in store for Italy's constructors? Ferrari's 360 Modena Spider was introduced at the 2000 Geneva

Ferrari's 360 Modena Spider may well be the world's most exhilarating open-air car. Like its coupe brethren, it comes with a six-speed manual transmission or Ferrari's highly regarded Formula 1-inspired F1 semi-automatic gearbox.

Auto Show and will go on sale in the second half of the year. Its coupe brethren has been a runaway success, with demand so great that at the time of this book's publication cars are selling for more than $60,000 over list price in America's secondary market.

Ferrari is also planning to introduce another open-air model: a limited-production 550 Maranello "barchetta." By 2003, a 456 successor, and a new hyper-performance Ferrari that is often dubbed the "FX" or "F60," will be in production.

In a bid to challenge Ferrari's market leadership role, Volkswagen is infusing Lamborghini with unheard of amounts of capital. The factory is undergoing a major facelift, and a Diablo successor is being developed, as is a 360 Modena competitor.

So serious is VW/Audi about Lamborghini's future that the central Italian grapevine was buzzing in early 1999 that the two companies had purchased not one, but three of every Ferrari model. These were then being reverse-engineered in an effort to make Lamborghinis that are faster, better, and less expensive than the corresponding Ferrari.

Qvale Modena and Pagani are also looking forward. Their current platforms provide an excellent basis for additional models, making it no surprise that both firms have new cars in the pipeline.

Maserati is not sitting still, either. It will launch a new 3200 Spider in 2001/2002 and use this model as a springboard to return the American market. Unlike the European 3200s, U.S. cars will likely use a normally aspirated 4-liter V-8. After this model is introduced, Maserati will debut a new, Pininfarina-styled four-door.

Alfa Romeo will also return to America, thanks to General Motors taking a 20 percent stake in its parent company Fiat. Shortly after the deal was completed, it was announced that Alfa's new Spider will debut in 2003–2004 and be homologated for the U.S. market.

Lamborghini offered an optional Jota engine package that was available only to owners of the limited-production Diablo SE. Thanks to its air-induction system and other modifications, it pushed power output more than 550 horsepower. Just 14 customers chose the Jota option.

Bibliography

Several books were extremely important when researching this project. For anyone interested in the vast array of Alfa Romeo models, *Alfa Romeo Production Cars* (Giorgio Nada Editore) is your solution.

Ferrari cars are a different and more complex matter. The six books that seem to always be on my desk were the incomparable *Le Ferrari di Pininfarina* by Angelo Tito Anselmi, Godfry Eaton's *The Complete Ferrari*, Stanley Nowak's *Ferrari on the Road*, Keith Bluemel's *Original Ferrari V8*, and Giorgio Nada Editore's *Ferrari 1947-1997* and *Guida all'Identificazione Ferrari*.

There were several people that I was fortunate enough to interview, but passed away before we completed our talks. Thankfully, they had biographies or autobiographies that covered some of the areas we had yet to tackle. Those books are Oscar Orefici's *Carlo Chiti: Sinfonia Ruggente*, Dante Giacosa's *40 Years of Design with Fiat*, and Luciano Greggio's tome, *Bertone*.

Additionally, Battista Pininfarina's *Born with the Automobile* and Gioachino Colombo's *Origins of the Ferrari Legend* were invaluable for letting those two men tell the story in their own words. *Una Vita Per L'Automobile* was a wonderful source for quotes from Enzo Ferrari.

Books frequently referenced on the coachbuilders were Automobilia's *Pininfarina Catalogue Raisonne* and *Giugiaro Catalogue Raisonne*, the aforementioned *Bertone*, Angelo Tito Anselmi's *Carrozzeria Touring*, and *Carrozzeria Italiana: Advancing the Art & Science of Automobile Design* (Automobilia).

The importance of period publications cannot be overlooked, especially in understanding a car's impact at the time it was new. From the late 1940s through the 1970s, *Road & Track* is the most quoted, simply because they tested (and covered) sports cars and Italy's sports car scene better and more frequently than anyone else. Other invaluable periodicals were *Style Auto*, and the annuals *Automobile Year* and *World Car Catalogue/World Cars*.

Additional magazines and periodicals referenced from the author's library were *Autocar*, *Autosport*, *Automobile*, *Automobile Quarterly*, *Cavallino*, *CAR*, *Car and Driver*, *Fast Lane*, *FORZA*, *Motor*, *Motorsport*, *Motor Trend*, *Quattroroute*, *Performance Car*, *Road Test*, *Speed Age*, *Sports Car Graphic*, *Sports Car Illustrated*, *Sports Car International*. To supplement these publications, the Brooklands series of article reprints were a valuable source.

Alfieri, Bruno (editor). *Ferrari America Superamerica Superfast*. Milan: Automobila, 1996.

—. *Giugiaro Ital Design*. Milan: Automobilia, 1987.

—. *Pininfarina Catalogue Raisonne*. Milan: Automobilia, 1990.

Anderloni, Carlo Felice Bianchi; Anselmi, Angelo Tito. *Carrozzeria Touring*. Rome: Ediztione Autocritica, 1982.

—. Moretti, Valerio. *Ferrari 166 MM Barchetta*. Milan: Automobilia, 1991.

Anselmi, Angelo Tito. *Alfa Romeo 6C 2500*. Mazzo di Rho: EditorialeDomus, 1993.

—. *Automobili Fiat*. Milan: Libreria dell'Autombile, 1986.

—. *Le Ferrari di Pininfarina*. Edizioni Graifche Mazzucchelli SpA, 1988.

— (editor). *Tipo 166 The Original Sports Ferrari*. Sparkford: Haynes Publishing Group, 1985.

Automobile Quarterly (editors). *The American Car since 1775*. Kutztown: Kutztown Publishing Co., 1971.

Automobili Lamborghini. *Automobili Lamborghini Yearbook*. Sant' Agata: Automobili Lamborghini, 1989-1994.

Automobilia. Carrozzeria Italiana: *Advancing the Art and Science of Automobile Design*. Milan: Automobila, 1980.

Baldwin, Nick; Georgano, G. N.; Sedgwick, Michael; Laban, Brian. *The World Guide to Automobile Manufacturers*. London: Macdonald & Co., Ltd., 1987.

Balestra, Nino; De Agostini, Cesare. *Cisitalia Catalogue Raisonne*. Milan: Automobilia, 1991.

Baselt, Randall. *Ferrari Brochures and Sales Literature 1968-1989*. Foster City: Via Emilia Publications, 1991.

Bellu, Serge. *Guida All'Identificazione Ferrari*. Milan: Gorgio Nada Editore, 1992.

—. *Lamborghini Le Grande GT all'Italiana*. Milan: Giorgio Nada Editore, 1988.

Benson, Joe. *Illustrated Alfa Romeo Buyer's Guide*. Osceola, WI: MBI Publishing Company, 1992.

Bersani, Alberto; Fissore, Paolo. *Dal Disegno al Design*. Ivrea: Pruili & Verlucca, 1999.

—. Costantino; Augusto. *Il Salone dell'Automobile dal Valentino al Lingotto*. Turin: Daniela Piazza Editore, 1985.

Bluemel, Keith. *Original Ferrari V8*. Bideford: Bay View Books/MBI, 1997.

Boccafolgi, Roberto. *Ferrari Century*. Milan: SEP Editrice, 1997.

Borel, Jean-Marc. *Lamborghini*. Sant'Agata: Nuova Automobili Ferruccio Lamborghini SpA, 1981.

Braden, Pat; Roush, Gerald. *Ferrari 365 GTB/4 Daytona*. London: Osprey Publishing Ltd., 1982.

Breslauer, Ken. *Sebring The Official History of America's Great Sports Car Race*. Cambridge: David Bull Publishing, 1995.

Burgess-Wise, David. *Ghia Ford's Carrozzeria*. London: Soprey Publishing Ltd., 1985.

Cancellieri, Gianni (editor). *Maserati Catalogue Raisonne*. Milan: Automobilia, 1984.

Candini, Dante; Manicardi, Nunzia. *Stanguellini l'artigiano automobilistico modenese*. Modena: Edizioni il Fiorino, 1998.

—. De Agostini, Ceare. *Polvere e Gloria*. Milan: Giorgio Nada Editore, 2000.

Car Styling. *Bertone: Car Styling Special Number 19*. Tokyo: Car Styling Publishing Co., 1977.

—. *Giugiaro & Italdesign*. Tokyo: Car Styling Publishing Co., 1981.

Casucci, Piero. *Chiti Grand Prix*. Milan: Automobilia, 1987.

—. *Enzo Ferrari 50 Years of Motoring*. Milan: Arnoldo Mondadori Editore, 1980.

Ciferri, Luca. *Italdesign Thirty Years on the Road*. Turin: Formagrafica sas, 1998.

Cimarosti, Adriano. *Carrera Panamericana Mexico*. Milan: Automobilia, 1987.

Clarke, R. M. *Abarth Gold Portfolio 1950-1971*. Surrey: Brooklands Books Ltd.

—. *De Tomaso Collection No. 1*. Surrey: Brooklands Books Ltd.

—. *Ferrari cars 1946-1956*. Surrey: Brooklands Books Ltd.

—. *Ferrari 1947-1957 Limited Edition*. Surrey: Brooklands Books Ltd.

—. *Ferrari cars 1957-1962*. Surrey: Brooklands Books Ltd.

—. *Ferrari 1958-1963 Limited Edition*. Surrey: Brooklands Books Ltd.

—. *Ferrari cars 1962-1966*. Surrey: Brooklands Books Ltd.

—. *Ferrari Dino 1965-1974*. Surrey: Brooklands Books Ltd.

—. *Ferrari cars 1966-1969*. Surrey: Brooklands Books Ltd.

—. *Ferrari cars 1969-1973*. Surrey: Brooklands Books Ltd.

—. *Ferrari cars 1973-1977*. Surrey: Brooklands Books Ltd.

—. *Ferrari Collection No. 1*. Surrey: Brooklands Books Ltd.

—. *Ferrari Dino 308 & Mondial Gold Protfolio 1974-1985*. Surrey: Brooklands Books Ltd.

—. *Ferrari 328, 348 & Mondial Gold Portfolio 1986-1994*. Surrey: Brooklands Books Ltd.

—. *Ferrari 328, 348 Mondial Ultimate Portfolio 1986-1994*. Surrey: Brooklands Books Ltd.

—. *Fiat-Pininfarina 124 & 2000 Spider 1968-1985*. Surrey: Brooklands Books Ltd.

—. *Lamborghini Cars 1964-1970*. Surrey: Brooklands Books Ltd.

—. *Lamborghini Cars 1970-1975*. Surrey: Brooklands Books Ltd.

—. *Lamborghini Countach 1971-1982*. Surrey: Brooklands Books Ltd.

—. *Lamborghini Countach and Urraco 1974-1980*. Surrey: Brooklands Books Ltd.

—. *Lamborghini Countach and Jalpa 1980-1985*. Surrey: Brooklands Books Ltd.

—. *Lancia Stratos 1972-1985*. Surrey: Brooklands Books Ltd.

—. *Maserati 1965-1970*. Surrey: Brooklands Books Ltd.

—. *Pantera & Mangusta 1969-1974*. Surrey: Brooklands Books Ltd.

—. *Pantera 1970-1973*. Surrey: Brooklands Books Ltd.

—. *Pantera Gold Portfolio 1970-1989*. Surrey: Brooklands Books Ltd.

Colombo, Gioachino. *Origins of the Ferrari Legend*. Yeovil: Haynes Publishing Group, 1987.

Coltrin, Peter; Marchet, Jean-Francis. *Lamborghini Miura*. London: Osprey Publishing Ltd., 1982.

Cornil, Etienne. *Ferrari by Pininfarina*. Milan: Giorgio Nada Editore, 1998.

Consumers Guide (auto editors); *Lamborghini*. Lincolnwood: Publications International, Ltd., 1991.

Cosentino, Alfred. *Abarth Guide*. Tokyo: Nigensha Publishing Co., Ltd., 1984.

Costantino, Augusto (editor). *Ferrari Catalogue Raisonne*. Milan: Automobilia, 1987.

Cristiani, Bettina; Alfieri, Ippolito (editors). *Lancia Catalogue Raisonne*. Milan: Automobilia, 1990.

Crump, Richard; De la Rive Box, Rob. *Maserati Road Cars*. London: Osprey Publishing Ltd., 1979.

—. *Maserati Sports, Racing & GT Cars 1926-1975*. Sparkford: GT Foulis & Co. Ltd., 1975.

Cutter, Robert; Fendell, Bob. *The Encyclopedia of Auto Racing Greats*. Englewood Cliffs, NJ: Prentice-Hall, Inc., 1973.

D'Amico, Stefano; Tabucchi, Maurizio. *Alfa Romeo Production Cars 1910-1996*. Milan: Giorgio Nada Editore, 1996.

De la Rive Box, Rob; Crump, Richard. *The Automotive Art of Bertone*. Sparkford: Haynes Publishing Group, 1984.

—. *Lamborghini The Cars from Sant' Agata*. London: Osprey Publishing Ltd., 1981.

—. Stone, Matt. *Illustrated Pantera Buyers Guide*. Osceola, WI: MBI Publishing Company, 1991.

Deschenaux, Claude-Michele (editor). *Marlboro Grand Prix Guide 1950-92*. Marlboro, 1993.

Dregni, Michael. *Inside Ferrari*. Osceola, WI: MBI Publishing Company, 1990.

Drexel, John (editor). *The Facts on File Encyclopedia of the 20th Century*. New York: Facts on File, Inc., 1991.

Eaton, Godfry. *The Complete Ferrari*. London: Cadogan Books Ltd., 1986.

Edita, S. A. *Annual Automobile Review*. Lausanne: Edita S.A. Numbers 1-3, 1953-1956.

—. Automobile Year. *Automobile Year*. Lausanne: Edita S.A. Numbers 4-21, 30, 32, 38, 1957-1974, 1982, 1984, 1990.

—. Moity, Christian. *The Le Mans 24-Hour Race*. Lausanne: Edita S.A., 1974.

Editoriale Domus. *All the Fiats 1899-1999*. Rho: Editoriale Domus, 1999.

Editrice Telesio. *Maranello*. Milan: Editrice Telesio, 1996.

Ettore Bugatti s.r.l, *Ettore Bugatti*. Ora: Ettore Bugatti s.r.l., Numbers 0-2, 1990-1991.

Felicioli, Riccardo. *Lancia L'armonia e l'invenzione*. Milan: Alessandra Chiti, 1996.

Ferrari, Aldo. *Maserati From Origins to Biturbo*. Modena: Edizioni Rebecchi Modena,1985.

Ferrari, Enzo. *Una Vita Per L'Automobile*. San Lazzaro di Savena: Conti Editore SpA, 1998.

Ferrari SpA. *F50*. Modena: Ferrari SpA, 1995.

Fissore, Paolo. *Carrozzeria Fissore*. Milan: Giorgio Nada Editore s.r.l., 1991.

Fitzgerald, Warren; Merritt, Richard; Thompson, Jonathan. *Ferrari The Sports and Gran Turismo Cars*. New York: W. W. Norton & Company, Inc., 1979.

Foresti, Fabio; Facchinato, Daniela. *La Fucina del Toro*. Bologna: GEM s.r.l., 1993.

Forstick, Michael. *Pinin Farina Master Coachbuilder*. London: Dalton Watson Ltd., 1977.

Gabriel, Jean-Pierre. *Dino Le altre Ferrari*. Milan: Giorgio Nada Editore, 1989.

Gauld, Graham. *Modena Racing Memories*. Osceola, WI: MBI Publishing Company, 1999.

Georgano, G. N. (editor). *The New Encyclopedia of Automobiles 1885 to the Present*. New York: Crescent Books, 1986.

Giacosa, Dante. *Forty Years of Design with Fiat*. Milan: Automobila, 1979.

Giorgio Nada Editore. *Ferrari 1947-1997*. Milan: Giorgio Nada Editore, 1997.

—. *Mille Miglia 1947-1957*. Milan: Giorgio Nada Editore, 1997.

Goodfellow, Winston. *ISORIVOLTA The Men The Machines*. Milan: Giorgio Nada Editore, 1995.

Grayson, Stan (editor). *Ferrari The Man The Machines*. Princeton: Princeton Publishing, Inc., 1975.

Greggio, Luciano. *Bertone*. Milan: Giorgio Nada Editore s.r.l., 1992.

Hallwig S.A. *Illustrierte Automobil Revue*. Bern: Hallwig S.A., 1952-1957.

Halbertsam, David. *The Reckoning*. New York: William Morrow and Company, Inc., 1986.

Henry, Alan. *Ferrari Dino 246, 308 and 328*. Croydon: Motor Racing Publications, Ltd., 1996.

Higham, Peter. *The Guinness Guide to International Motor Racing*. Enfield: Guinness Publishing, 1995.

Jenkinson, Denis. *Sports Car Racing*. Lausanne: Edita S.A., 1982.

Lawrence, Mike. *AZ of Sports Cars since 1945*. Bideford: Bay View Books/MBI, 1991.

L'Editrice dell'Automobile. *World Car Catalogue*. Rome: L'Editrice dell'Automobile, 1962-1971.

—. *World Cars*. Rome: L'Editrice dell'Automobile, 1972-1985.

Lewis, Peter. *Alf Francis Racing Mechanic*. Yeovil: GT Foulis & Co. Ltd., 1957.

Logoz, Arthur (editor). *Auto Parade*. Philadelphia: Chilton Company. Volumes 2-6, 1959-1963.

Luranni, Giovanni. *La Storia Della Mille Miglia*. Novara: Istituto Geografico De Agostini, 1979.

Lyons, Pete. *The Complete Book of Lamborghini*. Lincolnwood: Publications International Ltd., 1988.

Marchet, Jean-Francois; Peter Coltrin. *Lamborghini Countach*. London: Osprey Publishing Ltd., 1986.

—. *Lamborghini Urraco and the V8s*. London: Osprey Publishing Ltd., 1983.

Marchiano, Michele. *Le Zagato Fiat 8VZ & Alfa 1900 SSZ*. Milan: Libreria dell'Automobile, 1987.

—. *Zagato*. Milan: Automobilia, 1984.

—. *Zagato: Seventy Years in the Fast Lane*. Milan: Giorgio Nada Editore, 1989.

Marzotto, Giannino. *Le Ferrari alla Mille Miglia*. Rome: Edizione di Autocritica, 1987.

Maserati SpA. *Maserati in Pista e su Strada*. Modena: Maserati SpA, 1991.

Massini, Marcel. *Ferrari by Vignale*. Milan: Giorgio Nada Editore, 1993.

Merritt, Richard. *Ferrari Brochures and Sales Literature 1946-1967*. Scarsdale: John W. Barnes Jr. Publishing, Inc., 1976.

Miller, Peter. *Conte Maggi's Mille Miglia*. New York: St. Martin's Press, 1988.

Minerbi, Marcello. *Alfa Romeo-Zagato SZ TZ*. Brescia: La Mille Migla Editrice, 1985.

Miska, Kurt. *The Berlinetta Lusso A Ferrari of Unusual Elegance*. Scarsdale: John W. Barnes Jr. Publishing, Inc., 1978.

Moretti, Valerio. *Ghia Catalogue Raisonne*. Milan: Automobilia. 1991.

Morris, Mike. *Fiat Dino Ferrari by Another Name*. Oxfordshire: Bookmarque Publishing, 1989.

Nixon, Chris. *Mon Ami Mate*. Isleworth: Transport Bookman Publications, 1991.

Nowak, Stanley. *Ferrari on the Road*. Belton: Dalton Watson Books, 1993.

—. Carrick, George; Gilberton, Ed. *Ferrari Spyder California*. Milan: Automobilia, 1990.

Oleski, Frank. *World Sports Cars Series-Built from 1945-1980*. Basel: Motor Classic Verlag, 1987.

Orefici, Oscar. *Carlo Chiti: Sinfonia Ruggente*. Rome: Autocritica Edizioni s.r.l., 1991.

Orsini, Luigi; Zagari, Franco. *Maserati*. Milan: Libreria dell'Automobile, 1980.

—. *OSCA La Rivincita dei Maserati*. Milan: Giorgio Nada Editore, 1989.

Pascal, Dominique. *Ferraris at Le Mans*. Yeovil: Haynes Publishing Group, 1986.

Pasini, Stefano. *Famous Car Factories Lamborghini*. Gothenburg: AB Nordbok, 1991.

Pellegrini, Daniele (editor). *Rivista Maserati*. Milan: Giorgio Nada Editore. Numbers 1-2, 1998-1999.

—. *Lamborghini Catalogue Raisonne*. Milan: Automobilia, 1998.

Piatti, Roberto. *Alfa Romeo S.Z.* Milan: Giorgio Nada Editore, 1989.

Picard, Jean-Rodolphe. *Dream Cars*. Lausanne: Edita S.A., 1981.

Pininfarina, Battista; Caballo, Ernesto. *Pininfarina Born with the Automobile*. Milan: Automobilia, 1993.

Pininfarina Public Relations Office. *Pininfarina Since 1930*. Turin: Pininfarina, 1981.

Porsche, Ferry. *Cars Are My Life*. Wellingborough: Patrick Stephens Limited, 1989.

Pourret, Jess. *The Ferrari Legend 250 GT Competition*. Scarsdale: John W. Barnes Jr. Publishing, Inc., 1977.

Prunet, Antoine. *The Ferrari Legend: The Road Cars*. Paris: Editions E.P.A., 1980.

Puttini, Sergio (editor). *Carrozzeria Boneschi*. Milan: Giorgio Nada Editore s.r.l., 1989.

Rancati, Gino. *Ferrari A Memory*. Osceola, WI: MBI Publishing Company, 1989.

Robson, Graham. *European Sports & GT Cars from 1961*. Yeovil: Haynes Publishing Group, 1980.

—. *Fiat Sports Cars*. London: Osprey Publishing Ltd., 1984.

Rogliatti, Gianni. *Maranello Ferrari e La Sua Gente*. Maranello: Puntografico SpA.

Routeclassiche Libri. *Ferrari Che Gente*. Milan: Editoriale Internazionale Milano, 1996.

—. *Ferrari Che Macchine*. Milan: Editoriale Internazionale Milano, 1996.

Ruberi, Mario. *Moretti*. Turin: Tipografia Egizia, Turin.

Sinek, Jeremy (editor). *Supercars The World's Finest Performance Automobiles*. Northbrook: Domus Books, 1979.

Small, Steve. *The Guinness Complete Grand Prix Who's Who*. Enfield: Guinness Publishing, 1994.

Stanguellini SpA. *Stanguellini*. Modena: Stanguellini SpA, 1995.

Style Auto Editrice s.n.c. *Style Auto*. Milan: Style Auto Editrice s.n.c. Volumes 1-36, 1962-1978.

Tanner, Hans. *Ferrari*. London: G.T. Foulis & Co., Ltd. 1968.

Temple Press Books Ltd. *The Motor Road Tests*. London: Temple Press Books, Ltd., 1951-1970, 1981.

Tipler, John. *The World's Great Automobile Stylists*. London: Apple Press, 1990.

Transport Motor Books. *Lamborghini Countach, Urraco, Jalpa, 002, Diablo*. Ipswich: Transport Source Books.

—. *Lancia Aurelia, Flaminia, and Appia*. Ipswich: Transport Source Books.

Trow, Nigel. *Lancia Stratos*. London: Osprey Publishing Ltd., 1990.

Unique Motor Books. *Alfa Romeo 1300-1600-1750*. Hockley: Unique Motor Books.

—. *Ferrari Cars 1949-1963*. Hockley: Unique Motor Books.

—. *Ferrari F355, 360, 456, 550*. Hockley: Unique Motor Books.

Varisco, Franco. *Nardi A Story of Cars and Steering Wheels*. Milan: Libreria dell' Automobile, 1987.

—. *815 The Genesis of Ferrari*. London: Hyde Park Group, 1990.

Wimpffen, Janos. *Time and Two Seats Five Decades of Long Distance Racing*. Redmond: Motorsport Research Group, 1999.

Wise, David Burgess. *The New Illustrated Encyclopedia of Automobiles*. Edison: Wellfleet Press, 1994.

Wood, Jonathan. *Great Marques of Italy*. London: Octopus Books Limited, 1987.

Wyss, Wallace. *De Tomaso Automobiles*. London: Osprey Publishing, 1981.

Yates, Brock. *Enzo Ferrari The Man, The Cars, The Races*. New York: Doubleday, 1991.

Yergin, Daniel. *The Prize*. New York: Touchstone, 1992.

Appendices

Appendix A: Sigificant Postwar Sportscar Manufacturers and Models

The following is a list of Italy's notable postwar sports car manufacturers and their significant models; by no means is this inclusive of all of the country's constructors, or its sports and GT cars.

Each entry starts with the years of the company's existence, its location, and a brief overview of its history.

The significant street models are listed chronologically by date of introduction; sometimes this date was several years before production began. For example (and an extreme one at that), Alfa's Montreal was first shown in 1967, but production did not begin until 1971. The second date is when production finished. When known, the total number built is listed.

As most of the companies had additional models, the reader is encouraged to contact specific marque club(s), reference book(s) included in the Bibliography, and visit prevalent web sites.

Abarth

1950–present; Turin. Carlo Abarth first started with Cisitalia in 1947, then formed his own company when Cisitalia encountered financial difficulties. Although his start was modest, over the next two decades Abarth would produce a dizzying and seemingly never-ending array of sports and racing cars. His machines scored countless class victories around the world. Abarth also had a prosperous performance parts business. In 1971 he sold his company to Fiat. The name is still used by Fiat to signify a high-performance version of a production car.

- 205A (1950–51; 3)
- 207A (1955; 12)
- 750 Zagato "Double Bubble" (1956– c. 1960; unknown)

Alfa Romeo

1910-present; Milan. Italy's oldest sports car manufacturer is among its most famous. The company first produced both touring and competition cars, and won a number of endurance and grand prix world championships prior to the war. After winning the Formula 1 world championship in 1951, the company withdrew from F1 competition for 28 years. Since the mid-1970s, Alfa has concentrated primarily on the production of mass-produced street cars. Currently, the company is owned by Fiat.

- 1900 C Sprint/1900 Super Sprint (1951–54/1954–58; 657/1,136)
- 1900 SSZ (1954–1958; 39)
- Giulietta Sprint/Sprint Veloce (1954–65/1956–63; 24,084/3,058)
- Giulietta Spyder/Spyder Veloce (1955–62/1956–62; 14,300/2,796)
- Giulietta Sprint Speciale (1957–62; 1,251)
- 2000 Spyder (1958–61; 3,459)
- Giulietta SZ (Round Tail) (1959–61; 169)
- Giulia Sprint (1962–63; 6,998)
- Giulia Spyder/Spyder Veloce (1962–65/1964–65; 9,256/1,092)
- 2600 Sprint (Coupe) (1962–66; 6,998)
- 2600 Spider (1962–65; 2,257)
- 2600 SZ (1963–1968; 103)
- Giulia Sprint Speciale (1963–66; 1,377)
- Giulia Sprint GT (1963–66; 22,671)
- 1300 & 1600 GT Jr. (1966–75; 106,352)
- 1600 Spider (Duetto) (1966–1967; 6,325)
- 1750 Spider Veloce/2000 Spider Veloce (1967–71/1971–93; 4,674/98,463)
- 1750 GTV/2000 GTV (1968–72/1971–75; 47,512/32,288)

- 33 Stradale (1967–1969; 18)
- Junior Zagato 1300/1600 (1970–1975/1972–1975; 1,108/402)
- Montreal (1967–77; 3,925)
- Alfetta GT/GTV 2000/GTV 6 (1974–76/1976–85/1980–86; 21,948/75,022/22,381)
- SZ (ES30) & RZ (1989–91/1992–93; 1,035/241)
- GTV (1994; still in production)
- Spider (1994; still in production)

ASA

1961–1967; Milan. ASA was born from Enzo Ferrari's desire to produce a small, four-cylinder GT. The engine was first shown in 1959 and, after approaching a number of parties to back the project, Ferrari sold the rights to produce it to Milan's wealthy De Nora family. To boost its exposure, ASA supplemented its street car production with a handful of competition cars.
- 1000 GT (1961–66; approximately 40)
- 1000 GT Spider (1963–66; approximately 10)

ATS

1962–1964; Pontecchio Marconi (Bologna). ATS was a direct result of the infamous Ferrari "Walkout" of 1961. The company attempted to emulate Ferrari by making a Formula 1 race car, and the 2500 GT. The F1 effort proved to be a disaster, as bad as the road car was good.
- 2500 GT/GTS (1963–64; approximately 8)

Bizzarrini

1965–1969; Livorno. Giotto Bizzarrini was the father of Ferrari's famed 250 GTO endurance racer, and the man behind the company that bore his name. After leaving Ferrari, he worked with a number of manufacturers, including Iso. When his consulting and manufacturing agreement with Iso ended in 1965, he continued producing cars under his own name. Almost all Bizzarrinis used Chevrolet Corvette engines.
- Strada 5300/GT America 5300 (1965–69; 139; this figure includes approximately 25 Iso Grifo A3 and A3/C)
- GT1900 Europa (1966–69; approximately 12)

Bugatti

c. 1989–1995; Campogalliano (Modena). The Bugatti renaissance was the dream of Romano Artioli, a successful Italian entreprenuer. Artioli desired to re-create the ambiance and technical excellence of the world's most famous prewar marque. The resulting factory was unlike any other, and the mid-engine, V-12, powered EB110 was likely the world's most sophisticated street car when it was introduced.
- EB110 (1991–95; approximately 140, this figure includes the EB110 SS)

Cisitalia

1945–1965; Turin. The car that truly captivated Italy immediately following the war was Piero Dusio's Cisitalia. The prominent industrialist's company first manufactured successful single-seat and competition racers that used Fiat-based mechanicals. Yet, Cisitalia's most famous model was the seminal 202 by Pinin Farina, the starting point for all subsequent postwar fastback designs; one resides in New York's Museum of Modern Art. Although the Cisitalia name survived into the mid-1960s, its most dynamic years were 1945–1952.
- 202 Coupe (1947–52; 153)
- 202 Cabriolet (1947–52; 17)

Cizeta

c. 1987–1992; Modena. Cizeta was the dream of Claudio Zampolli, a former Lamborghini employee who was a fixture in the southern California exotic car scene. The car was renowned for being the first to use a V-16 since the 1930s.
- V16T (1989–22; 7)

De Tomaso

1959–present; Modena. De Tomaso was founded by ex-pat Argentinean Alessandro De Tomaso. For the first several years, the company made Formula Jr. and Formula 2 cars, then graduated to street car production in 1963/64. De Tomasos often have sensational styling, and primarily use American V-8s. In addition to its midengine cars De Tomaso also manufactured a luxurious sedan, and a 2+2.
- Vallelunga (1963–67; approximately 55)
- Mangusta (1967–71; 401)
- Pantera (1971–94; approximately 8,000)

Ferrari

1947–present; Maranello. The most famous of Italy's (and likely the world's) sports car manufacturers is Ferrari. Named after Enzo Ferrari, the firm is the only concern that has participated in every postwar Formula 1 race, where it has won nine constructors' championships, and nine driver's championships. From 1949 to 1967, Ferrari gained even greater fame in endurance racing, when it won 12 world championships and dominated Le Mans. This had great rub off on its street cars, which are recognized for their performance, style, and engineering. A number of the firm's models were true "dual-purpose"cars—those that could be driven to a race, compete (and often win), and then driven home. In 1969, Enzo Ferrari sold 50% of the company to Fiat. Upon his death in 1988, Fiat purchased another 40%. Today, Ferrari remains the benchmark for all other sports car manufacturers.
- 166 MM Barchetta (1948–53; 25)
- 250 Europa (1953–54; 20)
- 250 GT Cabriolet (1957–62; 241)
- 250 Spider California (1958–63; 104; includes both long-wheelbase, short-wheelbase, and aluminum competition cars)
- 250 GT (1958–60; 350)
- 250 SWB (1959–62; 165)
- 250 GTE 2+2 (1960–63; 955)
- 275 GTB (1964–66; 440)
- 275 GTB/4 (1966–68; 330)
- 330 GTC & GTS (1966–68; 600/100)
- 206 GT (Dino) (1966–69; 154)
- 246 GT/GTS (Dino) (1969–73; 2,487/1972–74; 1,274)
- 365 GTB/4 "Daytona" (1968–74; 1,383)
- 365 GTS/4 "Daytona Spider" (1969–74; 121)
- 365/512/512BBi "Berlinetta Boxer" (1971–84; 387/929/1,007)
- 308 GT4 (1973–80; 2,824)
- 308 GTB/GTS (1975–80/1977–80; 2,897/3,219; both models continued into 1985 with fuel-injected engines)
- Testarossa (1984–91; 7,177)
- 288 GTO (1984–86; 272)
- 328 GTB/GTS (1985–89; 1,344/6,068)
- F40 (1987–92; 1,315)
- 348 tb/ts/Spider (1989–94/1989–94/1993–95; 2,895/4,230/1,090)
- 456 GT/GTA/GTM (1992/1994/1997; still in production)
- 355 GTB/GTS/Spyder/F1 (1994–99/1994–99/1995-99/1997–99; 3,938/2,048/2,663/2,624)
- F50 (1995–97; 349)
- 550 Maranello (1996; still in production)
- 360 Modena (1999; still in production)
- 360 Modena Spider (2000; still in production)

Fiat

1899–present; Turin. Fiat is the largest of Italy's industrial concerns, and has such economic clout that many consider Turin (population, 1.1+ million) to be a "company town." While Fiat is most famous for its manufacture of economy cars and family sedans, its sports car heritage can be traced back to its earliest days when the firm frequently (and successfully) participated in international competition. Almost all its postwar sports cars have mechanicals based upon its mainstream offerings, and a number of smaller manufacturer's existence depended on the availability of Fiat components. Today, the company is 20% owned by America's General Motors.

- 8V (1952–55; 114; this figure includes all custom coachwork versions)
- 1200/1500/1600S (1959–63/1960–66/1960–66; 11,851/20,420/2,275)
- 2300S (1961–68; unknown)
- 850 Coupe & Spyder (1965–73; 342,873/124,660)
- 124/2000 Spider (1965–86; approximately 130,000 for all versions)
- Dino Coupe and Spider 2000 & 2400 (2 Liter: 1965–69; 3,670 coupes, 1,163 spiders/2.4 liter: 1969–73; 2,398 coupes; 420 spiders)
- X1/9 (1972–89; approximately 180,000)
- Barchetta; (1994; still in production)
- Coupe (1994; still in production)

Intermeccanica

1959–1975; Turin. Frank Reisner's Intermeccanica started in a fashion similar to a number of other Italian manufacturers: constructing performance kits. After building the dimutive Imp, Reisner teamed with Apollo out of California, making the American-powered GT's coachwork and interior. This set the formula for Intermeccanica's own cars: sleek Italian bodies and chassis, powered by reliable V-8 engines. After Intermeccanica went under during the oil crisis, Reisner moved to America, and had success for a number of years making replica Porsche Speedsters.

- Griffith/Omega/Torino/Italia (1966–71; approximately 500)
- Indra Coupe/Convertible/2+2 (1971–74; 125 in total)

Iso

1962–1974; Milan. After the War, Iso patriarch Renzo Rivolta made a fortune in motorscooter and motorcycle production, and licensing the production of his Isetta bubblecar. He decided to enter the sports/GT world by offering Ferrari looks and performance combined with American reliability. The result was likely the best and most refined of all American-powered GTs, thanks in great part to its proprietary steel platform chassis. Iso saw some success in endurance racing in 1964-65, and competed in F1 for two seasons in the early 1970s. After the Rivolta family sold out to an American financier in 1973, the company was another casualty of the oil crisis, and closed its doors in late 1974. An attempt to revive the marque in 1990 proved stillborn.

- Rivolta GT 2+2 (1962–70; 801)
- Grifo (1963–74; 322, all models with Chevrolet small blocks and Ford V-8s)
- Grifo 7 Liter/Can Am (1968–70/1970-1972; 66/24)
- Varedo (1972; 1)

Isotta-Fraschini

1900–1949; Milan. Isotta-Fraschini began as a partnership between Cesare Isotta and Vincenzo Fraschini. Although the firm was better known for its luxury cars, it was one of Italy's sports car pioneers. An attempt to ressuscitate the marque immediately following World War II saw several intriguing, avant-garde GT and four door prototypes, but no production. In the late 1990s, the name was once again revived, this time outside of Turin. Like the effort five decades earlier, only a handful of cars were made before the firm went under.

- Monterosa 8C (1948–49; approximately 5)

Lamborghini

1963–present; Sant' Agata Bolognese (Bologna). Ferruccio Lamborghini was an immensely successful tractor and air conditioning manufacturer who decided to start producing his own GT car in the heady days of the early 1960s. His target was obviously

Ferrari, for anything Enzo did on the street, Lamborghini was determined to do better. His first V-12s featured four cams when Ferrari's cars only had two, and he beat Ferrari's first midengine offering (the six-cylinder Dino) to market by two years with the 12-cylinder Miura. After Ferruccio sold his remaining interest in the company in 1974, the firm encountered only brief periods of financial stability, drifting from one owner to another. Such uncertainty disappeared in 1998 when Germany's Volkswagen AG purchased the firm.

- 350 GT (1964–67; 120)
- Miura (1966–72; 765)
- Espada (1968–78; 1,223)
- Urraco (all models) (1970–79; 791)
- Countach (all models) (1971–90; approximately 1,969)
- Diablo (1990; still in production)

Lancia

1906-present; Turin. The company is named after its founder, Vincenzo Lancia. For decades, the firm's products were known for their engineering excellence and sterling build quality, not surprising since Lancia was a test driver and racer during Fiat's earliest years. The Lancia family owned the company until 1955, at which time it was sold to Italian industrialist Carlo Presenti. He owned Lancia for 14 years, then sold it to Fiat. Lancia successfully competed in Formula 1 in the mid-1950s, and produced a number of world rally championship cars in the 1970s and 1980s. Today, the company remains a Fiat subsidiary.

- Aurelia B20GT/2500 GT (all series) (1951–57; 3,111)
- Aurelia B24 Spyder/Convertible (1955–58; 240/521)
- Appia Coupe, Convertible & Sport (1957–62; 3,884 for all models)
- Flavia Sport (1962–67; 640)
- Flavia Convertible (1962–69; 1,644)
- Flaminia GT & GTL (1959–67; 2,068)
- Flaminia Convertible (all variations, including 3C) (1959–67; 847)
- Flaminia Sport & Supersport (1959–67; 599)
- Fulvia Coupe (includes all types of Rallye, HF, Montecarlo and Safari) (1965–76; 139,799)
- Fulvia Sport & Fulvia Sport S (1965–73; 8,102)
- Stratos (1971–75; 492)
- Beta Montecarlo (1975-84; 7,595)
- 037 Rally (1982–83; 200)

LMX

1968–1972; Milan. LMX was formed by Italo-Argentinean Michel Liprandi, a specialist in fiberglass construction. His Sirex models used a proprietary spine chassis, and Ford V-6 engines that had a supercharger and turbocharger options. The Sirex was a basic, front engine sports car, rather than a refined GT.

- Sirex coupe & spider (1970–72; estimated 25–40 in total)

Maserati

1926–present; Modena. Maserati is one of the most revered names in Italy's competition and sports car history. The company was founded in 1926 by the Maserati brothers in Bologna. After primarily producing race cars for ten years, they sold the firm to Modenese industrialist Adolfo Orsi. Maserati competed in Formula 1 and endurance racing through 1957, winning the F1 championship that year, and narrowly missing the endurance crown. From 1958 to 1980, the firm concentrated on performance GTs that were typically more luxurious than their Ferrari and Lamborghini counterparts. Through much of the 1980s and 1990s, Maserati strayed from its GT roots, making the mass-produced Biturbo and 425/430 models, and their derivatives. Today, the company is owned by former crosstown rival Ferrari, and has returned to its GT heritage with its current model lineup.

- A6 (1946–50; 61)
- A6GCS/53 (1953–55; 52; this figure includes competition and street cars)

- A6G/54 (1954–57; 60)
- 3500 GT coupe & spyder (1957–64/1959–64; 1,972/242)
- 5000 GT (1959-65; 34)
- Mistral coupe & spyder (1963–70/1964–70; 828/120)
- Ghibli coupe & spyder (1966-73/1969–73; 1,149/125; these figures include the SS models)
- Bora (1971–79; 495)
- Merak/Merak SS/Merak 2000 (1972-80; approximately 1,535)
- 3200 GT (1998; still in production)

Moretti

1927–present; Turin. Giovanni Moretti's company initially concentrated on motorcycle production, then small vans and cars. In 1945, Moretti began producing sportier offerings that featured proprietary styling and small-displacement engines. By the mid-1950s, the company supplemented its sports and racing car production with a small sedan and station wagon. Moretti signed a contract with Fiat in the late 1950s/early 1960s, and has acted as a coachbuilder since that time, making sports cars and other vehicles on Fiat platforms.
- 750 Berlinetta (c. 1953–c. 1956; unknown)
- 750 Cabriolet (c. 1958–c. 1960; approximately 1,000)
- Sportiva (1967–69; unknown)

Nardi

1947–c. 1963; Turin. Enrico Nardi was a famous test driver and racer prior to World War II. In 1947 he teamed with Renato Danese to form Nardi & Danesi, and they began producing small displacement competition cars. Nardi took control of the firm in 1950, and produced a number of interesting cars into the early 1960s, with most being one-offs. Nardi gained considerably more fame as a tuner and constructor of steering wheels, with the latter item being used by Ferrari, Iso, and a number of other manufacturers.
- 2500 (1949; 1)
- Blue Ray (1955; 1)

OSCA

1947–1966; Bologna. When Adolfo Orsi bought Maserati in 1937, the Maserati brothers signed a ten-year contract that tied them to the company. In 1947 they returned to their home-town of Bologna, and formed OSCA. The company specialized in four-cylinder competition cars, using proprietary engines and chassis. OSCA also made a number of cars for the street, using the competition machines as their base. In September 1963 the brothers sold the firm to motorcycle manufacturer MV Agusta. Although OSCAs were built for three more years, these Fiat-based specials bore little resemblance to their ancestors.
- MT4 (1948–56; 78—the most famous were the Morelli-bodied spiders constructed from 1953 to 1956; 25)
- 1600 GTS (1960–63; 128 in total)

Pagani

1998–present, San Cesario sul Panaro (Modena). This company is an off-shoot of Horacio Pagani's Modena Design carbon fiber and composites manufacturing concern. The firm produces exclusive Mercedes-Benz V-12 powered midengine supercars that represent Horacio Pagani's singular vision. Other than the engine, Pagani designs and builds most everything in-house.
- Zonda C12/C12S (1999/2000; still in production)

Qvale Modena

1999–present; Modena. California's Qvale family used to own England's Jensen, and has six decades of experience in constructing, distributing, and selling sports and performance cars. In 1998 they entered into an agreement with De Tomaso to produce the Mangusta, a front-engine machine that was originally called the Bigua. In April 2000 they ended their relationship with De Tomaso, and are selling cars under their own name. Qvale Modena's products use a proprietary chassis and Ford engines.
- Mangusta (1999; still in production)

Scaglietti

1958–1960; Modena. Sergio Scaglietti is best known as an extraordinary coachbuilder for Ferrari; his machines include a number of world champion endurance racers, and masterpieces for the street. In 1958, Scaglietti was approached by American Gary Laughlin to design and construct a small series of special-bodied Corvettes. By the time Laughlin received the first car, he had lost interest in the project. Today, Sergio Scaglietti is retired, while Carrozzeria Scaglietti is a wholly owned subsidiary of Fiat for Ferrari.
- Corvette (1958–60; 3)

Siata

1926–1970; Turin. Giorgio Ambrosini founded Siata to manufacture performance parts for Fiat and other makes. After World War II, the company began producing cars under its own name. These models typically used proprietary chassis, and a modified Fiat drivetrain and suspension. A number of the firm's offerings were successful as competition cars, particularly in America. After the company ran into financial trouble in the mid-1950s, subsequent models did not have the luster of the earlier cars.
- 1400 Gran Sport (1951–52; unknown)
- 208S (1952– c. 1955; approximately 100)

Stanguellini

1929–1965; Modena. Celso Stanguellini first entered the automotive field was as a Fiat dealer. The company began offering performance parts and modifications in the late 1920s, which led to the formation of its own racing team in the late 1930s. After the War, Stanguellini began modifying and rebodying Fiats to participate in Italy's burgeoning competition scene. The company also made a handful of sports cars, and had its greatest success in the late 1950s as a manufacturer of Formula Jr. single seaters.
- 750 Sport & 1100 Bialbero Sport (1953– c. 1957; unknown)

Appendix B: A Brief Guide to Italy's Postwar Designers, Engineers, Entrepreneurs, and Managers

Following are thumbnail sketches of a number of the major figures in Italy's postwar sports car universe. By no means is this list all-inclusive.

Some, such as Piero Dusio, were not on the scene for a long period of time. Since they had such an impact that the spotlight primarily focused on them, they are included here.

The listed engineers' contributions are obvious, and thus easy to quantify. The work of designers and stylists can be more hazy, and thus more difficult to ascertain. Yet, there is no question Italy's postwar sports cars were as well known (and perhaps better known) for their beautiful styling as much as they were for their engineering excellence. All one has to do is look at the industry today, for numerous designers continue to draw on those shapes Italy made 30+ years ago for inspiration and direction.

Carlo Abarth

1908-1979. Abarth was born in Vienna. Since his father was Italian, he became an Italian citizen in 1918. After a successful motorcycle-racing career in the 1920s and '30s, during the war he managed an engineering factory in Yugoslavia. After the war, he represented Porsche in Italy, then worked for Cisitalia in the late 1940s. He started his own company in 1950, and produced an incredible variety of competition machines, and street-going sports cars. He also had a successful performance parts business. In 1971 he sold his company to Fiat.

Gianni Agnelli

Born 1921. A native of Turin, Agnelli is the son of Fiat founder Giovanni Agnelli. He studied law, and learned the automotive industry by working closely with Vittorio Valletta. He became managing director of Fiat in 1963, then company president in 1966. Agnelli was intimately involved in Fiat's purchase of Ferrari in 1969. An avid auto enthusiast, over the years he has commissioned a number of one-off Ferraris. He remains one of the most powerful men in Italy.

Giulio Alfieri

Born 1924. Giulio Alfieri is one of Italy's most brilliant postwar engineers. The son of an accountant, he first worked for Innocenti and Lambretta, then joined Maserati in 1953. He became the company's chief engineer in the mid-1950s, and was responsible for its championship winning 250F, a number of its most memorable endurance racers, and its most famous GT models. He left the company in 1975, and soon found himself the president of Honda in Italy. In the late 1970s, he became Lamborghini's chief engineer, a position he held until 1988. He currently has his own electronics firm. Contrary to popular belief, he is not related to engineer Gian Paolo Dallara.

Carlo Felice Bianchi Anderloni

Born 1916. The son of Carrozzeria Touring co-founder Felice Bianchi Anderloni, Carlo Anderloni is one of Italy's most likable and respected figures. In 1948 he was thrown into the design hot seat when his father unexpectedly passed away. He responded to the challenge beautifully, for his first project was the immortal Ferrari 166 MM "Barchetta." His resume as diverse as it is impressive, with subsequent works including Alfa's famed Disco Volantes and Lamborghini's 350 GT. After Touring went under in the mid-1960s, Anderloni was a consultant for Alfa Romeo.

Romano Artioli

Born 1932. A true auto enthusiast, Artioli began a love affair with Bugatti in the early 1950s. He harbored a lifelong dream to bring the company back to life, something he was able to tackle in the late 1980s, thanks to his success as an auto dealer and importer. Although Bugatti was the center of Italy's performance car universe through much of the early 1990s, even Artioli's impressive financial resources were not enough, and the company declared bankruptcy in 1995. In the late 1990s, Artioli sold the Bugatti name to Volkswagen. He is still part owner of England's Lotus.

Giotto Bizzarrini

Born 1926. The son of a wealthy landowner in Livorno, Bizzarrini's name is associated with a number of Italy's great sports, racing, and GT cars. The fiery engineer-test driver started his career at Alfa Romeo, then went to Ferrari in 1957. Here, he had his hand in the 250 SWB and Testa Rossa, among others, and is widely recognized as father of the immortal 250 GTO. After the Ferrari "Walkout" in 1961, he consulted with Iso, ASA, and Lamborghini, for whom he designed the now-legendary V-12. From 1965 to 1969, he built a number of cars under his own name, then worked with America's AMC on its startling midengine AMX/3. He currently consults with Japanese motorcycle manufacturers, among other clients.

Nuccio Bertone

1914-1997. The son of Carrozzeria Bertone founder Giovanni Bertone, Nuccio was brought up in the coachbuilding business. He began working for the firm full time in the 1930s, then started managing it in the early 1950s. Thanks to his great business acumen, courage, and a keen sense of style, in less than a decade he transformed the company into one of Italy's preeminent coachbuilders. Further, his critical role in the Alfa Giulietta story was key to transforming the coachbuilding industry. Bertone was actively involved in the styling of his cars, and worked closely with three of his greatest "finds," designers Franco Scaglione, Giorgetto Giugiaro, and Marcello Gandini.

Carlo Chiti

1924-1994. Carlo Chiti's exuberance and imposing presence make him one of Italy's most memorable engineers. The son of a civil engineer, he started with Alfa Romeo in 1952 in its testing department, and was then lured to Ferrari in 1957. He was its chief engineer

from 1958 to 1961, where he designed and developed championship-winning Formula 1 and endurance racers. As one who left Ferrari in the Walkout in 1961, he was the linchpin of ATS. When ATS floundered in 1964, Chiti joined Autodelta, which was soon overseeing Alfa Romeo's return to sports car competition; here, he masterminded a number of Alfa's most memorable models. He remained with Alfa through 1984, then started his Motori Moderni firm that designed and constructed racing engines.

Gioachino Colombo

1903-1987. Colombo was born outside Milan, and is most famous for designing the first Ferrari V-12. His career began at Alfa Romeo in 1924, and he became head of the company's technical department within four years. In the summer and fall of 1945, he worked with Enzo Ferrari, and was then rehired by Alfa Romeo. In 1948 he returned to Ferrari for three years, then went back to Alfa. A stint at Maserati from 1952 to 1953 was followed by three years with France's Bugatti, which was unsuccessfully attempting to regain its prewar glory. He then worked with Abarth, developing the 750 twincam engine. He also designed numerous projects for MV Agusta, and worked with Zagato on an electric car, the Zele.

Gian Paolo Dallara

Born 1933. Gian Paolo Dallara is considered by many to be Italy's finest postwar chassis engineer. After graduating from college in 1959, he joined Ferrari. He remained there for only 18 months, and was then lured to Maserati by acquaintance (and not a relative, as is often reported) Giulio Alfieri. Dallara then joined upstart Lamborghini, where he would go on to achieve great fame as the father of the landmark Miura. He left Lamborghini in 1968 to join De Tomaso. In 1972 he founded Dallara Automobili, a research, design, and production concern; subsequent clients included Lancia, Fiat, Iso, Lamborghini, and Ferrari. Today, Dallara primarily designs, develops, and produces open wheel race cars. His cars are multiple time winners at America's Indy 500.

Alessandro De Tomaso

Born 1928. Although he was born in Buenos Aires, De Tomaso's family roots are Italian. He came to Italy in the mid-1950s, and was initially a test driver for OSCA. After marrying American Isabelle Haskell, the two began racing Maseratis and OSCAs. By the late 1950s, De Tomaso was building single seat race cars. He branched out into street sports cars that used American engines in 1963. In 1967 he masterminded the purchase of Carrozzeria Ghia with the Haskells' Rowan Industries Corporation. His close association with Lee Iacocca and Ford in 1969 led to his most famous car, the Pantera; four years later, the American company would complete its purchase of Carrozzeria Ghia from De Tomaso. In the mid-1970s, De Tomaso bought auto manufacturers Maserati and Innocenti; in the late 1980s and 1990s, he sold them both to Fiat.

Piero Dusio

1889-1975. The man behind Cisitalia, Piero Dusio was in the right place at the right time. In the 1930s, the lively, athletic Turin-based industrialist started his racing career, competing with Alfa Romeos and Maseratis; he placed third at 1938's Mille Miglia, and won the Stelvio race. Cisitalia was born during the war, and was at the center of Italy's postwar sports car universe in the late 1940s. Financial troubles caused him to immigrate to Argentina in 1951 in an attempt to find additional capital for Cisitalia; this would prove unsuccessful. He died in Argentina in 1975.

Antonio Fessia

1901-1968. A mechanical engineer who was born in Turin, Fessia started his career in Fiat in 1923. He quickly worked through the ranks of the company, first in the aeronautics department, then directing the mechanical engineering offices. He left the firm in 1946, and worked for Ducati, Pirelli, and others. He went to Lancia in 1955, and eventually became its technical director. Fessia was responsible for the Flaminia, Flavia, and Fulvia cars.

Enzo Ferrari

1898-1988. The most famous name in sports car history was originally a racing driver. Ferrari joined Alfa Romeo in 1920, and raced through much of the decade. By 1930 he was managing the Scuderia Ferrari, a racing organization based in Modena that worked closely with Alfa. Ferrari parted ways with Alfa in 1938, and formed Auto Avio Costruzioni; the firm made two cars before World War II. After the War, Ferrari's company started using his name. An incredible variety of world-famous competition and street machines followed. Ferrari was an autocratic figure, a master at extracting the most out of his people. So great was his stature that, late in life, he did not go see the Pope; instead, the Pope came to see him in Maranello.

Leonardo Fioravanti

Born 1938. Born in Milan, Leonardo Fioravanti graduated with a degree in engineering, then started his career at Pininfarina in 1964. Elegant and cultured, the famed coachbuilding firm was the perfect place for his talents, as Fioravanti was involved in styling many of the most famous Ferraris. His resume includes the 206/246 Dino, Daytona, Boxer, 308 GTB/ GTS, and the 288 GTO. He was the firm's Director of Research for 15 years, starting in 1972. In 1987 he founded Fioravanti s.r.l., a design and consulting company in automotive design and architecture.

Mauro Forghieri

Born 1935. Among the most prominent in a long list of Ferrari engineers, Forghieri joined the company in 1959 after graduating with an engineering degree. At the young age of 27, he was thrust into the role of Ferrari's chief engineer following the infamous "Walk-out" of 1961. With Ferrari making it clear his was 100% behind the green engineer, Forghieri went on a tear, as his designs won a number of championships. He considers the "flat 12" engine one of his greatest accomplishments. He remained with Ferrari until 1987, then joined Lamborghini's fledging competition department. He stayed for several years, then left to form his own company, Oral Engineering.

Marcello Gandini

Born 1938. Along with Nuccio Bertone, if any individual could claim to be father of the wedge design, it would be Marcello Gandini. After working on and off in the automotive industry for the first half of the 1960s, his break came when Nuccio Bertone hired him as chief stylist in the fall of 1965. One of Gandini's first designs was 1966's legendary Lamborghini Miura. He followed this up with a number of sensational creations, culminating with Lamborghini's other seminal model, the Countach LP400. Gandini remained with Bertone into 1979, then went out on his own and worked closely with Renault for five years. Many of the late 1980s most famous supercars were created in his design studio outside Turin.

Dante Giacosa

1905-1996. The indomitable spirit of Dante Giacosa can be found in many of Fiat's sports cars—often facing a reluctant management, his equanimity, will, and wit brought them into being. After his career began at SPA in 1928, he joined parent company Fiat the following year. He rose rapidly through the ranks, and became the company's Director of Engineering in 1946. Giacosa loved to tinker in the effort to gain additional performance, and was frequently found at the wind tunnel, or out in the field with his test drivers. He remained Fiat's Director of Engineering through 1970, at which time he retired.

Giorgetto Giugiaro

Born 1938. Giorgetto Giugiaro's artistic familial line undoubtedly played a role in his being named "Designer of the Century." The immensely talented and driven man's career began innocuously in the Fiat Styling Center in 1956. He was then brought to the attention of Nuccio Bertone, and was hired in 1959 as the carrozzeria's chief stylist. For the next six years, he and Bertone astounded the world with one magnificent creation after another. Giugiaro left in 1965, and was quickly hired by Carrozzeria Ghia as its chief stylist. Giugiaro didn't miss a beat, churning out a number of memorable shapes. In 1968 he joined forces with Aldo Montovani, the former head of Fiat's Body Engineering Department. The result

was Ital Design, and suddenly Turin had a third major coachbuilding force. Today, the Giugiaro name is world renown, and Ital Design's clients cover all corners of the globe.

Vittorio Jano

1891-1965. Jano was born in Turin, so it should be no surprise that early in his career he was employed by Fiat. He remained with the company for 12 years, and was then lured to Alfa Romeo in 1923 by a persuasive Enzo Ferrari. Jano quickly had his hand in a number of the company's most famous models, including the dominant P2 single seater and the 6C series of sports and racing cars. He left the company in 1937, and ended up working for Lancia 15+ years later, where he would design the famed D 50 single seater. After Lancia withdrew from competition that year, he followed the D 50s down to Maranello and Ferrari. He worked closely with Ferrari into 1965—engineers such as Carlo Chiti claim it was he who designed Ferrari's V-6 Dino engine, and not Ferrari's son Dino. Following the death of his own son Giorgio, Jano took his own life in 1965.

Aurelio Lampredi

1917-c.1989. Aurelio Lampredi is another of the legendary names that sprinkles early Ferrari history. Yet, there was much more to his resume than designing "long-block" V-12 engines. His career began in 1937, working in the aeronautics field. His first stint at Ferrari went from October 1946 to March 1947; he then left for several months to work with Isotta-Fraschini in Milan. He returned to Ferrari that November, and remained with the company through 1955 as its head of design and testing. In September, he started work as Fiat's director of engine development, a position he held through 1977. He also worked with Abarth from 1972 to 1982, and remained a consultant to Fiat after he retired.

Ferruccio Lamborghini

1916-1993. Ferruccio Lamborghini was a typical Italian postwar success story. He grew up in the countryside between Modena and Bologna, then went to a technical school in Bologna. He was drafted into the war, where he reportedly demonstrated a true mechanical "touch." In the late 1940s, Lamborghini founded his successful tractor company. A little more than a decade later, he hit another financial home run with his heating and air conditioning concern. He formed Automobili Lamborghini in early 1963, and would remain the company's guiding light into the early 1970s. After financial difficulties forced him to sell his shares in the first half of the decade, he took up producing wine. In the late 1980s/early 1990s, Lamborghini's name was often linked with Romano Artioli's Bugatti effort.

Giovanni Michelotti

1921-c.1988. Giovanni Michelotti is likely the greatest stylist people have never heard of. As Italy's most prolific postwar designer, Michelotti's career began at Carrozzeria Farina in 1937. Over the next decade, he learned all phases of the coachbuilding industry. In 1949 he went out on his own as a freelance designer, and was soon working for a number of major firms. In the first half of the 1950s, he teamed with Alfredo Vignale's carrozzeria to create an incredibly diverse and imaginative series of Ferraris. He soon started receiving commissions from abroad, most notably from England's Triumph. In 1960 he formed his own coachbuilding company to manufacture his own creations.

Adolfo Orsi

1988-1972. Adolfo Orsi was born in Modena, the oldest of five children. His poor background caused him to leave school at a young age to help the family subsist. He became a scrap dealer, and soon built these modest beginnings into a thriving business. When he was in his 40s he owned his own foundries, railway lines, a car dealership, and had 2,000 employees. In 1937 he purchased Maserati from the Maserati brothers, and moved the company to Modena. Even though the Maserati brothers left in 1947 to form OSCA, Orsi's leadership and business acumen would make it Modena's largest producer of GT cars in the 1960s. The company also won the Formula 1 world championship in 1957. In 1968 he sold Maserati to France's Citroen.

Battista Pininfarina

1893-1966. Born Battista Farina, "Pinin" was the nickname by which he became known. He started his career working at his brother Giovanni's Carrozzeria Farina. Pinin visited America in the 1920s, where he learned much about mass production techniques. He formed Carrozzeria Pinin Farina in 1930, 31 years before the company and his name became "Pininfarina." He is likely the automotive world's greatest master of elegant shapes, proportions, and forms, and one of (if not *the*) largest influences on postwar styling. His company's most famous client remains Ferrari, a relationship Pinin started in 1952.

Sergio Pininfarina

Born 1926. The son of Battista Pininfarina, Sergio graduated with a degree in mechanical engineering in 1950, and immediately began working at his father's company. After Battista and Enzo Ferrari came to their historic accord in 1952, it was young Sergio who managed the account, and made it what it is today. As the 1950s progressed, he became more and more involved in managing the company, while maintaining a hand in its styling. When Pinin passed away in 1966, Sergio was named the company's president. He was president of the Turin Industrialists' Union in the second half of the 1970s, and played in integral role in the city's business world during that tumultuous period. Among numerous other honors, he was elected to Europe's Parliament.

Frank Reisner

Born 1932. Reisner was born in Hungary, the son of a successful industrialist. His family settled in Canada in the 1950s, and Frank went to Italy in the late 1950s with wife Paula to pursue a career in the country's burgeoning automotive industry. He founded Intermeccanica in 1959, and began building the small, rear-engine Imp. A collaboration with America's Apollo followed. In 1965, Reisner was constructing his own cars, selling them under the Intermeccanica name; all Intermeccanicas featured American-based powerplants. Shortly after the first oil crisis, he moved to California, and eventually returned to Canada.

Renzo Rivolta

1908-1966. Rivolta was the quintessential Milanese industrialist: hard charging, always interested in the bottom line, and continually mindful of the well-being of his employees. Immediately after the war, he sensed Italy would need inexpensive transportation, so his Iso company began producing motorscooters. When people's incomes increased, he began making motorcycles and the Isetta "bubblecar." In the early 1960s, his company underwent another transformation when it entered the world of exclusive 140-mph GTs with the Iso Rivolta 2+2, then the Iso Grifo. Rivolta was an avid sportsman who loved nature.

Piero Rivolta

Born 1941. The son of Renzo Rivolta, Piero Rivolta became the world's youngest automotive producer when his father unexpectedly passed away in 1966. He had been groomed for the job, and oversaw the design and production of new Iso models such as the Grifo Targa and 7 Liter, S4 and Fidia luxury sedans, and 2+2 Lele. In the late 1960s, he correctly predicted the ramifications of the economic and political uncertainties, and purposely downsized his company. After taking Iso public in 1972 on America's over-the-counter market, in 1973 he sold the family holdings to Italo-American financier Ivo Pera. Rivolta is currently a shareholder in Zagato.

Sergio Scaglietti

Born 1920. At age 13, Modena native Sergio Scaglietti was forced to enter the coachbuilding industry when his father suddenly passed away. In the 1950s he would gain worldwide fame as a coachbuilder for Ferrari, creating a number of the firm's most successful and memorable endurance racers. Amazingly, he never sketched one design, preferring to do everything "by the eyes alone." In the late 1950s, his company began producing Pininfarina-designed Ferraris, the talented coachbuilder often making his own design "tweaks" with Pininfarina's consent. In 1969 his company was bought by Fiat at the same time it purchased Ferrari. Scaglietti continued to manage the firm until his retirement in the mid-1980s.

Franco Scaglione

1917-1994. Perhaps the most mercurial figure in Italy's styling world, Scaglione was undoubtedly one of its greatest artists. He was originally hired by Nuccio Bertone in 1952, and worked closely with the coachbuilder for the next seven years. His most famous pieces of work from this creative period are undoubtedly the Alfa Romeo BATs. He went out on his own in 1959; his subsequent designs include 1963's Lamborghini's 350 GTV prototype. He also worked closely with Frank Reisner and Intermeccanica throughout the 1960s and the first half of the 1970s, where his last sports car design was Intermeccanica's rakish Indra.

Paolo Stanzani

Born 1936. Stanzani was hardly a year out of college when he was contacted by Ferruccio Lamborghini to come work for the upstart firm. With engineering degree in hand, Stanzani accepted, and started under Gian Paolo Dallara, the firm's chief engineer. When Dallara left Lamborghini in 1968, Stanzani was promoted to fill the position. Additionally, he became the company manager, and had an outstanding knack of bringing out the best in those who worked for him. He would oversee the design and development of a number of Lamborghini cars, his most famous being the Countach LP400. Stanzani left Lamborghini in 1975. Ten-plus years later, he would work for upstart Bugatti. Today, he is a freelance engineer.

Tom Tjaarda

Born 1934. The son of stylist John Tjaarda, Tom graduated from the University of Michigan with a degree in architecture. Thanks to a class thesis for a sports station wagon, Ghia immediately hired him in 1959. He would work there for three years, then move to Pininfarina, where he remained until 1966. After a brief stint at OSI, he became chief stylist at Ghia in 1968. He also had stints as head of the Fiat Styling Center and Carrozzeria Fissore. He opened his own design studio in 1986. Tjaarda's most famous sports cars are the Fiat 124 Spider, and De Tomaso Pantera.

Vittorio Valletta

1883-1967. His name is not attached to any particular sports car, but Valletta's behind-the-scenes role as a Fiat executive undoubtedly had a tremendous impact on Italy's sports car scene. He joined the company in 1921 with a background in economics and banking. His rise through Fiat's ranks was enormous, and he was made company president in 1946. Many feel he is one the most important people in the company's lengthy history, typified by Dante Giacosa christening him one of the leading forces behind the firm's great postwar success in the 1950s and '60s.

Ugo Zagato

1890-1968. Ugo Zagato started working at age 15 when he went to Cologne to work in a machine shop. He returned to Italy four years later, and got a job at Carrozzeria Varesina. During World War I, he constructed airplanes, the experience prompting him to form Carrozzeria Zagato in Milan after the war. For the balance of his career, Zagato relied on lightweight construction techniques and aeronautical ideas for design inspiration. The firm's close association with Alfa in the late 1920s vaulted the coachbuilder to prominence. After World War II, Zagato-bodied creations frequented the winner's circle of numerous events, thanks to their wind-cheating forms and light weight. In the 1950s and '60s, his firm made numerous production cars for constructors such as Lancia and Alfa Romeo.

Elio Zagato

Born 1921. Elio was the older of Ugo Zagato's two sons. He gained notoriety in the late 1940s/early 1950s as a racing driver, where he learned that "what wins on Sunday, sells on Monday." Elio used this experience in a number of Zagato products, constantly improving their performance. In the 1950s he became involved in the management of the firm, and had an active role in the creation of many Zagato cars. He became managing director of the company in 1966, and chairman upon his father's death in 1968. Assisting him in managing the company was his younger brother Gianni. Today, Elio is retired, and his son Andrea is actively running the firm.

Index

Abarth, Carlo, 42, 59, 61
Agnelli, Gianni, 118
Agnelli, Giovanni, 11, 90
Alfieri, Giulio, 67, 68, 69, 77, 91-93, 99, 100, 105, 107, 115, 130
Ambrosini, Giorgio, 21, 41
Anderloni, Felice Bianchi, 18, 19, 24, 38
Anderloni and Touring, 19
Anderloni, Carlo Felice Bianchi, 13, 18, 19, 24, 28, 30, 38, 39, 44, 64, 67, 68, 78
Anderloni, Emilio, 18
Anderloni, Linda, 18
Artioli, Romano, 133–135
Ascari, Antonio, 14
Baghetti, Giancarlo, 74, 75
Balboni, Valentino, 131, 132, 138
Banca Nazionale di Sconto, 22
Bazzi, Luigi, 14, 37
Bellei, Angelo, 107
Bellentani, Vittorio, 39
Benedetti, Giampaolo, 134
Beretta, Piero, 74
Bergman, Ingrid, 52
Bertocchi, Aurelio, 67
Bertocchi, Gino, 39
Bertocchi, Guerino, 39, 67, 69
Bertone, Giovanni, 20
Bertone, Nuccio, 20, 29, 32, 41, 45, 53, 55, 59, 76, 84, 85, 88, 95, 101, 102, 107–109, 118
Billi, Giorgio, 72, 134
Bizzarrini, Giotto, 29, 52, 71, 65, 72, 77, 79, 80, 92, 94, 135
Boano, Mario Felice, 54, 84
Bolster, John, 65, 92, 116
Bondurant, Bob, 79
Bono, Gaudenzio, 90
Borgeson, Griff, 30, 74, 134
Brock, Pete, 92
Brown, Milt, 81, 114
Busso, Guiseppe, 31, 37, 43
Cahier, Bernard, 61, 65, 74, 84
Campari, Guiseppe, 14
Canestrini, Giovanni, 12, 39
Caniato, Alfredo, 15
Caniato, Augusto, 15
Caproni, Giovani, 22
Carrozzeria Bertone, 20, 29, 53, 84
Carrozzeria Boneschi, 29, 44, 62
Carrozzeria Colli, 44
Carrozzeria Falco, 18
Carrozzeria Farina, 13, 19, 51
Carrozzeria Fissore, 29, 62, 82
Carrozzeria Ghia, 21, 44, 46, 73, 85, 89, 92, 104

Carrozzeria Intermeccanica, 81
Carrozzeria Pavesi, 128
Carrozzeria Savio, 21
Carrozzeria Speciale, 44
Carrozzeria Touring, 18, 24, 29, 38, 43, 44, 67, 75, 78
Carrozzeria Varesina, 14
Carrozzeria Vignale, 114, 115
Carrozzeria Viotti, 22
Carrozzeria Zagato, 14, 15
Casarini, Giordano, 50, 115, 120, 122, 142, 144
Chinetti, Luigi, 75
Chiti, Carlo, 71, 72, 83
Ciferri, Luca, 133
Colombini, Augustina, 30
Colombini, Dante, 30
Colombo, Gioachino, 30, 31, 37, 38, 43, 51, 121
Cortese, Franco, 38
Cozza, Emanno, 39
Cumberford, Robert, 114
Cunningham, Briggs, 39
Dallara, Gian Paolo, 75, 77, 78, 79, 94, 95, 101, 105, 143
Danese, Renato, 41
De Nora, Oronzio, 74
De Tomaso, Alessandro, 81, 104, 114, 120, 144
De Tomaso, Santiago, 143, 144
Di Biase, Venazio, 105
Di Virgilio, Francesco, 45
Dreyfus, Rene, 23
Dusio, Carlo, 35
Dusio, Piero, 33, 34, 35
Farina, Giovanni, 13, 19
Farina, Guiseppe, 40
Farina, Sergio Pinin,
Ferrari, Enzo, 15, 17, 22, 23, 30-32, 65, 69, 71, 72, 94, 100, 103, 109, 130
Ferrari, Piero, 138
Fessia, Antonio, 152
Finmeccanica, 54
Fioravanti, Leonardo, 102, 103
Fiorio, Cesare, 106
Fittipaldi, Emerson, 116
Fochi, Luciano, 31
Forghieri, Mauro, 82, 83, 109
Formenti, Federico, 24
Fraschini, Antonio, 18
Fraschini, Vincenzo, 18
Frére, Paul, 54, 92, 93, 132, 134
Gallo, Pasquale, 32
Gandini, Marcello, 94-96, 99-101, 107, 109, 110, 116, 134, 138, 143, 144

Gardini, Girolamo, 30, 52, 65, 72, 74
Gauld, Graham, 74
Ghia, Giacinto, 29
Giacosa, Dante, 21, 22, 27, 29, 33, 34, 41, 42, 44, 46, 84, 90, 153
Giugiaro, Giorgetto, 79, 84, 85, 88, 90, 92, 93, 100, 104, 113, 144
Gobbato, Ugo, 22, 23, 32, 37
Grant, Gregor, 74
Greggio, Luciano, 12, 18, 32, 84, 88, 118
Griffith, Jack, 114
Gruppo Orsi, 22, 23, 31, 39, 56
Guidotti, Giovanbattista, 15
Haskell, Isabelle, 82
Held, Jean-Francis, 111
Hill, Phil, 132, 134
Hispano-Suiza, 28
Hoare, Colonel Ronnie, 82
Hoffman, Max, 34, 54
Hruska, Rudolf, 54
Iacocca, Lee, 104, 105
Innocenti, Ferdinando, 40
Institute of Industrial Reconstruction (IRI), 22
Intermeccanica, 114
ISO Industries, 114
Isotta, Cesare, 18
Isotta-Fraschini, 18, 22, 46
Ital Design, 104
Jano, Vittorio, 14, 15, 23, 30, 45
Kaiser, Henry, 34
Lamborghini Trattrici, 77
Lamborghini, Ferruccio, 76, 77, 79, 94, 109
Lampredi, Aurelio, 75, 153
Lancia, Gianni, 45
Lawrence, Brandon, 134, 135
Leimer, Rene, 114
Lini, Franco, 77
Livanos, Peter, 129
Luraghi, Guiseppe, 102
Lurani, Count Giovanni, 29, 80
Lutz, Bob, 114
Manney, Henry, 73, 79, 91, 94
Marchiano, Michele, 15
Marmiroli, Luigi, 132
Martinengo, Franco, 89
Maserati, Alfieri, 22
Maserati, Bindo, 18, 22, 38
Maserati, Ernesto, 22, 39, 63
Maserati, Ettore, 22, 39
Massimino, Alberto, 24, 39, 74
Michelotti, Giovanni, 51
Miles, Ken, 88
Mille Miglia, 12, 13, 15, 17, 20-22, 24, 32-34, 38, 41, 42, 45, 51

Miller, Ron, 132
Mimram, Patrick, 122
Modena Design, 143
Molinari, Giorgio, 71, 72
Montabone, Oscar, 118
Monteverdi, Peter, 115
Montezemolo, Luca Cordero di, 138, 142
Moretti, Giovanni, 55
Moto Guzzi, 115
Mussolini, Benito, 11-12, 14, 15, 22, 24, 29, 30
Nardi e Danese, 41
Nardi, Enrico, 31, 32, 40, 41
Nasi, Angelo, 31
Needell, Tiff, 140
Nichols, Mel, 104, 119
Norbye, Jan P., 113
Novaro, Emile, 132
Nuvolari, Tazio, 31, 34, 42
Nye, Doug, 129
Orsi, Adolfo, 22, 23, 31, 39, 66-68, 92, 93
Orsini, Luigi, 17, 39
Pagani, Horacio, 131, 142, 143
Patino, Jaime Oritz, 72
Pera, Ivo, 114
Perini, Giancarlo, 133
Plescia, Ron, 81
Pininfarina, Giovanni Battista, 13, 19-21, 27, 29, 31, 33-35, 37, 65, 89
Pininfarina, Sergio, 19,29, 45, 49, 50, 52, 65, 66, 84, 92, 94, 95, 104, 109, 113, 119, 121, 129, 138, 142
Pizzi, Giuliano, 78
Ponzoni, Gaetano, 18, 38
Porsche, Dr. Ferdinand, 31, 34, 42, 54
Pozzo, Josette, 19
Prearo, Enzo, 99, 116
Purdy, Ken, 95
Qvale, Bruce, 143
Qvale, Kjell, 143
Raggi, Pierluigi, 79, 80, 85
Ramaciotti, Lorenzo, 141
Rancati, Gino, 24
Rapi, Fabio Luigi, 46, 60
Reisner, Frank, 114
Renzi, Carlo, 84
Revelli, Mario, 21
Ricart, Wilfredo, 23
Rivolta, Piero, 28, 63, 76, 78, 91, 92, 99, 100, 110, 111, 113, 114, 135
Rivolta, Renzo, 28, 40, 63, 77, 79, 81, 154
Robinson, Peter, 119
Romeo, Nicola, 13
Rosinski, Jose, 133

Rossellini, Roberto, 52
Rossetti, Georges-Henri, 110
Salamano, Carlo, 45, 47
Salvarani, Walter, 50
Santorelli, Sergio, 85
Sapino, Filippo, 29, 46, 85
Savonuzzi, Giovanni, 34, 35
Scagliarini, Armando, 42
Scaglietti, Sergio, 15, 29, 31, 40, 66, 100
Scaglione, Franco, 53, 54, 59, 78, 81, 84, 104, 114
Scarzi, Ubaldo, 117
Scuderia Ferrari, 15, 17
Segre, Luigi, 89
Spada, Ercole, 111
Squazzini, Giovanni, 129
Stabilimenti Farina, 39
Stanguellini, Celso, 41
Stanzani, Paolo, 94, 101, 107, 108, 114
Tavoni, Romolo, 71, 72
Tjaarda, John, 89, 90
Tjaarda, Tom, 49, 87, 91, 104, 105, 106, 118–121, 129
Turati, Arturo, 12
Vaccarino, Guiseppe, 45
Vignale, Alfredo, 51
Volpi, Count Giovanni, 72, 74
Von Newmann, Johnny, 65
Walkout, 72, 77, 82
Wallace, Bob, 77, 94, 95, 107, 114, 117, 131
Weymann, Charles, 13
Zagato, Elio, 28, 29, 47, 61
Zagato, Ugo, 14, 15, 28
Zampolli, Claudio, 135

Models
Abarth, 41, 42
    205A, 41, 42
    207-A Spyder Corsa, 59
    207-A, 60
    Cisitalia 1100, 42
    Fiat-Abarth 750 Zagato, 60
Abarth and Company, 42
Alfa-Zagato, 15
    1750, 49
    1750 GS, 15
Alfa Romeo, 13, 14, 17, 19, 22, 23, 30, 32, 37, 38, 42, 49, 52, 64, 72
    1750 GS, 19
    1750, 30
    1900, 44, 45, 54
    1900 C Super Sprint, 42, 43
    1900 SSZ, 61, 148
    20 ES Sport, 15
    2000 GT Veloce, 88

2300, 30
256 Berlinetta, 30
2600, 75
2600 Bertone coupe, 74
2600 Touring Spider, 74
2900, 30
30 ES Sport, 15
3500 Spider Super Sport, 89
6C 1750, 23
6C 2300 Pescara Coupe
    Aerodinamico, 19
6C 2500 Sport, 32, 33
6C 2500, 28, 42, 43
8C 2300, 18, 19
8C 2900 B, 19, 29
8C 2900, 17, 20, 32
Alfa 1750, 17, 18
Alfetta 158, 32
Berlinetta Aerodinamica Tecnica 5
    (BAT 5), 53
Canguro, 85, 90
Duetto, 88, 91
Flying Star, 18, 19, 23
Giulia GTA, 87
Giulia Sprint, 75, 88
Giulia Sprint GT, 87, 88
Giulietta, 64, 88
Giulietta Speciale, 64
Giulietta Sprint, 53, 54, 64
Giulietta Spyder, 55, 64
GTV, 140
Normale, 14
P2, 30
R.L. Sports, 14
R.L., 14
RLSS, 15
SC 2900, 24
Spider, 119
Spider Speciale Aerodinamico, 89
SZ, 64
Tipo 33 Stradale, 104
Tipo Corsa 13
TZ-1, 85
Apollo, 81
    GT, 81
Autocostruzioni SA (ASA), 74, 76
    1000 GT, 73, 77, 85
    1000 GT Spider, 73, 75
Automobili Turismo Sport (ATS), 74, 76, 134
    2500 GT, 71-73
Auto Avio Costruzioni, 24, 30
    815, 22, 24, 30
Bertone, 20, 51, 69, 100
    Sprint Speciale, 61
Bizzarrini, 149
    Grifo, 81
    Grifo A3, 80
    Strada, 80, 81, 95
Boneschi, 20

Bugatti, 133, 135
    EB110, 134
Cisitalia (Compagnia Industriale Sportivo
    Italiana), 32, 37, 42
    202 MM Spyder Nuvolari, 35
    202 MM, 34, 35
    202, 43
    360, 35
    D46, 34
    Type 360, 54
De Tomaso, 149
    Guara, 143
    Mangusta, 92-94, 143
    Pantera, 105, 106, 145
    Pantera GT5, 128
    Vallelunga, 82
Ferrari, 37, 51, 52, 67
    166 MM, 38, 39
    166 SC, 37
    206 GT (Dino), 103, 104
    246 GTS (Dino), 105
    250 GT, 64, 65, 77
    250 GTL, 82-84
    250 Cabriolet, 62, 65
    250 Europa, 52
    250 GT, 64, 66, 82
    250 GTE, 82, 83
    250 Spyder California, 62, 65, 66
    250 Testa Rossa, 66
    250 SWB, 65, 66, 85
    275 GTB, 83, 84, 85
    275 GTB/4, 83, 102, 103
    275 GTS, 83
    288 GTO, 129, 130, 134, 138
    308 GT4, 115
    308 GTB, 122, 123
    308 GTBi, 123
    308 GTS, 122, 123
    308 Quattrovalvole, 127
    330 GTC, 95, 102
    330 GTS, 102
    340 MM, 51
    342 America, 52
    348, 131, 132
    348 GTS, 132
    355, 137, 142
    360 Modena Spider, 144
    360 Modena, 141, 142
    365 Boxer, 119
    365 California, 87, 90
    365 GTB/4, 102, 103
    365 GTS/4, 103
    365 GT/4 BB, 106, 107, 119
    375 America, 52
    375 MM, 52
    375 Plus, 52
    410 SA (Superamerica), 66, 69
    456 GT, 137, 138
    512 BB, 123

512 TR, 132, 133
550 Maranello, 138, 145
Dino 308 GT4, 113
Europa GT, 52
F40, 130, 131, 133, 134, 138
F50, 138
Mondial Cabriolet, 124
Testarossa, 129
Type 125, 37
Fiat, 11, 13, 15, 19, 29, 32, 34, 37, 38,
    41, 42, 49
    1100 Sedan, 42
    1100 S, 41, 42
    1100, 60
    1200 Roadster, 61
    1200, 74
    124, 150
    124 Spider, 89, 91, 120, 121
    1500 Roadster, 61
    1500 Spyder, 63
    1500, 21, 22, 32
    1600S, 61, 64
    230 S, 85
    2300S, 73, 75
    2800, 29, 32
    508C MM, 21, 22, 42
    508, 21
    508C, 24,
    508S Balilla Sport, 21
    514CA, 21
    514S, 21
    600, 59, 61
    6C 1500, 20
    750 Testadoro, 60
    750 Fiat-Abarth Zagato, 62
    850 Coupe, 88
    850 Spyder, 90, 96
    8V, 44
    Balilla Sport, 21
    BV, 45, 46, 47, 61
    Coupe, 140
    Dino, 91, 92, 96, 104
    Dino Coupe, 150
    X1/9, 118, 121
    X1/20, 118
Ghia, 20, 29, 47, 51, 69, 82
    450 SS, 85
Innocenti
    950 Spyder, 89
Iso
    Grifo A3/L, 76-78, 79
    Grifo A3/L Spider, 85
    Grifo 7 Liter, 99
    Grifo Can Am, 99
    Grifo, 95, 101
    Grifo GL, 80
    Rivolta GT, 76, 79
    Varedo, 111
Isotta-Fraschini, 11

8A, 19
8C, 38
KM4, 11, 12
Lamborghini, 76, 108, 143
    350 GT, 75, 79
    350 GTV, 78
    350 Spider, 84
    400 GT, 75
    400 2+2, 75
    Countach, 107, 109, 110
    Countach LP400, 119, 123
    Countach LP500, 108
    Countach LP500 S, 121, 123
    Countach Quattrovalvole, 130
    Diablo, 132, 133, 140
    Diablo GT, 141, 143
    Diablo SE, 139, 140, 143
    Espada, 101, 150
    Jalpa, 122, 123
    Miura, 94, 95, 102
    Miura Roadster, 96
    Miura S, 103
    Miura SV, 109
    Silhouette, 117
    Urraco, 117
Lancia, 19, 31, 32, 38, 49
    037 Rally, 150
    Aprilia Berlinetta Aerodinamica, 19, 20
    Aprilia, 31, 32
    Aurelia B10, 45
    Aurelia B20 Elaborazione, 45, 59
    Aurelia B24 Spyder, 54, 55
    Austura Berlina Aerodinamica, 20
    Austura, 19
    B20 GT, 43
    Beta Montecarlo, 118
    Flaminia, 64, 88
    Flaminia GT, 64
    Flavia Coupe, 90
    Fulvia, 88, 89, 106, 107
    Fulvia Coupe, 88
    Fulvia Sport S, 88
    Rally 037, 123
    Scorpion, 118
    Stratos, 106-108
    SZ (Zagato), 64
Maserati, 31, 39, 68
    2+2 Mexico, 91
    3200 GT, 144, 151
    3500 GT, 67-69, 91
    6CS/46, 31
    A6, 30, 32, 37, 38, 41
    A6 1500, 31
    A6 2000, 61
    A6G/54, 51
    A6GCS, 51
    Biturbo, 120, 121
    Bora, 105-107
    Ghibli, 92-95, 105

Ghibli spider, 100, 101
Ghibli SS, 101
Merak, 116, 122
Mistral, 85, 93
Quattroporte, 91
Moretti, 56
    Gran Sport, 56
OSCA (Officine Specializzate
    Construzione Automobilli), 39, 56
    1500, 63
    1600 GT, 62
    MT4, 39, 56
Pagani
    Zonda C12, 142, 143
Qvale Modena, 143, 144
    Qvale Mangusta, 142
Siata (Societa Italiana Auto
Trasformazione Accessori), 41, 44, 56
    1400 Gran Sport, 41
    208S Spider, 55
    Amica, 39, 41
    Daina, 39, 41
    Gran Sport, 41
    Tipo TC, 41
Zagato, 29, 46, 47, 49, 51, 56, 60
    8V, 47
    Isotta-Fraschini, 60